1st Ed 1250

D0989537

AIR BOMBARDMENT

AIR BOMBARDMENT

the story of its development

by Air Marshal Sir Robert Saundby

HARPER & BROTHERS, NEW YORK

Copyright © 1961 by Robert Saundby
Printed in the United States of America

All rights reserved.
No part of the book may be used or reproduced in any manner whatsoever without
written permission except in the case of
brief quotations embodied in critical articles
and reviews. For information address
Harper & Brothers,
49 East 33rd Street, New York 16, N.Y.

FIRST EDITION

F-L

Library of Congress catalog card number: 61-10226

To the youth of today who, if they will accept the scientific evolution of war and go forward with courage, can build a world free from strife, with equity and justice for all under the rule of law.

Contents

List of Illustrations

Introduction

Much has been written about air warfare. There are excellent official histories of the First World War, and many volumes of the history of the second one have already appeared. Accounts are available, or soon will be available, describing almost every air operation that has ever taken place. It might be thought that the subject has been so adequately recorded that there is no need for a book on the history of air bombardment.

But air bombardment is the basic element of air power, and the story of its development, from small beginnings to a position of dominance, has never yet been properly presented to the public. Various misconceptions about the way in which it works are still commonly met with, and remarkable misstatements frequently occur in speeches, articles, and letters to the press.

It might be supposed that the general lack of enlightenment on this subject is due to an absence of interest in it, but that hardly seems to be tenable in view of the readiness of most people to express their opinions, and even to lay down the law, about these matters. There is therefore reason to believe that a connected story of the development of air bombardment—from the roc to the rocket, as it were—will have some value and interest.

It has been imperative, in order to deal with so vast a subject within a reasonable compass, to exclude much that might have been of service to my theme. I have had to adhere closely to the essentials of my story, while trying to avoid the fault of oversimplification. Only so much of the political and military background has been sketched in as I have judged to be necessary to put the subject into its proper perspective, to make decisions intelligible, and to explain the course of events.

I hope that I have been fair to those who hold views which I believe to be misguided. I have not, however, shirked the task of pointing out what seem to me to be mistakes and wrong decisions, though I have endeavored to support my contentions with evidence and reasoned argument.

It is my earnest wish that this book may assist in bringing to a juster frame of mind some of those who at present are unsympathetic to the idea of air bombardment and skeptical of its achievements. As long as war exists the Free World must be prepared to defend itself. If war is horrible—and I for one do not doubt that it is—then that is a reason for striving to abolish it, but not, as Clausewitz pointed out, "for making the sword we wear blunter and blunter by degrees from feelings of humanity, until someone steps in with one that is sharp and lops off the arm from the body."

ROBERT SAUNDBY

Part I

THE FIRST WORLD WAR

1   The Dawn of Military Aviation

Long before it became possible for him to do so in reality, man has
flown through the skies in his imagination. There have been many
legends of human flight—the magic flying carpet of Bisnagar;
Daedalus and his son Icarus, flying from Crete to the mainland
with wings of feathers; Swift's flying island of Laputa; Robert
Paltock's English classic, *Peter Wilkins*, and others.

The remarkable thing about these imaginary tales is that they have
so often come near to the truth, as revealed by modern scientific
development. We now have something not unlike the flying carpet
in the hovercraft; Icarus was killed as a result of a technical weakness about which he had been warned, but in the exhilaration of
flight he forgot what he had been told. Few people with any experience of flying have not come across a similar tragedy. And Laputa is
very like a manned satellite. Paltock, in his story of the flying
"Indians," shows a remarkable awareness of the possibilities of
gliding flight.

The story of the Sindbad the Sailor, in the *Arabian Nights*, gives a
legendary account of an air–sea battle. Sindbad relates that when he
was in his ship he saw the two rocs, which were giant birds,

*flying towards us, carrying great stones, or rather rocks, in their fearful
claws. They hovered just over the ship, and then one of them let
fall a stone which, however, missed the ship and fell into the sea,*

3

which dashed up like a great wall of water. But the other roc, un-
happily, aimed better, and dropping his enormous stone into the
very middle of the ship, splintered her into a thousand pieces.

The ship sank immediately, throwing the crew into the water, while
the victorious birds flew away and were soon out of sight. This incident, which is the earliest known reference to air bombardment, has
set the pattern for almost every air-sea battle since.

Man had always envied the birds and longed to fly, and by the
eighteenth century he had gained enough knowledge to bring human
flight within the bounds of possibility. The first means of aerial
navigation open to man was the balloon, in the beginning lifted by
hot air. In June 1783, the Montgolfier brothers released from the
market square at Annonay in France a hot-air balloon, which reached
the remarkable height of 6,500 ft. in a few minutes. Very soon other
ascents had been made, carrying into the air various animals, which
returned to earth unharmed. It is a pity that the Montgolfier brothers
did not take the opportunity of ascending in their own balloon, and
so of becoming the first men to fly. This honor belongs to two bold
Frenchmen, de Rozier and d'Arlandes, who, in November 1783,
ascended in a hot-air balloon from Paris and made a very successful
and uneventful flight.

A new era had begun and progress at first was rapid. In 1804 a
manned balloon went up to over 23,000 ft. This record was not
beaten until 1862, when a balloon released in England ascended
to 34,400 ft., to the great discomfort of the aeronauts, who suffered
severely from frostbite and lack of oxygen. But although man was
no longer earth-bound, a balloon could only drift with the wind. And
so the idea of a dirigible balloon or airship began to take shape. But
there was as yet no suitable engine to drive such a craft. Several
steam engines were designed for the purpose, but they were all too
heavy and insufficiently powerful.

Inventors began to turn their minds to mechanical flying machines.
As early as 1863 fixed wing and helicopter aircraft had been designed
and some had even been built, but they still awaited a power plant
light enough to raise them into the air. Practical experiments, therefore, were confined to gliding flight without power. An ingenious
German, Otto Lilienthal, began gliding in 1890, and by 1894 had
mastered the problems sufficiently to enable him to rise to a greater

height than the point from which he had started. He succeeded in
flying a distance of 1,500 ft., but was unfortunately killed in an
accident to one of his gliders in 1896.

Meanwhile development was also going on in the United States.
From 1880 Langley had been experimenting with successful models
powered by compressed air or elastic motors, and in 1896 he built
a full-scale airplane driven by a remarkable gasoline engine that developed 52 h.p. with a weight of only 250 lbs. This machine actually
took off but crashed into the Potomac River and was lost. Hiram
Maxim also built an airplane, and gave much attention to the development of lightweight steam engines. He never tried to fly this
machine, but contented himself with running it along between two
rails and measuring its lifting power.

In the meantime there had been a parallel development of lighter-
than-air craft. The Brazilian engineer, Santos-Dumont, built a series
of small airships, powered by gasoline engines, which were very
successful. In 1901 he won the Deutsch prize of 125,000 francs[1] by
flying from St. Cloud round the Eiffel Tower and back again. His
airship was well known in Paris, as he used to fly low around the
city, and many people believed that the future of air transport was
to be found in the dirigible airship. The later rigid airships, pioneered
by Count Zeppelin, seemed for a time likely to fulfill this promise.

Armies were not much interested in airships, as they considered
that they were too vulnerable to antiaircraft fire to be much use in
the battle zone. But navies were attracted by their qualities of long
endurance, and believed that they would prove valuable for sea
reconnaissance. The military development of airships, therefore, was
mainly along the lines of naval cooperation.

For a long time aviation seemed to have mainly peaceful uses,
and its first military applications were ancillary and inoffensive. At
the siege of Paris in 1870, during the Franco-Prussian War, balloons
were used for conveying messages and, on occasions, people in and
out of the beleaguered city. And during the war in South Africa
in 1899-1901, the British used man-lifting kites in order to see, as
General Sir Edward Swinton put it, the other side of the hill. One
of the curbs on the development of aviation had been the fear of its
misuse by the wicked. In the latter part of the seventeenth century,
Francesco de Lana, a Jesuit monk, warned the world that an airship

[1] Then worth about £10,000 or $40,000.

might be able to cause "a ship to capsize by flinging down pieces of iron, kill the crew and set the ship ablaze with artificial fire, with bullets and with bombs. Not only ships, but also houses, castles and towns might be served in this way, without risk to those who cast down such objects from immeasurable heights." And the great Dr. Johnson recorded his view that the security of the good would be gravely imperiled, if the wicked were able to attack them from the air at will.

In 1900, Wilbur and Orville Wright, basing their work on the experiments of Lilienthal and the American inventor Octave Chanute, built a number of gliders with which they studied the problems of stability and control. Their success was largely due to the fact that they realized that the main problem was not so much to get a machine into the air as to be able to control and guide it once it was airborne. At last in December 1903, with a power-driven biplane equipped with elevator, rudder, and warping wings, they solved the problem of deliberate, controlled flight.

This epoch-making event did not cause the excitement it deserved. Most people regarded it much as they did Blondin's crossing over the Niagara Falls on a tightrope—as a wonderful achievement, but one hardly likely to have much effect on the course of human affairs. Flying became the passion of a few enthusiasts in many countries, but it was mainly confined to displays and demonstrations. The crossing of the English Channel by Blériot in 1909 had some effect, as it was a breach of the traditional insular security of Britain. But the fighting services were everywhere slow to grasp the significance of aviation.

Italy was first in the field. The Army had an aeronautical section as early as 1884, and had used balloons for reconnaissance in the Eritrean War in 1887-1888. During the army maneuvers in Libya in 1911 five airplanes and two small dirigible airships were used for reconnaissance purposes with a good deal of success. Shortly after the end of these maneuvers a quarrel between Italy and Turkey came to a head, and early in October war broke out. The Italians occupied Tripoli, and a fortnight later the Turks counterattacked. On October 23, 1911, Captain Piazza, who had the imposing title of Commander of the Air Fleet, took off in an airplane for the first wartime flight. He flew over the enemy encampments, causing surprise and consternation in the Turkish ranks. On October 25 Captain Moizo, when on a reconnaissance flight, had the wings of his machine pierced by rifle bullets fired from the ground without causing any damage to the structure. A further remarkable development occurred on November 1, 1911, when Lieutenant Gavotti dropped four bombs on enemy targets. These bombs were apparently modified hand grenades of Swedish manufacture, weighing 2 kilograms, or about 4½ lbs. each. As the days went by several more bombs were dropped and it was not long before Turkey protested at the bombardment of a hospital at Ain Zara by Italian airplanes. In fact, inquiries could not establish the existence of a hospital at that place, but some of the Turkish military tents there may have been used to shelter the sick and wounded. The Italians pointed out that their warships had bombarded the encampment at Ain Zara with 152 heavy shells without any protest from the Turks. Almost the very first use of bombs from the air resulted in an illogical protest, suggesting that a few small aerial bombs were far more potent and destructive than a large number of shells fired by naval guns. There followed a considerable discussion in the Turkish, Italian, and neutral press about the ethics of air bombardment, which was the first example of a long series of such controversies.

The performance of the six aircraft engaged in this campaign was encouraging to those who believed in the future of military aviation. The Italian airmen seem to have handled their machines with courage and skill and, in spite of many difficulties, to have been of considerable service to the Army.

In Britain, the first unit of military aviation was formed in 1911. This was the Air Battalion of the Royal Engineers, which had one company of man-lifting kites, one company of airships, one of balloons, and one of airplanes. A few progressive young naval and army officers had seen the possibilities of military aviation and had learned to fly at their own expense. When, in 1912, the Royal Flying Corps was formed, they were naturally drawn into it. This corps was a joint service, with military and naval wings, and a central flying school manned by officers and men of both Services.

The British had a very clear, if also very limited, idea of the purpose of military aviation. It was to be reconnaissance, pure and simple. The generals hoped that their airplanes would be able to fly over the enemy's rear areas reporting the location of troops, dumps, depots, and the movements of traffic. From these reports the Intelligence staff, with their other sources of information, would be in a better position to estimate the enemy's intentions and to locate his main forces. The admirals hoped that airships and airplanes would be able to search rapidly great areas of sea, and by keeping an eye on the whereabouts of the enemy's battle fleet, enable them to maintain a favorable tactical position at sea and avoid being surprised.

In the United States, the Army Air Arm came officially into being as early as 1907, but progress was very slow. On August 1 of that year, the Signal Corps established an Aviation Division, responsible for all matters connected with "balloons, air machines, and kindred subjects." At first the division possessed nothing but balloons, but in 1908 a small dirigible airship was taken on to its strength. It was not until August 1909, that the first airplane, a Wright biplane, was delivered to the United States Army. For eighteen months this airplane represented the total strength of the Army Air Arm, but early in 1911 another airplane was lent to it by the generosity of Mr. Robert J. Collier. It was not until later in the year that the United States Congress specifically provided funds for aviation.

It is interesting to note that as early as 1911 a former Army officer, Riley E. Scott, invented a bombsight and offered it to the War Department. Although the sight was quite promising, the War Department declined to purchase it. The inventor then took it to Europe and entered it in a competition, at which it won a substantial money prize.

The United States Army pilots very early showed some restiveness at being commanded and administered by the Signal Corps. There were several incidents, and an angry chief signal officer described them as being "deficient in discipline and the proper knowledge of the customs of the Service and the duties of an officer." Indeed, in almost all the embryo air forces of the world, the pilots were regarded with some apprehension by the older Regular Army and Navy officers.

In December 1913, a Signal Corps aviation school was set up at North Island, San Diego. But progress was still very slow and by 1914, when the First World War began, the Army Air Arm had only some twenty airplanes on its strength. It is strange that the United States, which saw the inception of powered flight at Kitty Hawk in

1903, should at this stage have fallen so far behind Britain, France, Germany, Italy, and even Russia.

In July 1914, legislation gave permanent status to the Aviation Section of the Signal Corps, with an authorized strength of 60 officers and 260 other ranks.

By 1914, the United States Navy also possessed a small air arm.

In France, although some individual members of the fighting Services were enthusiastic aviators, the Army and Navy chiefs were apathetic. The French General Staff did not believe that aviation could do much to assist the Army, nor were the French naval authorities optimistic about the uses of aircraft in sea warfare. Both Services possessed a small air arm, but so little thought had been given to the way in which it should be used that it would almost seem that they had not grasped the importance of *applied* flying, as distinct from *pure* flying. It is reported that General Foch, who had commanded the École Superieur de la Guerre, and was regarded as unusually progressive and open-minded, said "Aviation is good sport, but for the Army it is useless."

The Germans also set up corps of military and naval aviation, but appeared to be somewhat uncertain about their military uses. The Army Air Service was placed under the Inspector-General of Military Transport, which seems to suggest that it may have been vaguely regarded as a means of transport. There is evidence of some attempt to train the pilots and observers in reconnaissance work, but most of the generals appear to have been skeptical of the value of airplanes in this role.

The German naval air service tended to specialize in airships, and even before the war it possessed several large Zeppelin and Schütte-Lanz vessels. The trial flight of the first Zeppelin airship took place as early as 1900, but it was not very satisfactory. It was not until 1905 that a second ship was built, which was very soon taken over by the German Government. The long range and great lifting power of these ships put them, in those days, in a class by themselves, but they were always very vulnerable to incendiary bullets and anti-aircraft shells.

It will have been noted that, in all these incipient military air forces, Britain alone had set up a unified Service, with military and naval wings, intended to supply the needs of both the Army and the Navy. This organization, however, did not last long. In July 1914, only some six weeks before the outbreak of the First World War, the British Admiralty decided to break away and form its own air service. And so the Royal Naval Air Service came into being, and the Royal Flying Corps was given the status of a corps of the Army. Before the split occurred the Royal Flying Corps could muster just over 2,000 officers and men; after it, at the beginning of the war, the Royal Flying Corps was able to send four squadrons to France in support of the British Expeditionary Force, and the Royal Naval Air Service had a total of 54 aircraft on its strength.

To sum up, on the outbreak of war, military air forces were new and largely untried, and the generals and admirals had, for the most part, only a vague idea of the tasks they expected them to perform. Where their ideas were more clearly defined, they looked to aircraft to provide them with up-to-date reconnaissance reports. But it is true to say that the two older Services had no great faith in the ability of aircraft to further the course of land or sea operations, and none at all in their offensive power.

2　Air Bombardment in World War I

For some months after the outbreak of the First World War all military aircraft were used primarily for reconnaissance. Before long it was realized that airplanes and captive balloons were able to spot the fall of shells with great accuracy, and so could be used to correct and even, on occasions, to control the fire of artillery. So great became the demand for these services that the military aviation of all the belligerent nations began to expand as rapidly as circumstances would allow, and every new unit was immediately absorbed into the work of reconnaissance and artillery spotting.

Soon after the war began, the Royal Flying Corps in France was organized into wings, each wing being placed under the control of an army corps. This decentralization continued throughout the war. As the British Expeditionary Force expanded the corps became armies, and their wings became brigades. By 1916 each of the four armies in France had under its control a brigade of the R. F. C. The French, German, and Italian air forces were at this time also decentralized in much the same way.

All the air forces taking part in the war were equipped at the outset with rather slow two-seater types, but it was not long before fast single-seater airplanes, intended for longer range reconnaissance, began to appear. These aircraft were called "scouts," and they carried no armament. The Germans were the first to turn a "scout" into a "fighter" by equipping their Fokker airplane with a fixed ma-

11

chine-gun, firing forward in the line of flight. An interrupter gear was fitted to enable the bullets to pass between the blades of the revolving airscrew. Air fighting then began on a serious scale, as Britain, France, and Italy built various types of fighter aircraft. But in spite of the Italian experiments in North Africa in 1911, practically no bombing was done by any of the army air forces.

The naval air services were less heavily engaged in cooperation duties, and they were the first to carry out bombing raids. The German Zeppelins raided Britain, and the Royal Naval Air Service carried out five attacks against airship sheds in Germany toward the end of 1914. It was not until January 1915, that the Royal Flying Corps made its first bombing attacks, when Lille railway station and the airship sheds at Ghistelle were attacked. No further attempts at bombing were made by the R. F. C. until just before the Battle of Neuve Chapelle in March.

At this time there was no bombsight available. Bombs were dropped in horizontal flight from as low a level as possible, and were aimed merely by eye. This point-blank bombing exposed the aircraft to machine-gun and rifle fire from the ground, and resulted in many casualties. As the same aircraft were used for bombing and for routine army cooperation work, General Headquarters were reluctant to lose valuable aircraft in this way. In the summer of 1915, R. F. C. Headquarters reviewed the results of bombing up to that time. It was found that while 141 attacks had been made on railway objectives, only three, according to the available evidence, had been successful. As a result of this review, General H. M. Trenchard,[1] commanding the R. F. C. in France, prevailed upon G. H. Q. to lay down

that the present spasmodic efforts against unsuitable or unimportant objects will be discontinued. Aeroplanes will not be used by Armies in attempts to influence local situations by bombing railway stations and junctions. Sustained attacks with a view to interrupting the enemy's railway communications will be ordered by G. H. Q. in conjunction with the main operations of the Allied Armies. Special squadrons are being trained for this purpose.

This appears to be the first, if rather indirect, allusion to the principle of concentration as applied to bombing, and also the first

[1] Later, Marshal of the Royal Air Force Viscount Trenchard.

reference to sustained attacks and specialized bomber squadrons. We can also see the first serious attempt by G. H. Q. to centralize the control of bombers in order to prevent their misuse by subordinate formations. Unfortunately this attempt was not successful.

Before the Battle of Loos in September 1915, an attempt was made to use a co-ordinated bombing effort to disorganize the German communications behind the battle zone. An ambitious plan was devised, which provided for the attack of the German railway system from La Fere northward to the Channel coast. For this, the efforts of the R. F. C., the R. N. A. S. at Dunkirk, and of the French aviation corps were to be co-ordinated. Some 35 targets were listed, and as the total weight of bombs dropped was no more than 5½ tons, there was certainly no concentration. A study of the German official archives shows that although numerous bombing attacks on railway stations, junctions, and sidings were recorded only two were successful. At Wallers station a local passenger train was hit and damaged, and at Valenciennes two ammunition trains were hit. Twenty wagons exploded and traffic was temporarily suspended.

The bombing attacks were unsuccessful in preventing the movement of reserves from the Lille-Valenciennes district to the Loos front. The German records admit that, in several instances, the transport of troops and material was made more difficult by these attacks, but these difficulties were overcome with comparative rapidity, and all units and formations called up to reinforce the battle area arrived at their destinations on time.

These results were not encouraging, but it must be remembered that air bombardment was still in its infancy. Each aircraft carried only one or two 112 lb. bombs, and each bomb, consisting of a heavy cast-iron casing and a small charge of explosive, did not do a great deal of damage. Although by now a simple type of bombsight was in use, the observer's view of the target was far from good and the standard of bombing accuracy was poor. But, even making allowances for all these shortcomings, the plan was not a success. Its chief fault was lack of concentration; far too many targets were attacked. If the whole weight of the attack—and 5½ tons is not a heavy attack by any standards—had been directed at the key point of the railway junction at Valenciennes, the results would no doubt have been better.

In December 1915, R. F. C. Headquarters issued a paper on bombing policy. It stated that

*the go-as-you-please methods have been abandoned definitely both by
the French and by ourselves in favour of attacks carried out by
swarms of aeroplanes. It is now an accepted principle that attacks on
all important objectives should be carried out by as many aeroplanes
as possible, all the aeroplanes flying together and reaching the objective together. . . . Attacks on trains in motion appear to be the single
exception to the swarm formation. . . . The French fly at varying
heights, and this undoubtedly increases the difficulties of the A. A.
gunner. Varying heights of 6000 ft. and over have proved satisfactory.
The chances of one areoplane bombing another one are so small as
to be neglible.*

The leader of the swarm was equipped with a simple bombsight[2]
but the rest were generally without one, and simply dropped their
bombs when they saw the leader drop his. This resulted in the bombs
falling in a very wide pattern, suitable only for large targets.

By the spring of 1916 the armies were taking a greater interest
in bombing, and were demanding more of it. There was a growing
tendency to divert aircraft from their normal task of army cooperation which, if the objectives had been well chosen, might not have
been a bad thing. Unfortunately the targets were usually too small
and too numerous to produce good results. Matters were brought to
a head by a disastrous attempt to bomb a small, and quite unimportant, railway junction at Carvin on March 9, 1916. It took place in
bad weather; little or no damage was done to the target, and of the
31 aircraft taking part, only five regained their airfields. The remainder
were shot down or made forced landings; many crashed in northern
France, two in the Channel, and one actually in southern England.
Shortly after this, restrictions were imposed by G. H. Q. which put
a stop to organized bombing until the preparations for the Somme
battle in July 1916.

These restrictions further reduced the possibility of conducting
experiments in bombing, and made it more difficult to effect improvements in technique or tactics. But the Army had become so dependent on air cooperation for reconnaissance and artillery spotting that
it required the employment of every aircraft available; bombing

[2] See Appendix C.

attacks could only be made at the expense of that cooperation.

At the opening of the Battle of the Somme the R. F. C. was organized in four brigades—one allotted to each Army—and the 9th Wing, which was under the operational control of R. F. C. Headquarters. Each brigade consisted of two wings—one composed of army cooperation squadrons, and the other of fighter and bomber squadrons. The 9th Wing consisted of fighter and bomber squadrons, and was a centralized reserve which could be employed wherever it was most needed.

The German air force, which was excessively decentralized at the beginning of the war, had by now been reorganized and brought under the dircet control of their General Headquarters. But the French aviation corps was even more completely decentralized, under the control of subordinate military formations, than was the R. F. C.

The renewal of bombing which prefaced the Somme battle was not a success. There was no attempt at concentration in time or space, and indeed it was in many ways little more than a repetition of the attempts before Loos to disrupt the German railway communications. Twenty-eight aircraft were given the task of denying access by rail to the area in front of the 4th Army. Their primary object was to find and attack trains in motion, with the idea of blocking the lines by derailments and, if no trains could be found, to attack the railway stations at Cambrai, Busigny, and St. Quentin. This meant that single aircraft were wandering about well behind the front in search of trains, and the British fighter protection was insufficient. Ten aircraft were lost in the first three days and the plan was abandoned.

The German records show that there was no serious interruption to their movements as a result of this bombing. One aircraft, however, dropped its bombs on St. Quentin station when two battalions were detraining. The bombs hit an ammunition train which caused heavy explosions. A locally serious situation followed, as the troops dispersed rapidly. A large part of their equipment was lost, and they had to be sent back to their depot to refit.

It is obvious that the 28 aircraft, even if adequate fighter protection had been forthcoming, had been set a task far beyond their powers.

The failure to provide adequate fighter support for the bombers was a direct consequence of the decentralized organization of the

R. F. C. The Germans, having a centralized control of their air forces, were able quickly to concentrate a large part of their fighter strength in the battle zone, whereas the R. F. C. had in the area only the brigade allotted to the 4th Army, on whose front the battle was being fought. As time went on this situation became steadily worse, and the brigades belonging to the disengaged armies were ordered to carry out bombing attacks on their own fronts, in the hope of drawing off enemy fighters from the Somme area. This idea is clearly apparent from a report written by General Trenchard at this time:

There are very few German aircraft opposite the 1st, 2nd, and 3rd Army fronts (i.e. the disengaged fronts) but I hope the result of our air work during the last two days will induce the enemy to send some of his fighters back again.

His hopes were not fufilled; the Germans, very naturally, concentrated their air forces opposite the 4th Army front, where the battle was being fought, leaving as few aircraft as possible opposite the disengaged armies. The R. F. C. was unable to concentrate its own forces on the 4th Army front, because the armies, whether engaged or not, would not give up their aircraft. Since this decentralization destroyed the power of G. H. Q. to bring about concentrations of air effort, they had to fall back on the unsatisfactory expedient of ordering air activity on the disengaged fronts in the hope of inducing the Germans to disperse their own concentration.

The shortage of fighter aircraft on the 4th Army front moved G. H. Q. to ask the Admiralty to lend them some of the naval fighter squadrons, based around Dunkirk, which were almost without employment. The Admiralty agreed, and eight fighter squadrons of the R. N. A. S. were sent to the Somme, where they did much to restore the situation.

Soon after the beginning of the Somme battle there arrived in France several squadrons equipped with specialized long-distance bomber aircraft. In view of the unsatisfactory situation in the air at this time, they were mainly employed in attacks against enemy airfields. This is the first example of any serious attempt to use bombers to influence the air situation. Unfortunately, instead of concentrating against a few of the more important airfields, almost every known landing-ground seems to have been sprinkled, with the result that the German air force suffered little material or moral damage.

In March 1917, careful plans were made for an air offensive before the Battle of Arras. The object of these operations was twofold: to cause the enemy to withdraw his fighting aircraft from the battle front, and to interfere with his railway communications at a time when he was likely to be bringing up reinforcements. Here we see a divided policy; the R. F. C. wanted to use bombing for strategic effect, to draw off or pin down enemy fighters and throw the enemy air forces on to the defensive, while the Army commanders, who controlled the great majority of the squadrons capable of bombing, wanted to use them for tactical purposes on their own limited fronts. There was therefore a continuous conflict of policy between R. F. C. Headquarters and the armies, with the result that the bombers were never allowed to be concentrated on a task which was within their power to perform successfully.

At the third Battle of Ypres, the bombing was mainly directed against the enemy airfields. The idea seemed to be to keep as many airfields as possible under fire. For instance, on the day before the battle began, orders were given to attack fifteen airfields by four squadrons of fighters, and nine by three squadrons of bombers.

During the first three years of the war, whenever the enemy was troublesome in the air, there was a strong tendency to attack his airfields. The policy, however, never proved very successful.

There was nothing inherently wrong or unreasonable about the policy, though it is strategically defensive and justifiable only as a temporary diversion from the main offensive task. The failure was due to the fact that the policy was seldom properly implemented. Indeed on a few occasions in 1918 when German airfields—notably Boulay and Morange—were properly attacked by a combined bomber and fighter force, the results were good. And a well-planned and concentrated German attack on the airfield at Bertangles, near Amiens, in May 1918, put No. 48 Squadron out of the war for several weeks.

It is clear that by the end of the third year of the war, little progress had been made in the practice of air bombardment. Although R. F. C. Headquarters had realized the importance of concentration, the decentralized organization of the R. F. C. made its achievement impossible. The British Government was feeling far from satisfied that its air forces were organized in the most efficient way. Apart from the situation in France, there were two other aspects of British air organization which had proved defective, and were causing considerable anxiety.

The R. N. A. S. had been built up successfully to a very substantial size. It had few contacts with the enemy, and its casualty rate was low. Many of its squadrons were almost unemployed. The R. F. C., on the other hand, was more than fully employed. Its casualty rate was high, and it had been unable to expand rapidly enough to meet all its commitments. There was thus a surplus of air forces on the naval side, and a deficiency on the army side.

In addition, the Germans had been carrying out bombing attacks against targets in Britain, at first with Zeppelins by night, but later with airplanes in daylight as well. The air defenses had been relatively ineffective, and this had been the subject of a good deal of public criticism. The main difficulty was that there was no centralized authority responsible for air defense. It was shared between the Admiralty and the War Office, and each tended to blame the other when things went wrong.

In these circumstances the government decided to overhaul the organization of British air power, and they asked General Smuts, of South Africa, to survey the whole situation and make recommendations.

On August 17, 1917, General Smuts submitted his report to the British Government. He proposed that

an Air Ministry be instituted as soon as possible, consisting of a Minister with a consultative board on the lines of the Army Council or Admiralty Board, on which the several departmental activities of the Ministry will be represented. This Ministry to control and administer all matters in connection with aerial warfare of all kinds whatsoever, including lighter-than-air as well as heavier-than-air craft. . . . That the Air Ministry and Staff proceed to work out the arrangements necessary for the amalgamation of the Royal Naval Air Service and the Royal Flying Corps and the legal constitution and discipline of the new air service, and to prepare the necessary draft legislation and regulations. . . . That the air service remain in intimate touch with the Army and Navy by the closest liaison, or by direct representation of both on the Air Staff, and that, if necessary, the arrangements for close cooperation between the three services be revised from time to time.

The British Government accepted the report, and the Royal Air Force, under the control of an Air Ministry, came into being on April 1, 1918.

By this time the war was nearing its end, but during the last seven months several important changes in air organization were put into effect. Relatively idle units in the former R. N. A. S. were given active tasks, and British air power was more efficiently distributed. The effectiveness of British air defense was greatly improved, and raiding by German airships and airplanes soon ceased.

But by far the most important innovation was the setting up of a long-range bomber force, called the Independent Air Force. Its aim was the strategic air bombardment of enemy vital centers. It was situated in rear of the French armies to emphasize its independence from the control of G. H. Q., British Expeditionary Force, and the targets allocated to it were German centers of production and communication. Apart from the occasional attack of airship sheds by the R. N. A. S., this was the first time that targets in Germany itself had been attacked—hitherto, all targets had been in occupied France or Belgium.

The Independent Air Force was formed by an expansion of the 9th Wing, the old R. F. C. Headquarters reserve formation. It was placed under the command of General Trenchard, and Major-General J. M. Salmond[3] took over the command of the Royal Air Force at G. H. Q. Although there were great plans for the expansion of this force, there was not enough time for them to come to fruition, and by the end of the war it possessed only 11 squadrons. It was mainly equipped with variants of the D. H. 4. and D. H. 9., which had a radius of action of about 100 miles, and a bomb load of about 500 lbs. so that it was by no means a powerful force.

Some of its attacks against targets in the Ruhr and Rhineland were successful—far more successful than any previous attempts at air bombardment—but it cannot be said that it produced decisive, or even very positive, results. It irritated the German Government, had some effect on German morale, and drew off some of the fighter squadrons from the Western front to strengthen the German home defense.

Had the war not ended in November 1918, there were plans to bombard important centers in Germany, including Berlin, using

[3] Now Marshal of the R. A. F. Sir John Salmond.

long-range four-engined Handley Page bombers based in England,
each carrying a load of 2,000 lbs. of bombs or more. Larger bombs,
up to 1,650 lbs. in weight, were being developed. But this force
could not be made ready before the spring of 1919, and so it never
came into action.

The Russians, then as now, were secretive and rather un-coopera-
tive, and little was known about their ideas or their equipment. But
in general they relied on vast numbers, using weapons and transport
that were primitive even by the standards of 1914. They suffered
from bad leadership and worse administration. At the outset they
suffered a shattering defeat at the battles of Tannenberg and the
Masurian Lakes, and they never recovered the initiative. From the
beginning of the war until their final collapse in 1917, their air forces
carried out very little in the way of bombardment.

The French concentrated on short-range tactical bombing under
the control of subordinate military formations, and there is no reason to believe that their results in this field were any better than
were those of the R. F. C. The Germans did very little tactical bombing, but when they did so they always concentrated and were usually
successful.

When the United States entered the war in April 1917, their air
forces were still very small. But in 1916, foreseeing the possibility of
becoming involved in the war, Congress passed a National Defense
Act which increased the strength of the Aviation Section and established a reserve of officers and men. The War Department authorized
an increase of the Army Air Arm to seven squadrons, and shortly
before America entered the war a plan was prepared for an increase
to twenty squadrons.

Only when war broke out did the United States fully realize the
extent to which they had fallen behind Europe in the development
of military aviation. Not only was its air service small, but it had few
aircraft fit for war service. An enormous production plan was at
once put in hand, but it was not possible, in little more than eighteen
months, for it to be fully implemented. A considerable number of
pilots and observers were trained, but the most important American
contribution was undoubtedly the Liberty engine. It was produced
in great numbers, and was used as the power-plant of the British-
designed D. H. 9a. which was the best of the Allied bomber aircraft.

It was proposed that the United States air forces should be divided into two groups. One was to consist of squadrons engaged in close support of the Army, and the other was to undertake strategic operations at long range. The bomber and fighter—or, in American terminology, the bombardment and pursuit—units of this force were to have an independent mission, and were to carry the war into the skies over the enemy country. Although this excellent plan was accepted in principle, the war ended before it could be put into effect.

It took nearly a year for the United States air forces to reach the point at which they could provide air support for their armies and, like the newly formed Royal Air Force, it was in action for little more than seven months. During this period the United States bomber aircraft carried out 150 bombing attacks, dropping a total of 138 tons of bombs. Many of these raids were on distant targets, sometimes as far as 160 miles behind the front line.

The war ended without providing any convincing proof of the offensive power of aircraft. It had been shown that bombers could penetrate the enemy defenses, up to the limit of their radius of action, but it had proved impossible, owing to weather conditions and other factors, to achieve the concentrated and sustained attacks that could have been effective. The senior officers of the two older Services, in all countries, had no faith in the ability of aircraft successfully to carry out independent missions. They believed that air forces could make their most valuable contribution by acting in close support of sea and land operations.

Those who believed otherwise found it difficult to produce convincing evidence to support their views. Air bombardment had not, during the war, proved to be very effective. It is true that there were good reasons for this; most of the Allied bombing had suffered from lack of concentration, and from the selection of unsuitable targets. But few people were impressed by these arguments; the plain fact was that air bombardment had never, on any occasion, produced a decisive effect.

But those who believed in the offensive power of aircraft were able to quote the words of General Smuts, a very able man endowed with remarkable vision, who said in his report:

Air power can be used as an independent means of war operations. Nobody that witnessed the attack on London on 11th July (1917) could have any doubt on that point. Unlike artillery, an air fleet can conduct extensive operations far from, and independently of, both Army and Navy. As far as can at present be foreseen there is absolutely no limit to the scale of its future independent war use. And the day may not be far off when aerial operations with their devastation of enemy lands and destruction of industrial and populous centres on a vast scale may become the principal operations of war, to which the older forms of military operations may become secondary and subordinate.

These were truly prophetic words, and today they have been completely fulfilled; but in the difficult years that followed the end of the First World War that day, to many, must have seemed very far off indeed.

Part II

THE YEARS BETWEEN

3 The Third Dimension in War

It is not surprising that so radical a change as the introduction of the third dimension into war, by the development of submarines and aircraft, should have given rise to many urgent problems. The most pressing and obvious of these related to the organization and operation of these new weapons, but their influence on military strategy and on the psychology of civilian populations was profound and far-reaching.

War had been two-dimensional since its earliest beginnings, and a number of military doctrines had grown up which had been in existence for so long that they had usurped the status of principles. Chief among these was the doctrine which has become known as the classical doctrine, evolved by Napoleon and authoritatively put into words by Clausewitz.[1] It was fully accepted and supported by every military writer of importance from that time until the outbreak of the First World War.

This doctrine, as originally formulated, laid down that "the destruction of the enemy's military force was the leading principle in war." In more modern terms, it was taken to mean that the aim in war must always be the destruction of the armed forces of the enemy.

As long as war was fought in two dimensions the classical doctrine was completely valid. Since a fleet could operate only on the surface of the sea, it was not practicable for it to avoid the sea forces of

[1] General Karl von Clausewitz: 1780-1831.

25

the enemy and proceed to blockade an enemy's coasts or bombard his ports. If such action were attempted, a fleet might be caught in an unfavorable tactical position and destroyed. Similarly, an army, able to move only on the surface of the land, could not evade the opposing army and advance into enemy territory and occupy his key points. If an attempt were made to do so, an army would be exposed to dangerous flank attacks and its communications might be cut with disastrous results. Therefore neither fleets nor armies could achieve their objects until they had destroyed or crippled the opposing fleets or armies.

During the First World War the German High Command, making use of the weapons which could operate in three dimensions, began to depart from the classical doctrine. The campaign carried out by the German U-boats against the merchant shipping of the Allies, and not primarily against their warships, was one example. Attacks by Zeppelins and later airplanes against centers of war production or densely populated areas, were another. These were attacks, not against the armed forces of the Allies, but against the production and transport of their war materials. The operations of the British Independent Air Force against German industrial and railway centers in the Ruhr and Rhineland in 1918 had a similar object. Toward the end of the war the idea appeared of deliberately using air attacks in attempts to influence the morale of the enemy population.

All these operations were made possible because submarines and aircraft could make use of the third dimension to evade the enemy's armed forces and strike directly at any objective.

But it must not be supposed that the Allied war leaders realized the significance of these deviations from the classical doctrine, or that they had begun to question its validity. On the contrary, they insisted that it was unaffected by the introduction of forces capable of operating in three dimensions. The German departures from the strict application of the doctrine were condemned as unorthodox and unethical. They were regarded as breaches of the rules of war and offenses against international law.

It is worth pausing a moment here to inquire how these rules of war came into existence, and what is meant by the term "international law." In feudal times, when land was held in return for personal service under arms, resort to war could, and often did, have serious economic consequences. Food was seldom plentiful and, although the petty kings and dukes and counts were continually quarreling and trying to enlarge their domains at their neighbor's expense, they could not take farmers and peasants away from their tasks to serve in private armies without risking hardship, poverty, and even famine. These mischiefs might well outweigh anything that could be gained by continuing the fighting. Wars of long duration, therefore, usually occurred only when some important religious or ideological principle was involved. A good example of such a war is to be found in the Crusades, which so severely depleted the ranks of European chivalry.

The feudal system gradually merged into the monarchical order in Europe, and the state came into being. Its goverment commuted into money payments the obligations of its subjects to give personal military service. These payments, and other taxes, put into the hands of the government new wealth and power. To replace the former feudal liability for military service standing armies were created, which were mainly composed of professional soldiers—men who would sell their services to the highest bidder. Standing armies it was said—rather unkindly, perhaps, but not without truth—were recruited from all the indolent swashbucklers that governments could pick up in their own or any other country.

The standing army became an important and valuable piece of state property, the destruction of which was not lightly to be risked. It was regarded mainly as an instrument of policy, to strengthen the hands of the government in diplomatic negotiation, and as a security force, to prevent the erosion of the frontiers by land-hungry neighboring states.

With its garrisons, fortresses, and lines of defense, the standing army tended to become a state within a state, governed by strict conventions and, on the whole, keeping itself apart from the rest of the nation. The professional soldier, who lived by fighting, seldom had any ideological or other feelings about the war in which he might be engaged. He despised fanaticism, and had no intention of getting himself killed unnecessarily. He did not expect his commander to fight a pitched battle except in very favorable circumstances, and for a definite and important object. He was, of course, prepared to gamble on the fortunes of war, but he was usually a competent man-at-arms, with confidence in his own skill, and it should be remembered that the standard of personal security in any profession in those days was not very high.

The professional soldier was very particular about the proper observance of the conventions—the usages and disciplines of war. These conventions were rather like a set of trade union rules, designed to make the profession of soldiering tolerable. Campaigns were conducted during the summer months only, and armies went into winter quarters to escape the discomforts of snow, frost, and floods. The campaigns themselves were largely affairs of maneuver, of marches and countermarches, investitures and sieges, all conducted in a regular manner in accordance with strict and well-understood rules.

Generally speaking, it was against the conventions to attempt to take unfair advantage by unorthodox actions. For example, it was contrary to the usages of war to attack the baggage train or base camp of an enemy. A vivid illustration of the reaction of a professional soldier to a breach of the forms and disciplines of war is to be found in Captain Fluellen's indignant protest in Shakespeare's King Henry V.[2]

These usages, forms, and ceremonies of war were taken very seriously. It is strange, and even amusing, to read the rigid and punctillious instructions laid down by Jomini, Saxe, Bülow, and other leading exponents of the art of conventional warfare.

A very clear distinction was drawn between combatants and noncombatants. This was comparatively easy, because the ordinary people cared but little who won the war. They did their best to carry on with their normal affairs and keep out of trouble. But the professional soldier expected a bonus in the form of loot now and then, and there were occasions when the civilian inhabitants were plundered and even murdered. Cities were sometimes sacked and the countryside laid waste. But such lapses were exceptional and, on the whole, material destruction was avoided as far as possible and the rights of noncombatants were generally respected.

By the end of the eighteenth century a great change had occurred. The French Revolution, and the rise to power of Napoleon, made war the affair of the whole people, who were inspired by patriotic feelings and a fanatical devotion to their great leader. In France the small professional army, fighting on conventional lines, was replaced

[2] King Henry V, Act IV: Scene VII.

by the *levée en masse*, and the idea of the nation in arms was born. Napoleon's Grande Armée disregarded most of the conventions, and all over Europe it defeated the professional standing armies of other states. Napoleon became master of most of the Continent, until he was faced in the East by the vast spaces and land forces of Russia, and by the sea power of Britain in the West.

Napoleon's victorious campaigns put an end to the old-fashioned European professional standing armies. Britain alone, by virtue of her sea power and island situation, was able to dispense with a large conscript army. The whole system of conventional war was swept away, though some of the conventions survived. War became far more serious and pervaded the whole life of the nation, and a new and more realistic concept of military strategy made its appearance.

This drastic change in the character of war made a deep impression on contemporary students of military affairs. Clausewitz took the view that war had finally escaped the bonds of convention and that in the future, when fought between Great Powers, it would be total and absolute. He saw that total war would involve the whole nation, and that its prosecution, to be successful, must therefore be supported by public opinion. He had no faith in the reliability, in time of war, of international rules or agreements. He insisted that no nation, if faced by the probability of defeat, would allow itself to be bound by rules or restrictions of any kind. He maintained that war, whether anyone liked it or not, was a violent clash between nations in arms, which could never be humanized or civilized, and that if one side attempted to do so, it was likely to be defeated.

Clausewitz clothed in words the theory of war that Napoleon had originated and, in the German philosophic manner, carried it to its logical conclusion. His writings had a very powerful influence on political and military thought, especially in Germany. And today there is plenty of evidence of the truth of his views about the impossibility of making war more humane and less violent.

As long as the conduct of war was governed by the classical doctrine, any restrictions due to international law were relatively slight and unimportant. But when forces capable of using the third dimension became available it was possible, without destroying or crippling the enemy's armed forces, to strike directly at his centers of industry and population, and even at his capital city and seat of government. In fact, ever since the coming of war on a national scale, initiated by

Napoleon, all these things had been legitimate objectives, but in two-dimensional warfare they could not be attacked without first disposing of the enemy's armed forces. But once these forces had been dealt with, these vital centers were captured and occupied by the victorious army. War industries might be demolished or confiscated. Even as recently as 1945, the Russians removed most of the factory equipment and many of the workers from East Germany to the U. S. S. R., to assist in the rehabilitation and expansion of Soviet industry.

In the First World War, all the belligerents became nations in arms. Every fit person was drafted into the armed forces, or given war work of some kind. The distinction between combatants and non-combatants was becoming blurred, for it did not make sense to maintain that the man who drove an ammunition lorry behind the front was a combatant, while the man who made the ammunition or transported it to a theater of war was a noncombatant.

Strictly speaking, there is no such thing as international law. There are international treaties, conventions, and usages—which may be written or unwritten—but none has the force of law, because no sanctions exist to enforce them. Some attempts have been made since the First World War by the League of Nations, and more recently by the United Nations, to use various sanctions to enforce compliance with international law, but with no great success.

There are, however, certain usages, such as the treatment of prisoners of war in accordance with the Geneva Conventions, which it is normally in the interests of all the belligerents to observe. But the evidence seems to show that Clausewitz was right when he said that no nation would observe any rules if, by so doing, it risked defeat in a major war.

At the beginning of the First World War the German war leaders showed that they had accepted the idea of total war to a far greater extent than had those of Britain, France, or Italy. The Allies, in 1914, relied for the protection of their merchant shipping on the rule of international law that laid down that no merchant ship might be sunk at sea unless its crew had been put in a "place of safety," and it had been agreed that a ship's lifeboats were not a place of safety within the meaning of the rule. Had that rule been respected Allied shipping would have been safe from unrestricted attack by German U-boats. The German disregard of the rule found the Allied navies seriously unprepared, and it was not until 1917, after so great a tonnage had been sunk that the Allies were on the brink of disaster, that it was possible to organize an effective defense. The dropping from aircraft of explosive missiles on open towns and industrial centers was also a breach of the accepted rules of international law, as was the use of chlorine and phosgene gas against the Allied troops on the Western front.

Civilian populations, accustomed in two-dimensional warfare to the status of noncombatants, reacted strongly against the bombing from the air of centers of industry and transportation. This reaction was least marked in continental countries, which were used to the idea of wars fought in their territories, but was strong in the United States and strongest of all in Britain.

The island situation of the British people, and their successful reliance on sea power for so many centuries, had encouraged the idea that war was the business of the armed forces, in which the civilian population ought not to be involved. Since the Norman invasion in 1066 all their fighting, apart from a few civil wars—the last of which ended more than three hundred years ago—had been done on the high seas or in other people's countries. The British people were surprised and shocked when the German U-boats began to sink their merchant ships at sight, and they were shocked and angered by the German air attacks on London and other cities and towns. The German airmen were stigmatized as "baby-killers" in the British press, and the operations of the Independent Air Force were justified as reprisals.

Air bombardment, except for strictly tactical purposes, against targets close to the battle zone, was therefore regarded with a deep repugnance because it involved the civilian population in the operations of war. The British citizen took the view that the killing or wounding of uniformed soldiers and sailors in time of war was quite proper, but that the killing or injuring of civilian factory workers engaged in making weapons of war, or the crews of merchant vessels engaged in transporting them or other vital war materials, was wholly unjustifiable. If this is thought to be illogical, it may be pointed out that it is not more so than the acceptance of such weapons as shells, bayonets, bullets, and flame-throwers as legitimate while outlawing relatively humane weapons, such as mustard gas.

The alarm felt by civilian populations at the prospects of air attack was not lessened by the utterances of the prophets of air power. Prominent among these was General Giulio Douhet of the Italian air force, who published in 1921 a very advanced book called *The Command of the Air.* This book gravely offended not only civilians, but also soldiers and sailors throughout the world, and not least in Italy. Douhet laid down, first of all, that the Air Force must be independent of the Army and the Navy. He realized that war had become national and total, and that the entire population and resources of a nation would be "sucked into the maw of war." He saw that air forces could "go far behind the fortified lines of defense without first breaking through them." He understood the unity of the air ocean, and its freedom from all barriers and obstacles.

All the influences [he wrote] which have conditioned and character-ized warfare from the beginning are powerless to affect aerial action. No longer can areas exist in which life can be lived in safety and tranquillity, nor can the battlefield any longer be limited to actual combatants. The battlefield will be limited only by the boundaries of the nations at war, and all of their citizens will become combatants, since all of them will be exposed to the aerial offensives of the enemy. There will be no distinction any longer between soldiers and civilians.

Douhet realized the importance of gaining command of the air at the outset of a war. And he insisted that the classical doctrine, even if still valid for armies and navies, was not applicable to the operation of air forces. He also emphasized the powerful moral effect of heavy air attacks on capital cities and other vital centers.

He fully understood the value of concentration in air operations. He pointed out that during the First World War neither side subjected the other to a really heavy blow, concentrated in time and space. They nibbled at each other, the casualties adding up at the end of four years to an appalling total, but resembling in the manner of their application the Chinese "death of a thousand cuts." He believed that half the damage and casualties inflicted during the war would have sufficed to achieve victory for either side if they could have been accomplished in three months instead of four years. A quarter of it would have been sufficient if it had been inflicted in eight days.

He pointed out that air forces were ideally suited to concentrated attacks, and were well adapted to offensive action. He believed that effective air defenses would be costly and difficult to organize. He advocated concentrated and heavy air attacks against an enemy's centers of industry, transport, and administration, believing that by these means it was possible to bring about an almost complete paralysis of the enemy's power of waging war.

General Douhet suffered the fate of most prophets. He was fiercely attacked in his own country and elsewhere; scorn and ridicule were poured upon his writings, and even some airmen believed that he had gone too far. No doubt he was rather ahead of his time, but everything that has happened since he wrote his book has amply confirmed his theories.

In these circumstances statesmen in many countries began to think in terms of international agreements abolishing, or at least severely restricting, air bombardment except for tactical purposes in a battle zone. The next few years were to see several attempts to achieve a convention on these lines, seeking to curb the power of air forces to carry out independent long-range operations, and to subordinate their activities to the support of land or sea forces.

4 Peace and Its Problems

As soon as the Armistice was signed the Allies hastened to demobilize their greatly expanded armed forces, and to dismantle their improvised war machinery. Neither the British Admiralty nor the War Office thought of the Royal Air Force as anything more than a wartime expedient, and they confidently expected that the Air Ministry, like the Ministry of Munitions, would disappear. With the return to peacetime conditions they both showed a strong tendency to revert to the ideas and organizations prevailing before the war, and even the Tank Corps was severely cut down and neglected. They had little doubt that they would be allowed to divide British air power between them, and re-establish the Royal Flying Corps and the Royal Naval Air Service, in fact, if not in name.

But the Chief of the Air Staff, Air Marshal Sir Hugh Trenchard, held other views, and held them very strongly. During the next few years he had to fight hard for the continued existence of the Royal Air Force as a separate Service. He was perhaps fortunate in that the Admiralty and the War Office, which before 1914 had almost no experience of cooperating with each other, were still too independent to be able to stage a concerted attack on the Air Ministry. First one attacked and then the other, and the arguments they put forward were often contradictory and even tended to cancel each other. Nevertheless, during Trenchard's ten years as Chief of the Air Staff he had to face a long sequence of inquiries at ministerial level into the

34

continued autonomy of the Royal Air Force.

Trenchard's strongest argument was the need for centralized control of air forces, in order to concentrate them at the time and place where, at any given moment, they were most needed. The greatest asset of air forces, their remarkable flexibility, power of concentration, and offensive capacity, would be largely destroyed if they were divided and specialized for cooperation duties with the Army and Navy. As we have seen, it was precisely this weakness which, in the harsh reality of war, had brought about the formation of the Royal Air Force.

But the Admiralty and the War Office had no faith in the offensive power of aircraft. The Admiralty, in particular, refused to admit that aircraft were capable of sinking warships of any kind under operational conditions, and both the older Services took the view that air forces were of value only when used in close support of land or sea operations. They therefore strongly disagreed with Trenchard's idea of a separate air staff, trained at an Air Force Staff College, able to think out the new problems posed by the growth of air power, and to formulate new doctrines for the conduct of air operations.

The greatest weakness of Trenchard's position was that the Royal Air Force was superimposed on the older pattern of defense. Its existence did not make it possible to rely on a smaller Navy or Army, and its cost could not therefore be set off against economies on land or at sea. In these circumstances the taxpayer felt no urge to rally to its support. As soon as the war ended the government had drastically reduced its expenditure on the armed forces—especially the air force—and retrenchment and economy were the watchwords of the Treasury. It seemed probable that before long the government would decide that, however desirable it might be from the strategic point of view, Britain could no longer afford the luxury of a separate Air Ministry.

Trenchard saw clearly that unless the Air Force could find some way of taking over some of the responsibilities now allocated to the Army or the Navy, and so permit a reduction in land or sea forces to compensate for its cost, it would always be vulnerable, and liable to destruction in the pursuit of economy. The Army and the Navy, however, had no intention of allowing the Air Force to assume any of their responsibilities and indeed regarded the idea as ridiculous.

In 1920 the turn of events gave Trenchard the opportunity he was

seeking. Early in the First World War small military forces had been
sent to the Middle East to protect the two main British interests
there, the Anglo-Persian oil fields and their refinery at Abadan, and
the Suez Canal. Before very long the original defensive purpose was
forgotten, and an adventurous offensive policy was adopted. But the
forces available were too weak to support such a policy, and soon ran
into trouble. The Suez defense force, advancing into Palestine, was
sharply defeated at Gaza, while the force in southern Mesopotamia,[1]
thrusting northward along the Tigris, lost the initiative and became
besieged in the town of Kut-el-Amara. These reverses strengthened
the case for sending reinforcements to both theaters, and the British
Government was fascinated by the idea of a war of movement, where
results could be seen, in contrast to the deadly immobility of the
war in Europe. In consequence, the Middle East was strongly reinforced and advances continued on both fronts. Indeed, the Prime
Minister, Mr. Lloyd George, gave much attention to these side-
shows, and on one occasion urged General Allenby to capture Jerusalem "as a Christmas present to the British nation." What the
British nation would do with Jerusalem when they got it, or what
contribution its capture could make toward the defeat of Germany
—the only enemy that mattered—did not seem to have been considered.

The German General Staff were no doubt well satisfied with this
diversion of more than a million men to the Middle East. They were
happy to see their ally, Turkey, able to pin down so vast a force in
a secondary theater, where the war could neither be lost nor won.
When Ludendorff made his last desperate attack on the Western
front in March 1918, he hoped—not without reason—that the de-
nuded forces of the Allies would break under the impact, and that he
would reach the sea at the mouth of the River Somme. Had he succeeded in this, he would have effectively separated the American and
British armies in the north from the French armies in the south, with
the probability of an overwhelming disaster for the Western Allies.

Ludendorff just failed, and the situation was saved. This was
Germany's last throw, and with its failure they realized that they had
lost the war. The defeat of Germany brought about the collapse of
Turkey, but by that time the Allied forces—mainly British—had
conquered almost the whole of the territory, outside Turkey proper,

[1] Now Iraq.

formerly administered by the Ottoman sultans. The areas removed
from Turkish rule were formed into the new states of Palestine,
Transjordan, Iraq, Syria, the Lebanon, the Hejaz, and the Yemen.
Syria and the Lebanon were mandated to France by the League of
Nations, while Iraq, Palestine, and Transjordan came under British
control.

The mandate was a new idea. It meant that a Great Power would
be responsible for the defense, internal security, and the political
and economic development of a new state, and would nurse it until
it was ready for independent status. When this stage was reached,
the Mandatory Power had a duty to report the fact and sponsor its
membership in the League of Nations. After the admission of the
new state to the League, the Mandatory Power would be required
to withdraw its forces, and its future relations with its former protégé
would be defined, it was hoped, by a treaty of friendship and mutual
assistance.

All these countries were politically backward, poorly organized, and
economically weak, and no oil had yet been found anywhere in the
Middle East outside Persia. The new states were not acceptable to
Turkey or to Ibn Saud, then Sheik of Nejd and later King of Saudi
Arabia, and the policy of establishing a Jewish colony in Palestine
was already arousing suspicion and hostility in Arab quarters. In
addition, the peoples of some of the new countries were far from
satisfied with their new conditions, as they had expected too many
benefits to follow from the withdrawal of Turkish rule. They were
especially disgusted to find that it was still necessary to work for a
living.

The people of Britain were also deeply dissatisfied with the situation. They saw a large part of their forces overseas tied down in the
thankless task of defending hundreds of miles of disputed frontiers,
and maintaining law and order among peoples who confused their
new-found liberty with license to indulge in all sorts of crimes and
misdemeanors. The cost to Britain was very considerable, while the
advantages appeared to be insignificant.

When a serious rebellion broke out in Iraq in 1920, putting the
forces there in a position of some difficulty and even danger, there was
a strong outcry in the British press to hand back the mandates to
the League of Nations, evacuate the troops, and let the Middle East
go its own way. But the British Government was reluctant to with-

draw because it knew that if it did so the whole area would be submerged in a welter of war. It did not wish to expose the new countries to this ordeal, and in particular it was unwilling to abandon the vigorous and growing Jewish settlement in Palestine to expulsion or annihilation at the hands of the Arabs.

The dilemma was serious, and a ministerial conference, under Mr. Winston Churchill,[2] was convened in Cairo to investigate the situation and make recommendations. The estimate for the land forces needed to restore and keep order in the mandated territories would have made large demands on Britain's financial resources and manpower, and it was highly improbable that public support would be forthcoming for such a policy.

Trenchard offered a way out of the deadlock. He proposed that a system of air control of undeveloped countries should be instituted which promised, if successful, to cut the cost to a small fraction of that required by the army method of control, and which would make very minor demands on British manpower. The system was, however, untried and its adoption would involve some degree of risk.

The Cairo Conference decided to accept the risk and give the air control method a trial. It was agreed to make a start with Iraq and Transjordan and, if successful, to extend it to other suitable territories.

In 1922, the Air Force took over in Iraq and Transjordan. All British land forces, except one mixed brigade of British and Indian troops, some native levies, and a few squadrons of armored cars manned by the R. A. F., were withdrawn from the two countries.

The Royal Air Force allocated eight squadrons, including two long-range bomber-transport squadrons, which proved most valuable, to the garrison of Iraq, and one squadron to Transjordan. The air officer commanding in Iraq, and the senior Air Force officer in Transjordan, commanded all the forces in their respective countries. All land forces, except police, were reduced to the minimum and concentrated in central garrisons. The air forces were deployed on suitable airfields which could be protected against attacks on the ground. It was usually convenient, therefore, to station the troops at the air bases.

Under the old system of control, when disorders occurred that could not be dealt with by local police forces or military posts, a column of troops had to be sent from the nearest large cantonment

[2] At that time Secretary of State for War, and, temporarily, for Air also.

to the seat of the trouble. Since the cost of such an expedition was considerable, the decision to dispatch it was liable to be postponed until the disorders had reached dangerous proportions.

As soon as the column left it began to meet with opposition, because the inhabitants of the territories through which it had to pass in order to reach the scene of the disorders would usually oppose its passage. They did so partly because they had guilty consciences and feared that the troops intended to punish them, partly because they resented the intrusion of the troops on principle, and partly because they rather enjoyed fighting and hoped for loot in the form of rifles, ammunition, and so forth.

The troops therefore had to fight their way against people with whom they had no quarrel, and when after a slow and well-advertised journey they arrived at the offending village they would find the houses empty and everything of value removed. The sole means of punishing the offenders was to burn or destroy their houses, the only things they could not take away with them.

The column would then have to fight its way back home, and any serious miscalculation of ammunition or food supplies might—and sometimes did—bring about disaster. The military history of the North-West Frontier of India contains many examples of columns severely mauled and even annihilated.

Under the method of air control, when the police or the local political officer reported the beginnings of unrest, action could be taken at once at negligible cost and the trouble nipped in the bud. The offenders would be ordered to submit themselves for trial in a court of law. If they assented, well and good; but if they refused or committed further outrages a warning would be sent telling them that, on a certain date, their village would be bombed. They were told that they should evacuate their village and that it would not be safe for them to return until they were prepared to submit to the process of law.

On the day appointed the village would be bombed, but it was unnecessary, and indeed undesirable, to cause any serious damage. Occasionally the house or fort of a persistent malefactor would be selected for destruction, and this required a very high degree of bombing accuracy. An air blockade of the village, by means of intermittent light attacks—there was no need for heavy bombing—would then be instituted. Sooner or later the interruption of their daily life, the desire to return to the shelter of their homes and cultivate the land, and the impossibility of seeing any hope of ending their predicament, would bring about the surrender of the most intransigent lawbreakers. Then a body of police or troops would be flown in, accompanied by medical staff, to restore order, quell looting, bind up wounds, cure disease, distribute food, if necessary, and generally to rehabilitate the area.

Properly applied, air control never failed. Damage and casualties on both sides were negligible, and after the system had been in force for some time the threat of air action was usually sufficient to secure compliance with the law.

The opponents of air control had predicted that the use of the bomb, which they stigmatized as violent and brutal, would leave a legacy of hatred and ill-will. In fact, nothing of the sort happened, and airmen were held in great respect. No airman who fell into tribal hands during air control operations was killed or even ill-treated. And the author can testify, from personal experience, that the inhabitants of a village that had been bombed often took a lively pleasure in pointing out the results of accurate bomb-aiming, and that their whole attitude was entirely without rancor.

The truth is that the crews of aircraft engaged in air control operations, unlike columns of troops in tribal territory, enjoy so high a degree of security that they are never in a position of acute peril, or forced to fight for their lives. They are therefore able to adopt the ideal method of applying only the minimum force needed to achieve the object. Their operations, being free from the need for violence born of fear or despair, could be and were restrained, merciful, and reasonable. Moreover, because aircraft could fly freely over the heads of all the inhabitants of the country, they were not brought into conflict with any people not concerned in the dispute.

During the ten years of air control in Iraq, which ended with the surrender of the mandate and the entry of Iraq into the League of Nations, a standard of internal and external security, higher than the country had known for centuries, was maintained at a very low cost in lives, money, and effort. This genuine pacification brought growing prosperity, with irrigation schemes, improved communications, and finally the discovery of oil.

The success of air control in Iraq and Transjordan led to its extension to the Aden Protectorate. Since the end of the First World

War, the former Imam of Sana'a, who was installed as ruler of the Yemen after the withdrawal of the Turks in 1918, had been attacking and bullying the small sultanates and sheikdoms of the Protectorate, and even annexing parts of their territory. These rulers all had treaties of protection, mostly signed in Queen Victoria's reign, but it was proving impossible to give them the support which they had a right to expect. A plan was drawn up, but it required the provision of land forces on a scale, and at a cost, which neither the British nor the Indian governments would accept. A small air control operation was staged in 1925, which was very successful in checking an attempt at further encroachment by the Yemen, and in 1928 a system of air control under an air force commander was set up. This, with modifications, is still in force today.

The proved effectiveness and economy of air control in the areas in which it had been tried led to an attempt to employ it on the North-West Frontier of India where the conditions, apart from one difficulty, were ideally suited to it. But that difficulty proved insuperable. Although such operations as were entrusted to the Air Force were uniformly successful and economical, the Army and its system were far too deeply entrenched, and all the forces in India were under an Army commander-in-chief. The great majority of the experienced civilian administrators wished to adopt air control methods, but the Army consistently frustrated such attempts, and they came to nothing.

In general, the success of the system of air control of undeveloped countries was both immediate and lasting. Its efficacy and humanity attracted the support of the governors and administrators of such territories, while its marked economy made a strong appeal to the British Treasury.

The system was, however, bitterly attacked by many people who had an instinctive horror of air operations, and especially of bombing. Most of these people were honest and well-meaning, though hardly any of them had the faintest idea of how the system worked. They were reinforced by a group, less naïve, which had vested interests in the older methods of control by land forces. The air control system was often publicly condemned as unworthy of a civilized people, and accusations of quelling disorders by "indiscriminate bombing" were made by those who should, and indeed sometimes did, know better. But the demonstrable saving in lives and the improvement in public order where air control had been instituted, and the even more telling financial economy, blunted these attacks and the system was able to survive.

By finding work for the Air Force within the pattern of the British system of defense, which substituted air power for land power instead of merely adding to it, and which performed the task more humanely, efficiently, and economically, Trenchard's system of air control had a very powerful influence in stabilizing the position of the Royal Air Force as a separate Service. While this was of immense value, and had a vital bearing on Britain's ability to survive the opening phases of the Second World War, the system encouraged the specialization of the training and equipment of the Royal Air Force along lines that seriously prejudiced its effectiveness in a major war. The Air Ministry was too short of money to be able to keep bomber squadrons in being, except as part of the garrisons of air controlled territories. And so it came about that for a number of years all British bomber aircraft, bombsights, bombs, and the training of bomber crews, were specialized for use in air control operations. Since these operations were carried out from a low height, against no air opposition, little attention was paid to performance at high altitude or to defensive armament. No great efficiency was demanded from the small types of bomb that were adequate for air control purposes. The crews were trained to bomb into wind, taking a long straight run at the target, and they became used to tactical methods that would be out of the question in a major war. On the other hand map-reading, navigation, target identification, and bombing accuracy were all of great importance, and much valuable progress was made in these directions. The need for a good view for the bomb-aimer was early appreciated, and the prone position was developed in No. 45 Squadron in 1923 by Squadron Leader A. T. Harris.[3]

Since the air blockade could be maintained during the hours of darkness by the use of bombs fitted with delayed action fuses, night operations were also neglected although a certain number of night-bombing attacks in Iraq were undertaken, with some success, by No. 45 Squadron.

But if the preservation of the Royal Air Force as a separate Service had resulted in its bombing activities becoming specialized along the

[3] Now Marshal of the R. A. F. Sir Arthur Harris, Commander-in-Chief, Bomber Command, 1942-1945.

lines needed for successful air control operations, the development of military aviation in France and the United States was retarded by its subordination to the two older Services. French air power, divided into army and navy air forces, was specialized for the support of land or sea operations, and was strictly under the control of military and naval commanders. For example, in the Riff War in North Africa in 1924-1926, a tough campaign against a serious rebellion, nine squadrons of aircraft were used entirely in the close support of land forces. In the words of General Armengaud: "Their duty was to proceed en masse to the support of each mobile column whenever it was in difficulties—that is to say—whenever it moved." The air forces were used solely for the immediate protection of the columns, and on many occasions they were allocated tasks for which airplanes were unsuitable. Thus we find that large numbers of aircraft were continually employed on such duties as flank guards in the presence of thirteen squadrons of cavalry, and for short-range bombardment of enemy positions before an infantry attack in the presence of twenty-three batteries of artillery. Because the troops were allowed to become tactically dependent on close air support, the whole air force was dragged into the defensive. It was the only force at the disposal of Marshal Lyautey, the Commander-in-Chief, which was able to take and maintain the offensive, yet it was given a task that tied it by the leg to troops struggling as much against topography and the weather as against the enemy. Consequently the Air Force lost its liberty of action and offensive power, and, by becoming a rather indifferent substitute for cavalry and artillery, robbed itself of its power of influencing to any marked extent the course of the war.

This misemployment of aircraft was the main cause of the serious difficulties encountered by the French in this war, which in July 1925 became so critical that the Commander-in-Chief contemplated evacuating Fez and retiring on Rabat. Large land reinforcements were needed to restore the position, and the cost to the French, in lives and money, was very great. A study of the circumstances makes it clear that a properly planned use of the French bomber forces in an offensive role in the early stages would have brought the situation under control, and avoided the need for a long-drawn-out and expensive land campaign.

The explanation of Marshal Lyautey's failure to use his air forces offensively, and for his general misdirection of the air effort, may be found in the fact that he had no air staff officers at his headquarters, nor indeed at any level in the forces under his command. He and his subordinate commanders were unable to think about the employment of air forces, or air bombardment, except in terms of the close support of mobile columns.

In the United States the Navy Air Service does not appear to have chafed unduly at its subordination to the United States Navy, but the Army Air Corps took a very different view. Although it was a part of the United States Army, by the end of the First World War its leaders had begun to build up doctrines at variance with those of the War Department. There were three main trends discernible at this stage. First, the example of the Royal Air Force encouraged a desire to establish a separate air force. Secondly, mainly inspired by Brigadier-General "Billy" Mitchell, there was a deep appreciation of the value of strategic air bombardment, which in the autonomous Royal Air Force had largely been lost sight of owing to its preoccupation with the air control of undeveloped countries. Thirdly, there was a strong urge to develop a heavy long-range bomber capable of waging a strategic air offensive.

After the First World War the United States cut down its defense appropriations, with a consequent struggle between the Services for as large a share as possible. The Navy wanted a powerful fleet of modern battleships, while the War Department was determined to build a sound Regular Army capable of rapid expansion in an emergency. In this concept, the air forces were divided and allocated to the support of the land and sea forces. The able and enthusiastic younger leaders of the Air Corps were thoroughly dissatisfied with this organization, for they believed that their corps should be free to think out its own combat doctrines, develop its own equipment, and direct its own forces in battle. Such views were sternly discouraged by the War and Navy Departments.

The Army Air Corps found a powerful champion in Brigadier-General Mitchell, Assistant Chief of the Army Air Corps from 1919 to 1925, an experienced and practical airman of great ability and a very forcible personality. Recognizing the traditional importance of sea power in the United States defense organization, Mitchell concentrated his attacks mainly against the Navy. He claimed that aircraft could sink any warship by means of bombs or torpedoes, but his repeated requests for suitable target ships, against which to test his theories, met with no response. In 1920 the Navy, as an alternative, staged somewhat unconvincing tests under its own conditions, but mounting pressure from Congress compelled it to give way. In July 1921, three former German warships, the battleship *Ostfriesland*, the cruiser *Frankfurt*, and a destroyer, were allocated for bombing trials off the mouth of the Chesapeake. Mitchell hurriedly assembled a bomber force, and sank all three ships. There was much argument about the validity of these experiments—which had been directed by the Navy—but no one could deny the fact of the sinkings. Mitchell went on to conduct further tests, sinking the old U. S. battleships *Alabama* in September 1921, and *Virginia* and *New Jersey* in 1923.

These experiments aroused much interest, not only in the United States but throughout the world and especially in Britain. Mitchell made full use of them as a text for his continued agitation for the establishment of a separate air service, though he agreed that a unified Defense Department, controlling co-equal naval, land, and air forces would be acceptable. The violence of this agitation led, in 1925, to Mitchell's removal from the office of Assistant Chief and his banishment to the Eighth Corps Area at San Antonio. But Mitchell was too ardent to bear exile in patience, and he published a statement in the press, on the occasion of the loss of the naval airship *Shenandoah*, accusing Army and Navy chiefs of neglecting, and even sabotaging, military aviation. He was recalled to Washington and tried by general court martial on charges of insubordination. The trial aroused much heat and was given great publicity. Mitchell was found guilty and suspended from duty for five years, and before long he resigned from the Army.

This tragic end to a brilliant career, selflessly devoted to the interests of the Air Corps, removed Mitchell to the sidelines, but his ideas were not scotched. In his first book on air power *Our Air Force: The Keystone of National Defense* he had put forward, as early as 1921, the idea of strategic air bombardment, conducted independently of land or sea operations; and in his *Winged Defense*, published in 1925, he had insisted that air power had brought with it a new doctrine of war, and that the basis of air power was the bomber aircraft. In his last book, *Skyways*, written in 1930, Mitchell strongly attacked the classical doctrine that the object in war must always be the defeat or destruction of the armed forces of the enemy. He said:

The advent of air power which can go straight to the vital centers and entirely neutralize or destroy them has put a completely new complexion on the old system of war. It is now realized that the hostile main army in the field is a false objective and the real objectives are the vital centers. The old theory that victory meant the destruction of the hostile main army, is untenable.[4]

Mitchell was one of the great prophets of air power, and if he sometimes made claims that could not, at that time, be fully substantiated, his vision was true and his theories were sound. And his martyrdom in the cause of the development of air power did much to add force to his views and to make them more widely known.

[4] *Skyways*, by Brigadier-General W. Mitchell, p. 255.

5 The Years of Illusion

After the First World War the United States Air Service, like the Royal Air Force, went through a period of uncertainty regarding its status and organization. In 1923 the Lassiter Board, which was mainly composed of military members, had recommended the creation of a force capable of carrying out independent bombardment missions. It was visualized that this force would operate under the control of Army General Headquarters. The Lampert Committee of the House of Representatives, after a very thorough investigation that lasted nearly a year, recommended in 1925 a unified Air Force coequal with the Army and Navy, and the setting up of a Department of Defense to control all three fighting Services.

This caused alarm in the Navy and War departments, and President Coolidge appointed another board, under Dwight W. Morrow, to report on "the best means of developing and applying aircraft in national defense." After a brief study, the Morrow Board advised against a separate Air Force and a Department of Defense, but recommended that the Air Force be renamed the Air Corps. It also proposed that an Assistant Secretary of War should be appointed to look after air matters, and that the Air Corps should have a senior representative on the Army General Staff.

The recommendations of the Morrow Board were accepted by Congress, which gave effect to them by passing the Air Corps Act of July 1925.

Under this act the Air Corps was still wholly subordinated to the
Army. A five-year scheme of expansion was, however, authorized, but
owing to lack of funds no effective action was taken until July 1927.
But Air Corps training and logistics, which had been suffering from
lack of money since the end of the war, were put on a sounder basis.

All these measures, though they did something to strengthen the
Air Corps and improve its status, did not touch the real problem of
whether or not the Air Corps had an offensive power that would
justify its employment in an independent role, and thus warrant its
separation from the Army and the Navy. On this question the views
of the War and Navy Departments, and those of the Air Corps, were
irreconcilable.

The ideas implanted by Mitchell and others had a powerful influence on Air Corps doctrine, and the frustrations of army control
only strengthened the determination of the Air Corps to achieve
independence. Its leaders never ceased to press strongly for the creation of a force of long-range heavy bombers capable of undertaking
independent missions.

Meanwhile the Air Corps suffered from a surplus of obsolete aircraft and engines left over from the great production drive of 1918,
much of the output of which arrived too late to be used in the war.
In particular the large supply of Liberty engines had caused depression in the U. S. aircraft engine industry through lack of development
and production orders for new engines. In 1930 Congress forbade the
production of new aircraft designed to use Liberty engines. At this
date, the Air Corps still had more than $40 million worth of Liberty
engines in stock.

At last, in 1931, a step was taken which gave to the Air Corps
responsibility for the land-based air defense of the coasts of the
United States and its overseas possessions. In 1933 maneuvers were
held on the West Coast, during which the Air Corps proved that it
could concentrate quickly wherever it was required. The need for a
long-range force of reconnaissance and bomber aircraft was also
clearly apparent. The leaders of the Air Corps pressed the point, and
obtained authority to develop long-range bomber aircraft. This new
responsibility did for the Air Corps what Trenchard's system of
air control had done for the Royal Air Force; it gave it a task within

the framework of the defense system which it—and it alone—could perform.

In France the air force, though reduced after the end of the war, was not so severely cut down as in the United States or Britain. In fact, the French army—especially in North Africa—had become very dependent on air support of all kinds. If their air force was misused, as it was in the Riff War, it was not neglected. But it was trained and equipped for the close support of land and sea operations, and it possessed only short-range light bomber aircraft. There was no movement to create a long-range bomber force.

The Italian air force, the Regia Aeronautica, enjoyed a very high prestige and since the end of the war had been allowed a good deal of freedom of thought and action. In March 1923, it was constituted as a third and separate Service, under an Air Ministry. The views of its more advanced leaders, such as General Italo Balbo, who believed in long-range bombardment in independent operations, were in close accord with those of the Royal Air Force and the United States Air Corps. There was, however, some conflict of opinion in the Regia Aeronautica, as General Amadeo Mecozzi believed that air forces were of value mainly in support of armies and navies.

Soviet Russia was slowly recovering from the effects of the Bolshevik revolution. It was certain that the Russians had an air force at this time, but very little was known about it. They had no long-range bomber force, and very little experience of air bombardment of any kind.

The Germans had no air forces, but had built up a very efficient civil air line, Lufthansa, which helped them to train pilots and keep their aircraft industry alive. In addition, it was suspected that they were secretly helping to train the Russian air force.

Soon after the end of the First World War the British Government had given an undertaking that the Royal Air Force would possess a first-line strength equal to that of any other air force within striking distance of the country. A committee set up under Lord Salisbury in 1923 had reported in favor of creating a substantial home defense air force, but nothing was done about it at the time. In 1925 pressure was put on the government to fulfil its undertaking, as the French air force was relatively strong and the R. A. F. at home had been allowed to fall to a very low level. Indeed, apart from training schools, its total strength in the United Kingdom consisted of five army cooperation squadrons. There was not a single fighter or bomber squadron in Britain at that time. Overseas there were only two fighter squadrons, and some twenty squadrons equipped with light bomber or army cooperation types, stationed in Iraq, Egypt, Palestine, Trans-Jordan, the Sudan, Aden, India, and Singapore. The government decided to form a new Air Force Command, to be called the Air Defence of Great Britain (A. D. G. B.).

The composition of this force gave rise to a good deal of controversy. The two older Services strongly urged that all its squadrons should be armed with fighter aircraft, and that the whole force should be strictly defensive in character. This view was shared by an influential body of civilian opinion. It was argued that a purely defensive force of fighter squadrons would not be provocative, since it could threaten no other country, and that therefore it would not lead to competitive rearmament in the air.

Trenchard, on the other hand, took the view that a bomber force, capable of attacking an enemy's airfields and supply depots, his aircraft and engine factories, and his transport system, was an essential part of an air defense organization. The idea was well expressed by General Douhet when he wrote

it is not enough to shoot down all birds in flight if you want to wipe out the species; there remain the eggs and the nests. . . . Destroying an enemy's aeroplanes by seeking them out in the air is, while not entirely useless, the least effective method. A much better way is to destroy his airports, supply bases, and centres of production.[1]

But Trenchard went further; he maintained that the air war should not be fought over Britain, but in the skies over an enemy's country. He therefore advocated a bomber force strong enough to take the offensive and threaten an enemy's vital centers at the outset. This, he argued, would rob an enemy of the initiative and throw his air force on to the defensive. Offensive action of this kind would thus be the best way of reducing or even preventing an air attack on Britain's vital centers.

After a thorough investigation Trenchard's argument prevailed, and

[1] *The Command of the Air.*

the Air Ministry proposed that the new force should have a total of 52 squadrons, one third of which (17) should be fighter squadrons, and two-thirds (35) should be equipped with bombers. This proposal gave rise to much debate in Parliament, and argument in the press and elsewhere. Many views were put forward—often by those with the most rudimentary knowledge of the principles of air or any other form of warfare—as to the correct proportion of fighters to bombers. The Air Ministry was accused of trying to create a powerful offensive bomber force, which Britain's neighbors could not help regarding as a threat to their security, under the guise of a home defense organization.

From a purely defensive point of view the main considerations were the area to be defended in relation to the probable scale of attack, and the estimated bomber force needed to cripple the enemy's air offensive. But if the whole of Trenchard's argument was accepted, then obviously the defensive fighter force should be kept as small as was practicable, allowing the maximum resources to be allocated to the bombers, in the hope of being able to seize the initiative by powerful offensive action on the outbreak of war.

Trenchard's proposal was eventually accepted by the British Government, but the decision to divide the force into one-third fighters and two-thirds bombers was a purely arbitrary one, since no precise method was available for calculating the best ratio between bombers and fighters.

Although the decisions as to the size and composition of the force had been made, progress was very slow. Money was short, and it was impossible at that time to discern any real threat from the air to Britain's security. Germany had no air forces, the Italian Regia Aeronautica and any air forces the Russians might have were out of range, and no one in their senses believed that the French air force was likely to attack Britain. In addition, the British Government had accepted in 1924 what was known as the "Ten-year Rule," which was to have a most pernicious effect on British defense policy. This rule laid down the assumption that no major war would break out within the next ten years. This might not have been so harmful if, as each year went by, the period had been reduced, so that by 1930 it would have been reduced to four years. But each successive year was taken as the starting point of this harmonious epoch, and so the period always remained at ten years. When any new defense project was planned, the British Treasury would ask whether it could be completed within ten years. If the answer was that it could —and few projects in those days could take more than ten years— it was unlikely that authority would be given to start it that year. Under the operation of this rule British defenses sank to a very low level of unpreparedness for war.

Some progress was made with the formation of the fighter squadrons of A. D. G. B., but few bomber squadrons were formed. When the plan was authorized in 1925 it was the intention of the British Government that it should be completed in five years. But by 1930, although all 17 fighter squadrons were in existence—at least on paper—no more than 12 of the bomber squadrons had been formed. Of these 8 were short-range light day bombers, and 4 were longer range twin-engined night bombers.

The main reasons for the slow build-up of the bomber force, apart from the usual financial difficulties, were to be found in the reluctance of the British Government and people to appear to be building an aggressive force, and in their hopes of abolishing or limiting air bombardment, as part of a plan of general disarmament.

The Versailles Treaty, which ended the First World War, forbade Germany to have any armaments apart from a few small naval vessels for coastal patrol work, and an army of 100,000 men for internal security purposes. Submarines and military aircraft were entirely prohibited. But the treaty made it clear that this was intended to be a first step toward general European disarmament. As the years went by and Europe did not disarm to the level imposed on Germany, and indeed showed signs of increasing its armaments, the German Government and people became more and more dissatisfied. They pointed out, with some justice, that either their neighbors should honor their pledge to disarm or that Germany should be allowed some measure of rearmament.

In 1925 the League of Nations had set up a preparatory commission to explore the ground for a general disarmament conference. Neither the United States nor Russia were members of the League, but both had indicated their willingness to join in such a conference. But progress in disarmament is never rapid and the commission was soon involved in endless difficulties. In the meanwhile the United States Secretary of State, Mr. Frank B. Kellogg, proposed a pact renouncing war as an instrument of policy, which in 1928 was signed by fifteen nations. By the following year every state of importance, including Soviet Russia, had accepted its terms.

In Britain the pursuit of disarmament had been intensified when the first Labour Government came into office in 1924. The British Labour party had many pacifists and internationally minded socialists in its ranks, people who meant well enough but who had little or no knowledge of world affairs. The Labour Government favored an idealistic foreign policy, tending to rely on the League of Nations—on what was called collective security—rather than on its own strength. Its ambition was to lead the world toward a new era of disarmament and peace, and it believed that if it set a good example many nations would follow suit. In order to create a favorable atmosphere for international talks on disarmament, it postponed the construction of several warships, and suspended all work on the defenses of Singapore.

This question of the defense of Singapore had proved a very controversial one. While there was fairly general agreement among responsible people that Singapore must be defended, there was much argument about the best way of doing it. Soon after the end of the First World War, when it was decided to make Singapore the main base for the British Navy in Far Eastern waters, Trenchard had proposed that it should become a powerful air base. He contended that it could best be defended by an air striking force which could attack an enemy sea-borne expedition while it was yet far off, and could support the Army in the event of an attack overland through Malaya. The Navy disagreed with this view. It was part of their creed at this time that aircraft could not sink or even damage warships under operational conditions. They therefore proposed that any available money should be used to provide a powerful shore-based battery of 15-inch guns in concrete emplacements. The War Office took the view that the nature of the country would make any attack by way of a landing in Malaya and an advance southward through Johore exceptionally difficult, and that it could be ruled out as impossible. Both the War Office and the Admiralty insisted that any attack on Singapore Island must come from the sea. The British Government accepted this view.

The Air Ministry did not agree that an overland attack, though admittedly difficult, was impossible, or even improbable. But however that might be, Trenchard claimed that a force of reconnaissance aircraft, torpedo-bombers, and fighters, supplemented by 6-inch gun shore-based batteries, would provide a cheaper and more effective defense against a sea-borne expedition than would a battery of heavy guns. He pointed out that aircraft could find and attack an enemy force far beyond the range of any land-based artillery. Since aircraft were mobile all the air forces required for the defense of Singapore need not be permanently stationed there in time of peace. If the airfields and other facilities were provided, a part of such air forces could be stationed elsewhere and be rapidly moved to Singapore in time to deal with an attempted attack. In this way considerable economies in defense expenditure could be realized.

Before a firm decision on these controversial questions had been reached, the British Labour Government came into office in 1924, and decided to suspend the Singapore defense scheme in the hope of improving the prospects for general disarmament.

After a long period of indecision a new government decided in 1927 to proceed with the construction of a shore-based battery of three 15-inch guns, and left the question of substituting aircraft for the remaining heavy guns to be decided later. The second Labour Government under Mr. Ramsay MacDonald assumed office in 1929, and on the grounds that the Kellogg Pact had made a major war illegal, and therefore improbable, it offered to postpone the formation of further bomber squadrons in A. D. G. B., to reduce the strength of the British Navy, and to suspend all work on the Singapore Base pending the outcome of the League of Nations Disarmament Conference.

Its enthusiasm for cutting down on preparations for defense was increased by an acute financial crisis. The economic setback in the United States in 1929 had widespread repercussions in many other countries, and before long the British economy was in dire straits. All forms of government expenditure were drastically cut, and so serious a view was taken of the situation that Mr. Ramsay MacDonald and Mr. Phillip Snowden and some of their followers joined with the Conservative party in order to deal with it.

The League of Nations Disarmament Conference eventually assembled in Geneva in February 1932, and was soon engaged in discussing a wide range of proposals. Among these were two of great importance to the future of air power. The first of these was a proposal to prohibit entirely all forms of bombardment from the air, to which the British Government added a rider permitting the use of bombing for the air control of undeveloped countries. The proposal, thus amended, was on much the same lines as one discussed by an Oecumenical Council in the fourteenth century, which sought to forbid the use of gunpowder in war "except against infidels." Many other amendments were added, in an attempt to legitimize the bombing of strictly military targets in support of land or sea operations. It was eventually apparent that the difficulty of defining what was, and what was not, a legitimate target would make the proposal unworkable in practice. A second proposal was then tabled, limiting the unladen all-up weight of military aircraft to a maximum of 3,000 lbs.

If this had been accepted it would clearly have ruled out anything except the short-range light bomber, useful only for tactical purposes. It would have effectively curbed the offensive power of aircraft, and in practice confined them to the support of land or sea operations. This proposal was welcomed by the armies and navies of many countries, and for a time there seemed to be a chance that it might be generally accepted.

But by the time the Disarmament Conference got to grips with its task, the general situation had begun to deteriorate. In 1931 Japan, taking advantage of a carefully contrived incident in Manchuria, took hostile action against the Chinese. The situation in the Far East became rapidly worse, and in 1932 a Japanese expeditionary force landed on the coast of China only a few miles from the International Settlement of Shanghai. It was clear that the European positions in China and Malaya were threatened, and the British Chiefs of Staff were at last able to persuade the government to abandon the "Ten-year Rule", which had done so much to hamper British defense policy since 1924.

But these troubles in the Far East might not, in themselves, have wrecked the Disarmament Conference. It continued its wearisome efforts to reach agreement. In the way now so painfully familiar, proposals, counter-proposals, amendments, and attempts to reach a compromise followed each other laboriously, each one the subject of an exhaustive discussion that led to nothing. It was eventually clear that the German claims to equality of status and the French insistence upon security could not be reconciled. Indeed the German attitude tended to stiffen as the conference meandered on, and this tendency grew more marked after Hitler became Chancellor in January 1933.

By this time the League of Nations itself was beginning to disintegrate under the strains to which it had been subjected. Early in 1933 Japan gave notice of her intention to resign from membership of the League. In October of that year Germany walked out of the Disarmament Conference and withdrew from the League, and soon afterward Italy threatened to do the same. Since the United States and Soviet Russia had never been members, the League was thus practically destroyed. The conference struggled on for several months in the hope of saving something from the wreck, but it formally broke up in May 1934, without achieving any result whatever.

The policy which had guided successive British governments since 1924 was now finally discredited. British hopes of disarmament were shattered and all ideas of collective security, which had never had much reality, had to be abandoned. It was necessary to appreciate the new situation and to take such action as was needed to restore Britain's threadbare defenses.

In retrospect, it would appear that Britain was almost alone in hoping for great results from the League of Nations Disarmament Conference, and also in trying to set an example to the world by accepting a measure of unilateral disarmament. The failure of this policy was now manifest, and its results were dire. But it is doubtful if the lesson has yet been learned.

6   The Period of Rearmament: 1934-1939

With the rise to power of Adolf Hitler and the rearmament of
Germany, Europe moved from a postwar into a prewar era. Mr.
Lloyd George, the British Prime Minister during the last two years
of the First World War, had called it "the war to end war," and
many people all over the world hoped and even believed that he
was right. Much was expected from the League of Nations; it was
hoped that it would deter aggression and foster a new respect for
international law. Britain—with what were then called the self-
governing Dominions—and France, Italy, Belgium, Holland, the
Scandinavian, and many other countries had tried hard to make the
League a real force for peace in the world. It was strange that the
United States declined to join the League, for President Wilson had
been one of the first to put forward the idea and had helped to mold
its constitution. But after the end of the war the isolationist forces
in America gained the upper hand, and so the League was weakened
and handicapped from the outset by the absence of the leading
transatlantic Power.

Disarmament, as always, had proved difficult, because most nations coming to a disarmament conference are nervous of being led
into agreements that might prejudice their security. It has happened.
But even if no effective disarmament agreement had proved to be
possible, it was a fact that the Allies had drastically reduced their
armed forces at the end of the First World War, and there had
been very little effective rearmament since. At the beginning of 1934,

the military forces of almost every European Power were at a very low level, both from the point of view of quantity and quality. A possible exception was Soviet Russia, which had been steadily building up the Red Army into a large force, but it was trained and armed more for the purposes of internal security than for a major war. Its equipment was simple, and it still largely relied on horse transport.

The resurgence of Germany had coincided with an acute and widespread financial depression in Europe, when most governments felt obliged to reduce their expenditure, and the last thing they wanted to do was to increase their defense forces. At first, therefore, there was a tendency to minimize the seriousness of the political change in Germany, and to hope that Hitler would be satisfied with a modest increase in the German armed forces. This optimism was, however, unjustified and German rearmament proceeded further and more rapidly than even the pessimists had foreseen. There were several reasons for this. During the period when the Versailles Treaty was supposed to be in force—from the end of the war until the rise of Hitler—the Germans had displayed great ingenuity in minimizing and even evading the effect of its military provisions. Their army of 100,000 men had been used as a training corps to produce scores of thousands of potential officers and noncommissioned officers. In addition, they had made a secret arrangement with Soviet Russia, by means of which they trained the Russian air force. This enabled them to create and keep in flying practice a body of experienced German military pilots. They also set up many clubs to train young men to fly gliders. Their civil airline, Lufthansa, kept alive the nucleus of an aircraft industry, and had given their designers and producers an opportunity of creating big, fast, long-range aircraft with an up-to-date performance.

After the failure of the League of Nations Disarmament Conference and the partial collapse of the League itself, the United States had tended to become more aloof than ever from Europe and its problems. The United States Air Corps was chiefly concerned with the creation of a long-range bombardment force for coast defense, and to secure freedom from Army control.

The British Government was extremely reluctant to start rearming. The financial position had somewhat improved, but there was a strong antiwar movement in the country. There is little doubt that the appalling conditions of trench warfare on the Western front in the First World War, and the loss of nearly a million men in the armed forces, had created a horror and hatred of war that was deep and widespread. The threat of air bombardment of populated centers in any future war tended to increase this very natural aversion, and many worried people were inclined to take refuge in an unreasoning "antiwar" attitude. The genuine pacifists—those who believe that the way to keep the peace is to ignore the possibility of war and who label anyone who wishes to defend the country as a warmonger —were few in number, but the climate of opinion in Britain at that time tended to give more scope than usual to their activities. A body calling itself the Peace Pledge Union sent out a letter to a very large number of people, asking them to reply on an enclosed postcard to the question "Are you in favor of or against war?" The question was of course absurd; it was on a par with asking people if they were in favor of or against floods, earthquakes, or any other form of disaster. Naturally very few people would answer such a question by saying that they were in favor of war. Although many of those who received the letter did not answer it, the great majority of those who replied said that they were against war, and the Union gave much publicity to this evidence of British antiwar feeling.

It is never easy for a democratic government to estimate the strength of public opinion on any subject, unless it is specifically tested in a general election. A vociferous and well-organized minority will make a far greater impact than a relatively silent, apathetic majority. The British Conservative party did not make rearmament an issue in the general election of 1935 because its leaders feared, probably without reason, that if they did so they might have lost the election. If a Labour Government had come into power in 1935 it was most unlikely, judging by the record of previous Labour administrations, that it would have approved any effective program of rearmament. The Conservatives therefore thought it best not to make rearmament an issue in the election, but if returned to power to put in hand a modest program, which could be accelerated if the situation deteriorated.

The Conservative party won the election and proceeded to carry out this policy. Authority was given to form, as soon as possible, the remaining bomber squadrons in A. D. G. B., bringing its strength up to the 35 squadrons originally planned in 1925. As all the squad-

rons of the Auxiliary Air Force had been converted to fighters, these
bomber squadrons would all be regular units. During the period when
the League of Nations Disarmament Conference was in session the
government had not allowed the Air Ministry to formulate requirements for any military aircraft of a greater unladen weight than
3,000 lbs. In 1933, the Air Ministry was permitted to issue Air Staff
requirements for a high-performance fighter armed with six .303
Browning machine guns. Later this requirement was increased to
eight guns. These requirements produced, in due course, the Hurri-
can and Spitfire.

The bomber squadrons of A. D. G. B. were equipped with short-
range obsolescent types of aircraft that would have been of very
little value in a major war. After the breakup of the Disarmament
Conference in the spring of 1934, the Air Ministry was allowed to
issue requirements for a high-performance long-range bomber, which
produced the Whitley, the Hampden, and the Wellington. The
Whitley was a conversion from an existing design, in an effort to
save time in getting a more modern longer range aircraft into
service.

If Britain was reluctant to rearm, France was no less unwilling to
do so. Ever since the end of the First World War the French
had struggled to keep Germany disarmed. If, in the early twenties, the
nations of Europe had come together and negotiated a genuine and
substantial reduction of their armaments, it might have been possible
to avoid the rearmament of Germany. But they did not make the
attempt until it was too late. After the failure of the Disarmament
Conference and the resignation of Germany from the League, it was
impossible to prevent the Germans from rearming by any means short
of war. The French were profoundly disappointed by this failure,
and felt that they had not received the support to which they were
entitled from their former Allies.

In 1935 two events occurred which caused a serious worsening
of the political situation in Europe. Italy began hostilities against
Abyssinia[1] and, although the Italians undoubtedly had some grounds
for complaint against the Abyssinian Government, it was indisputable that Italy had fired the first shot. So, under the rules of the
League of Nations, Italy was named as an aggressor and an attempt

[1] Now Ethiopia.

was made to apply economic sanctions against her. These had little effect on the conduct of the war but they caused much ill-feeling. In resentment at this treatment Italy resigned from the League and turned to Germany for support. Hitler and Mussolini made common cause and thus the Rome-Berlin Axis came into existence. It is interesting to note that the one course of action which would have been effective—the closing of the Suez Canal to Italian shipping— was never even suggested. The canal, under the International Convention of 1888, was free to the ships of all nations in peace and war, and the British in Egypt saw to it that this freedom was strictly observed.

The second event was a revolution in Spain against an incompetent government that was showing a strong tendency toward communism. Germany sent armed forces and war material to assist the cause of General Franco and the insurgents, and Italy gave him weapons and naval support. The League of Nations agreed that all its members should adopt a policy of nonintervention. This resulted in a flood of "volunteers" from many countries—including Britain—coming to the aid of the Spanish Government. After a bitter civil war lasting nearly two years, during which German military forces tried out their new aircraft and weapons, the insurgents were victorious.

This prolonged struggle caused a deep division of opinion among the nations of Europe and further discredited the League. In addition, the differences between right-wing and left-wing political parties in many countries were painfully exacerbated.

The British Government was by now seriously alarmed at the state of international tension existing in Europe. It seemed clear that if the deterioration continued, the outbreak of full-scale war was probable. The alarm felt in Whitehall was increased when two British Ministers, Sir John Simon and Mr. Anthony Eden, returning from a visit to Germany, reported that the German air force had already reached parity with the Royal Air Force and intended to attain parity with the French air force, estimated at 2,000 first-line aircraft. A scheme for the immediate expansion of the R. A. F. was approved, followed by a more comprehensive one in February 1936.

By the time Hitler came to power much of the Versailles Treaty had been eroded away, and he proceeded to tear up what remained of it. When in March 1936 he decided to send German troops into the Ruhr and Rhineland, which under the treaty were demilitarized zones, the French wished to use force to prevent it. They felt that it would be intolerable to have, once more, German armed forces on their eastern frontier. Britain did not support France at this critical moment, and indeed the whole League of Nations was strongly against the use of force to restrain the Germans. It argued—with that peculiarly legalistic form of logic that has produced so many calamitous decisions in the last thirty years—that Germany, in moving troops within her own territory, was not committing aggression and that intervention would not be justified. It is now known that the Germans were in no position to resist such an intervention, which could have been safely and easily carried out by the French army. Hitler has recorded in his diary that he had staked everything on this move, and that if it had failed he would have committed suicide. However that may be, it is interesting to speculate on the effect that this intervention, if it had taken place, might have had on the subsequent history of Europe.

The Germans were allowed to remilitarize the Ruhr and the Rhineland, and the only action taken was to send diplomatic protests, which were coolly rejected. With this move one of the last provisions of the Treaty of Versailles disappeared. The French were alarmed, but they were also bitter and disillusioned. They felt that their last hope of security had vanished, for they had little confidence in their ability to withstand the onslaught of a fully rearmed Germany. In these circumstances they might have been stirred to put their defenses in order, but they were unable to rise to the occasion. In fairness to the French, it should be remembered that they had suffered very severe losses in the First World War. One and a half million men, among them the bravest and best to whom France might have looked for leadership in the days to come, were killed and many more were seriously disabled. In addition, the addiction of the French General Staff to the offensive, *"l'attaque, l'attaque, toujours l'attaque,"* had not survived the Army's terrible experiences in 1917. They had now swung to the other extreme and put their faith in a static defense system. They had built a fortified line—named after a French Minister of War, M. Maginot—along the Franco-German frontier. Unfortunately this line was never extended northward to the Channel coast. The difficulty was a political one. If the line were to be built along the Belgian-German frontier, the Belgians felt that any hopes they might have of remaining neutral would be destroyed, as it would be clear that they were included in a Franco-British military alliance. The French, on the other hand, could not bring themselves to extend the line northward along their frontier with Belgium, as this would have excluded Belgium from the Western defense system. The difficulty was never resolved, and so the northern part of the Maginot Line was never built. This was to prove a fatal defect when the German invasion of western Europe occurred in 1940.

The French air force was trained and equipped for the task for which it was designated—the close support of land operations. It was, however, deficient in modern fighters and had no properly organized system of air defense. Attempts by the British to persuade them to reorganize and modernize their air defenses were unsuccessful. The French General Staff, which controlled their air force, had even at this date no understanding of the right way to use air power. Their air forces were still cut up and decentralized under the orders of subordinate military formations. They had no belief in the offensive power of air forces acting independently, and no intention of creating a long-range bomber force.

Generally speaking, while the junior ranks were sound, keen, and efficient, the equipment of the French air force was obsolescent, its staff work bad, and its leadership inept.

The British Government now fully understood the seriousness of the situation in Europe, but little attempt was made to explain to the British people the peril in which they stood. Popular support for rearmament was therefore lukewarm, and indeed the Labour party, in opposition, obstructed every move to strengthen the country's defenses, and encouraged pacifist leanings.

In 1936 a major reorganization of the Royal Air Force was approved; A. D. G. B. was abolished and four new functional commands —Bomber, Fighter, Coastal, and Training Commands—were created. Also in 1936, the Air Staff issued new requirements for a long-range bomber, which produced the four-engined Stirling and Halifax, and the twin-engined Manchester.[2]

In October 1936 it was discovered that Germany was aiming at a first-line strength of 2,500 aircraft, including 1,700 bombers, and a new expansion scheme for the R. A. F. was approved. This provided

[2] Later converted to the four-engined Lancaster.

for a total of 2,387 first-line aircraft, excluding the Fleet Air Arm, which early in 1937 was separated from the R. A. F. and made the sole responsibility of the Admiralty. During 1937 schemes of expansion followed one another so rapidly that each scheme was superseded by a new one before much could be done to implement it.

On March 12, 1938, German troops entered Austria and precipitated a fresh crisis in Europe. The Air Staff was directed to do everything in its power to secure, during the next two years, the maximum possible expansion of British air power. New units were formed and the strength on paper of the R. A. F. increased, but most of these units were still equipped with obsolete or obsolescent types of aircraft.

In September 1938 another crisis occurred which brought Europe to the brink of war. The Treaty of Versailles had annexed to the new state of Czechoslovakia, carved out of the former Austria-Hungarian Empire, a strip of land containing some two million Germans. The object of this was to provide a topographically defensive frontier between Germany and Czechoslovakia. Hitler announced his intention of incorporating these Germans, and the territory in which they lived, into the German Reich. There was some justification for this action; it had been both wrong and foolish to separate the two million Germans from their homeland in an attempt to make the frontier more viable from a strategic point of view. But Hitler greatly exaggerated the miserable plight of these Germans living under Czech rule. Incidents were contrived and stories of atrocities fabricated, until the whole German nation became convinced of the justice and urgency of the need to liberate their fellow countrymen in Czechoslovakia.

Europe was becoming tired of Hitler's policy of seizing one piece of territory after another, each one his "last territorial claim in Europe," and was convinced that a halt must be called to Germany's aggressive policy. France and Britain threatened war if Hitler marched into Czechoslovakia, while Russia adopted an uncertain attitude and made vague promises. Hitler was not deterred, and mobilized his forces. Italy was alarmed, and tried to restrain Germany, and it is probable that Hitler was influenced to some extent by Mussolini's representations.

The British Prime Minister, Mr. Neville Chamberlain, arranged two meetings with Hitler, and an agreement was made at Munich whereby the German area of Czechoslovakia, known as the Sudeten-

land, would be returned to Germany, while Hitler promised not to
interfere with the remainder of Czechoslovakia, and indeed undertook to join with France and Britain in guaranteeing its future independence and security. This agreement was received at the time with
relief and acclamation in almost every country in Europe, and in
truth it was the best that could be hoped for in the circumstances.
In March 1939, Hitler broke his pledge and assimilated the whole
of Czechoslovakia into the rapidly expanding German Empire.

A few people at the time, and many afterward when Hitler broke
faith over Czechoslovakia, took the view that Britain and France
should have gone to war to keep the Sudeten Germans under Czech
rule. If they had done so they would not have had a very strong moral
case, for they would have been using force to perpetuate a dubious
decision. And their military weakness was such that they could not
have avoided defeat. While it was true that German rearmament was
far from complete, Hitler's forces were well-trained and equipped,
while scarcely any of the fruits of the British and French drive to
produce modern arms had yet been gathered. The R. A. F. possessed
less than a hundred Hurricanes and only six Spitfires, and weekly
production rates would not have replaced war wastage. The chain
of radar stations that was to play such a vital part when the test
came in 1940 was not yet complete, and no station was fully operational. The shortage of .303 ammunition was so acute that Fighter
Command could have operated at the estimated scale of war expenditure for little more than a month, and then only if Bomber
Command had required none at all. There were less than fifty modern
twin-engined bombers available, and no four-engined bombers at all.
The antiaircraft guns were few, and they also were very short of
ammunition.

The British army was in no better shape, and the navy, though
suffering less from neglect, was far from being ready to meet its
commitments. There just had not been time to recover from nearly
twenty years of grinding parsimony, and the effect of the "Ten-year
Rule." There is no reason to believe that the Czech army would have
lasted any longer than did the Polish army a year later. Britain and
France could have given them no direct military assistance, and
Czechoslovakia would have been overrun within a few weeks, leaving
Germany free to turn toward the West. It is as certain as anything
can be in military affairs that if war with Germany had come in

September 1938, France and Britain would have been ignominiously defeated. There is little doubt that Russia would have sat on the fence and joined the winning side.

It has been said by critics of the Munich Agreement that the military advantages claimed for it were never realized, because in fact the Germans made better use of the subsequent year to improve their armaments than did France and Britain. As far as air forces are concerned this is not true. The R. A. F. enormously increased its strength in relation to the German air force. And it must be remembered that it was the Battle of Britain, which the R. A. F. was just able to win, that robbed Hitler of victory in 1940. Had the battle been lost, Britain would have been invaded and defeated, and Germany would have been master of all Europe west and south of the frontier of the U. S. S. R.

But even if Germany had made better use of the year after Munich than did Britain, it does not follow that her relative advantage would have been increased. The arithmetic is simple. Suppose that at the time of Munich Britain possessed 200 modern aircraft and Germany 1,000—which was roughly the actual position—the odds against the R. A. F. would be 5 to 1. If the British built 300 and the Germans 500 between Munich and the outbreak of war a year later, then the R.A.F. would have 500 and the Germans 1,500. The odds have shortened to 3 to 1. Add another 500 each between the outbreak of war and the start of the Battle of Britain, and the R. A. F. would have 1,000 and the Germans 2,000. The odds would be 2 to 1. In fact, the position would be slightly better, because many of the German pre-Munich aircraft would be out of action being overhauled and reconditioned.

In addition, there were four factors of great importance. The British supply of small arms ammunition suitable for use in air gunnery was so inadequate as almost to be decisive in itself. Secondly, the whole system of radar-controlled interception, which was vital to the success of Fighter Command in the Battle of Britain, was not in working order at the time of Munich. Thirdly, the great self-governing dominions were by no means enthusiastically disposed toward war over this issue. And, finally, the crisis took the French and British people by surprise. It arose suddenly during the summer holidays, and only during the last few days was the gravity of the situation fully realized. The French and British were morally unprepared to go to war. Lulled by two decades of talk about "war to end war" and hopes of disarmament, and putting too much trust in the League of Nations, they were appalled by the idea of war—especially war over an issue in eastern Europe which few of them understood.

The extent of their moral unpreparedness can be measured by the flood of almost hysterical relief which everywhere greeted the news of the Munich Agreement.

The shocking weakness of Britain's defenses horrified those in a position to know the facts, but the government was in a difficulty. If the truth were revealed to the British people, in the hope of rousing them to make a great effort to re-arm as quickly as possible, it was felt that Hitler would precipitate a full-scale war in the spring of 1939, so as to take full advantage of the weakness of the Western Allies. If the truth were concealed as far as possible, it was hoped that the outbreak of war might be postponed until the autumn of 1939, or even the spring of 1940. Since much of the spade work had been done and the drive to produce modern armaments was now beginning to yield substantial results, the British and French governments agreed to adopt the latter course.

A new scheme of expansion for the R. A. F. was authorized and all financial restrictions were removed. In addition, approval was given to extend still further the aircraft manufacturing facilities: new factories were to be built and more use made of subcontracting. Ten new fighter squadrons were to be formed as soon as possible, for home defense, and the building of the chain of radar stations hastened. Further stations, to improve the radar cover, were authorized. The provision of trained aircrews and reserves of airmen was to be inceased, and training facilities extended. The possibility of obtaining supplies of military aircraft from the United States was to be explored, and a large number of British four-engined heavy bombers ordered.

The last British Air Estimates to be published before the outbreak of war reached a figure of nearly £221 million. During most of the years between the two World Wars, the Air Estimates were less than £20 million, and at their lowest point, in 1922, they dropped below £11 million. Money was now being poured out like water in an effort to catch up with the German air force, and to repair the damage done during the many years of folly and parsimony when Britain had starved and neglected the Royal Air Force.

The military impotence of Britain and France at the time of the Munich crisis, which made it impossible for them to stand up to Hitler, should have done much to dispel popular misconceptions in both countries. Unfortunately, since it was necessary to conceal the military weakness of the Allies, the facts were not very generally understood, even by some of those in the highest circles. British and French conduct was ascribed, not to military weakness, but to political cowardice and ineptitude. This was not so, and their leaders had to choose between political withdrawal and military defeat. Faced with this hard choice, they accepted withdrawal and made the best terms they could. And the course of events justified the policy adopted by the Western Allies after the crisis, for the Second World War did not start until Germany attacked Poland at the beginning of September 1939.

The Munich Agreement had succeeded in postponing the outbreak of war for nearly a year; a postponement the military value of which it is almost impossible to overestimate.

Part III

THE SECOND WORLD WAR: PREPARATION

7 Outbreak of World War II

When Hitler's forces marched on Prague and annexed the whole of Czechoslovakia into his new Germany, he extinguished any remaining hopes that he would content himself with removing what most Germans believed to be the injustices of the Treaty of Versailles. Not only had he, for the first time, broken his solemn word and torn up an agreement freely entered into, but he had brought under German rule a country inhabited by people who by no stretch of the imagination could be regarded as Germans. It was clear that all Germany's neighbors, especially those to the east and south, were threatened.

It was not difficult to foresee the Nazi Government's next move. After the First World War the Baltic port of Danzig had been made into a Free City, guaranteed by the League of Nations. Danzig contained many Poles as well as Germans, and it was Poland's natural and only outlet to the sea. The Free City was connected to Poland by the Danzig Corridor, a strip of Polish territory which cut right across East Prussia. The arrangement was clumsy and, to Germany, abhorrent, but in 1919 it had appeared to those responsible for settling the affairs of Europe to be the best compromise. The symptoms of impending trouble were already visible; stories were circulating in Germany about the intolerable plight of the Germans living in the Free City, and the great inconvenience caused by the Danzig Corridor. There could be little doubt that Hitler's next exploit would be the "liberation" of Danzig and the suppression of the Corridor.

Poland made it clear that she would resist any forcible attempt by Germany to change the *status quo*, and France and Britain assured Poland of their full support. They realized the geographical obstacles to the provision of direct military assistance to Poland, and in these circumstances they attempted to negotiate an agreement with Soviet Russia. If the Russians could be persuaded to join the Western Allies in guaranteeing the Free City and the Corridor, Hitler would, if he attacked Poland, be faced with a war on two fronts.

The negotiations with the Russians followed the usual course. At first they were encouraging and it seemed as if an agreement was within reach. As soon as the negotiators began to formulate precise commitments or define an agreed policy, the Russians raised difficulties. Although the Western Allies conceded one point after another, the talks dragged on interminably month after month with no firm agreement on anything. But the general attitude of the Russians was still not unsympathetic and the British Government hoped that the negotiations would eventually succeed.

Suddenly, on August 21, 1939, the signing of a nonaggression pact between Germany and Russia was announced. While the negotiations had been going on between France, Britain, and Russia, the Soviet and Nazi Foreign Ministers, Molotov and Ribbentrop, had arranged a secret meeting and come to terms. Hitler could now face war in the west over Danzig without the fear of having to deal with an attack on his eastern frontier. This deceitful act by the Russians gave the signal for the Second World War to begin.

On September 1 the German air force bombed Warsaw, the Polish capital, and German divisions crossed the Polish frontier. France and Britain, in accordance with their undertakings, declared war on Germany. Russia and Germany agreed to divide Poland between them, and the Red Army advanced into eastern Poland, from which it has never withdrawn. The Polish air force was destroyed in a few days, and in a few weeks all resistance ceased. France and Britain had been unable to do anything to help Poland, which was now wholly occupied by German or Russian troops.

Britain and France had expected a German air attack to follow their declaration of war, but Hitler was in no hurry to begin hostilities in the West. He hoped that the Western Allies would accept the fact that Poland was defeated and divided, and that the cause for which they had declared war no longer existed. He thought it probable that they would now make peace on terms which would leave him free to pursue his expansion toward the east. There was indeed some support in France for such a policy, but Britain would have none of it. The British Prime Minister, Mr. Neville Chamberlain, made it clear that the war would go on until either Britain or Germany was defeated.

Unrestricted submarine warfare against Allied merchant shipping began as soon as war was declared, but no other hostile action was taken by Germany in the West. Italy had not yet come into the war, and was waiting to see what would happen. The European winter was fast approaching, and hostilities, except at sea, died down.

Britain and France now took stock of their position. It was clear that it was necessary to postpone, for as long as possible, a trial of strength with Germany. In Britain, especially, new and up-to-date aircraft and weapons were coming off the production line in ever-increasing quantities. But it was also clear that the Allies had not the offensive power in the air to carry the war into the skies over Germany. An initial defensive phase, therefore, could not be avoided, and the crucial defensive battle in the air would be fought in Allied air space.

Ever since 1935 the British Government had given increasing priority to the requirements of air defense. The production of the eight-gun fighter, the training of fighter pilots, the development of radar for plotting the approach of enemy aircraft and for controlling interception, and the provision of fighter airfields for home defense, had all taken precedence over the requirements of the bomber force. In the circumstances this was inevitable, for it was essential that Britain, at least, should be able to survive the opening defensive phase of the war.

When war broke out Bomber Command consisted of fifty-five squadrons, but this apparent strength was illusory. The British Government, when authorizing the feverish expansion of the Royal Air Force, had insisted that everything should be "put in the shop-window." New squadrons were added, but there were no reserves of aircraft and no operational training organization. Behind this policy lay the hope that the apparent size of the force might act as a deterrent to Hitler and the Nazi Government. When war broke out, deterrent effect no longer had any value. The Command now had to operate against massive defenses, and provision must be made to replace war wastage in aircraft and crews. Ten squadrons of light bombers were earmarked to go to France in support of the British Field Force, and ten more squadrons were taken out of the front line to act as operational training units and provide reserves to replace lost crews or aircraft in the mobilized squadrons. These numbered 35, with a total first-line strength of 420 aircraft. Assuming a serviceability rate of 75 per cent, this would give a daily average of some 315 aircraft, but the position was not as good as this, because some of the squadrons were short of fully trained aircrews.

In contrast to this, the German air force had a first-line strength of some 1,500 long-range bombers. But these aircraft, though fast and generally well-designed, were deficient in defensive armament. The force was mainly intended to be used for tactical bombing in the support of land operations, or for long-range bombardment in countries like Poland, where air opposition would be slight or negligible.

The British Air Staff were anxious to test, in actual combat, the eight-gun fighters and long-range twin-engined bombers with their power-operated gun turrets. An Air Component of the Field Force (A. C. F. F.) and an Advanced Air Striking Force, (A. A. S. F.) were sent to France as soon as possible. The A. C. F. F. included a number of fighter squadrons equipped with Hurricanes, and the A. A. S. F. consisted of two wings of light bomber squadrons, equipped with Blenheims and Battles. The fighters gained a good deal of experience in action with German fighter and reconnaissance aircraft, and many valuable lessons were learned. The general conclusion was that the performance and armament of the Hurricane were satisfactory after a few modifications, such as a more concentrated alignment of the guns, had been made, and that the new tactics, worked out for the multi-gun fighters, were sound. But there were no targets available for the bombers, and their duties were limited to reconnaissance and training. Training in bombing and air gunnery was, however, seriously hampered by lack of suitable ranges, while exercises in long-distance cloud and night flying were almost impossible to organize owing to restrictions imposed by the French.

The remaining British bombers, based at home, were more fortunate. Although they, too, could find few targets, they were engaged in dropping propaganda leaflets over Germany. It was at first hoped that the leaflets might influence German opinion, and that the presence of British bombers in the night skies over Germany might give rise to numerous air raid warnings, causing some dislocation of German industry and civil life. Neither of these hopes was realized, but the leaflet raids provided a valuable form of operational training for the bomber crews.

It was still British and French policy to attack only military targets, situated in places where no errors or bad aiming could possibly cause civilian casualties. In these circumstances, Bomber Command was restricted to the attack of German warships at sea or at anchor in naval harbors. No attacks were allowed against ships in docks or alongside the jetties. Several minor attacks were made on ships at sea or at anchor without much success but on December 3, 1939, a force of twenty-four Wellingtons attacked two German cruisers lying at anchor off Heligoland. Not much damage was done, but the Wellingtons, though intercepted by a considerable force of German fighters, carried on a running fight with Messerschmitt 109's and 110's, and returned without loss. This encouraged the Air Staff to believe that the British bombers with their power-operated gun turrets could, as long as they maintained a close formation, successfully defend themselves against fighter attack.

On December 14 twelve Wellingtons attacked warships in the Schillig Roads, but during a running fight with the German Messerschmitts, five were shot down and one crashed on return to its base. On December 18 twenty-two Wellingtons attempted to attack warships in Wilhelmshaven, and were heavily engaged by German fighters. The Wellingtons got through to the target area, but all the warships were in dock or alongside the quays. Ten Wellingtons were shot down and three more crashed on returning to England.

There were two main reasons for this failure. It had been hoped that the new power-operated turrets would give the bombers a defense that would enable a well-handled formation to withstand fighter attack. But it had also been thought that, owing to the high speed of the bombers, all such attacks would come from astern. Indeed, in the earlier raids, when the German fighters attacked from astern, the Wellingtons were able to give a good account of themselves. But the raid of December 3 was the last of this phase. The Germans, after studying the fields of fire of a shot-down Wellington, realized that it was relatively defenseless against a beam attack from above. They therefore gave up attacks from astern in favor of beam attacks. The British had believed that such attacks would be ineffective owing to the large deflections in aiming that would be involved, but this did not prove to be so in practice.

The second weakness was the lack of self-sealing fuel tanks. Priorities for these tanks had rightly been given to the fighters, and it had not proved possible to equip the bombers by the end of 1939. One incendiary bullet striking a fuel tank could set a bomber on fire.

These early operations were, in themselves, of small importance, but they have been dealt with in some detail because they had a profound effect on British bombing policy for the next four years. Immediate steps were of course taken to provide all bombers with self-sealing tanks as soon as possible, and all were so equipped by the spring of 1940. The fields of fire of the Wellingtons were also modified to eliminate the inability to deal with beam attacks. But the most important consequence of these raids was a decision to concentrate on night bombing. The Air Staff had always hoped that daylight bombing of Germany, by long-range well-armed bombers flying in formation, would be practicable. They did not believe in the value of fighter escorts, and no provision had been made for a long-range fighter suitable for this task. They now came to the conclusion that Wellingtons and Hampdens would be unable to operate by day over Germany against fighter opposition. The Whitley was slower and less well-armed, and had always been regarded as a night bomber. This decision meant that the whole of the British long-range bomber force would henceforth operate only by night. Only the light bombers, the Blenheims and Battles, working under general fighter cover in support of the Field Force, would in future operate in daylight.

Although this decision was arrived at after a brief experience of German fighter opposition, and before the provision of self-sealing tanks and improved fields of fire had remedied the main defects of the Wellingtons, it was undoubtedly correct. Subsequent operations proved conclusively that long-range bombardment of targets in Germany by the R. A. F. in daylight would not have been practicable.

This alteration of policy was possible because the British Air Staff, while hoping that day bombing of German targets would prove to be feasible, had always envisaged the possibility of having to work by night. The aircraft were designed and the crews were trained for night as well as daylight bombing, although it is true that the difficulties of navigating and finding the target in darkness against heavy opposition had not been fully appreciated.

It is interesting to contrast this policy with that of the United States Air Corps. When in 1933 the Air Corps had been given the responsibility for the land-based air defense of American coasts, the way was open to the creation of a force of long-range bombers. This was called the G. H. Q. Air Force, and it came into existence on March 1, 1935.

In 1933 the Air Corps had organized a competition for the design of a multiengined long-range high altitude bomber, and this competition was won by the Boeing Airplane Company with a design largely based on that of a transport aircraft. This was accepted by the Air Corps and given the designation XB-17. Tested in 1935, the XB-17 had encouraged an order for a modified version, which was the well-known B-17, the Flying Fortress. But owing to opposition from the Army General Staff, the number ordered was no more than thirteen. For the next three years the Air Corps fought to get a substantial order placed for this promising aircraft, but with little success. The Army saw in the B-17 a symbol of the determination of the leaders of the Air Corps to build a long-range bomber capable of independent missions, and they were equally determined to prevent any such development. In 1938 the Secretary of War refused to allow any appropriations for bombers other than for light or medium types suitable for Army support.

In the summer of 1938 this struggle reached its climax. The Army General Staff were resolved to put the Air Corps back in what they regarded as its proper place. Its responsibility for coast defense was revoked, and it was forbidden to order any B-17's in addition to the forty then being built. Several of the Air Corps leaders were demoted or put on the retired list.

But the darkest hour is just before the dawn. The Munich crisis in September 1938 caused a dramatic change in the air policy of the United States. In October 1938 plans were prepared for a considerable expansion of the Air Corps. After four years of struggle the G. H. Q. Air Force was, on March 1, 1939, transferred from the control of the Army General Staff and placed directly under the

Chief of Air Corps, at that time Major-General H. H. Arnold. This
was a great step forward, and gave to the Air Corps the control of its
training and equipment shortly before the outbreak of war in Europe
set on foot a great expansion of American air power. When the war
began the Air Corps possessed only twenty-three serviceable B-17's,
but large orders were then placed and opposition to the creation of a
long-range bomber force was at last subdued.

The Air Corps believed that the B-17, carrying a large battery of
guns, would have sufficient defensive power to allow of deep penetra-
tration in daylight by well-drilled formations against massive fighter
opposition. For this reason, like the British Air Staff, they did not
consider the provision of long-range escort fighters necessary or even
practicable. Unlike the British, however, the Air Corps had designed
and trained its long-range bomber force solely for high altitude precision bombing in daylight. It relied on the fire-power of the B-17,
the high standard of training of the pilots and air gunners, and the
accuracy of the Norden bombsight.[1] This was a policy which could
not be altered nor reversed. The B-17 was unsuitable for night operations, and the crews were not trained to fly at night. Indeed, they
were not even trained to take off and land in the dark, which was
to prove a serious handicap during the short daylight hours of winter
in northwest Europe.

But there was no doubt that the B-17 was a magnificent airplane,
the Norden sight was the best of its kind, and the crews were well
trained. The Air Corps was committed to a policy of high altitude
daylight bombing, and it was determined to make a success of it.

Meanwhile the R. A. F. Bomber Command was carrying out its
leaflet raids over Germany, and building up its operational training
organization and its war reserves. As the spring of 1940 approached,
France and Britain waited for Hitler to move. Very good use had, on
the whole, been made of the eighteen months since the Munich
crisis. The French mood was changeable; it ranged from optimism to
apprehension and gloom, and they had not done all they could have
done to improve their training and equipment. In Britain the coming
struggle was awaited with considerable anxiety, but also with some
degree of confidence.

The frosts and snows of winter began to disperse and the period of
waiting was nearly over. The hour of trial was at hand.

[1] See Appendix C.

8 The Expedition to Norway

Germany's war industries were largely dependent on the import of iron ore. Before the war she had imported 60 per cent of her total consumption of this commodity, of which 40 per cent came from Sweden. The total of this Swedish ore amounted to some nine million tons a year, and after the outbreak of the war Germany would need even more, as some of her other sources, such as France and North Africa, would no longer be available. And the Swedish ore was especially valuable to Germany, as it is very rich in iron content.

There was a safe sea route through the Baltic from the Swedish port of Luleå, but the capacity of this route did not exceed five million tons a year, because Luleå was icebound during the winter months. When this route was out of action, the Germans shipped the ore from the ice-free port of Narvik in northern Norway. But this route was only practicable as long as the ore ships could evade the Allied blockade. In order to assist in this the Germans routed their ships as close as possible to the Norwegian coast. There are continuous sea passages, known as the Leads, between the fringe of innumerable islands—the Skerries—and the mainland. By using the Leads they kept as far away as they could from the Allied sea and air forces, and by keeping within Norwegian territorial waters—which was possible from a point well within the Arctic Circle to the entrance to the Skagerrak—they were immune from interception.

In November 1939, the British Government had decided to institute the Northern Barrage of minefields across the North Sea, which in the First World War had proved valuable in making it more difficult for German submarines and warships to gain access to the main Allied shipping routes. But as long as the Leads were free to German ships, the Northern Barrage would be ineffective. In December 1939, the British Admiralty pressed strongly for sea-mines to be laid in the Leads, and in January 1940, the Norwegian Government was asked for permission to do so. This was firmly refused.

Early in 1940 the British Government prepared a plan and collected resources for a military expedition to help Finland, which had been attacked by the Soviet Union in December 1939. The Allies had hoped that this attack on the Finns would cause the Scandinavian countries to interpret their neutrality in a manner more favorable to Allied interests, and that they would give facilities for this force to cross their territory in order to reach Finland. But the negotiations were still proceeding when, on March 13, the Finnish Government capitulated.

The Allies then decided to mine the Leads without Norwegian permission and plans were prepared to send the Expeditionary Force, which had been designed to help Finland, to seize and hold the port of Narvik if the Germans should react to the mining of the Leads by invading Norway.

On April 5 France and Britain sent a joint note to the governments of Norway and Sweden, reserving the right "to take such measures as might be necessary to prevent Germany from obtaining from Norway resources or facilities for war purposes." On the night of April 7 mines were laid in Norwegian territorial waters at West Fjord, Bud, and Stadlandet, with the object of forcing the German ore traffic to emerge from safety and become liable to interception. Normal shipping traffic would also have to leave territorial waters at these points, but that would only be a minor inconvenience. The purpose of this action was explained in a statement issued by the Allies on April 8.

The Germans had been planning the occupation of Denmark and Norway for some time. There were many advantages to Germany in an occupation of these two countries. Taking a short-term view, they hoped to divert Allied forces to a subsidiary theater of war, where they would be at a disadvantage, and thus weaken the Western front.

From a long-term point of view, the possession of the Norwegian coast would provide bases for submarines and surface raiders; air forces based in Norway could threaten the British naval base at Scapa Flow; and their ore traffic from Narvik could follow a safe route.

The Germans therefore prepared in great secrecy a plan to transport troops and equipment in warships, and in merchant vessels posing as ore ships and colliers, timed to bring about simultaneous landings at Oslo, Bergen, Kristiansand, Trondhjem, and Narvik. At least 1,000 aircraft were allocated to the support of this operation, and their main task was to destroy the Danish and Norwegian air forces, to seize the principal airfields in Denmark and southern Norway, and to attack Allied naval forces and other shipping attempting to approach Norwegian waters.

The plans were completed and everything was ready to launch this operation by the middle of March, but the Germans were looking for some justification for the attack on these two neutral countries. Some justification was needed, because Germany and Denmark had signed a pact of nonaggression as recently as May 1939. Hitler, in the hope of impressing public opinion in the United States and elsewhere, had offered to conclude such pacts with any small nations that felt themselves threatened by Germany. Denmark, conscious of the weakness of her position, was the only Scandinavian state to accept the offer. In this treaty, Germany and Denmark had agreed that they would in no circumstances resort to war or to any other form of violence against each other.

No excuse, however, could be found, but by early April Hitler was convinced that the Allies were about to take some action to impede the German ore traffic from Narvik, and he determined to forestall them. It was a mere coincidence that the German invasion began on April 9, the day after the Allied announcement that they had mined the Leads.

The essence of the German plan was surprise. Their sudden and powerful assault had a paralyzing effect on the government and people of Denmark. The country, militarily weak and morally disarmed by the nonaggression pact, offered no effective resistance. Norway was a different matter and, although the German surprise was complete, they encountered resistance in some places. Their naval losses were serious. Their newest cruiser, the *Blucher*, was

sunk in the approaches to Oslo, the pocket battleship *Lutzow* was
damaged, and the light cruiser *Koenigsberg* was sunk by aircraft of
the Fleet Air Arm operating from airfields in the isles of Orkney.
The British navy also suffered; the battleship *Rodney* and two light
cruisers were damaged by air attack, and the destroyer *Ghurka* sunk.
A naval battle also occurred off Narvik, in which two German destroyers and six transports were sunk, while the British lost two
destroyers. A second engagement a few days later, in which the battleship *Warspite* took part, completed the destruction of the German
ships and cut off their troops at Narvik from all supplies except such
as could be sent by air.

The Germans had lost in all one heavy and one light cruiser
and ten modern destroyers, and many other ships were damaged. The
British Admiralty considered that the naval situation would justify
the dispatch of the Expeditionary Force, originally intended to help
Finland, to the assistance of Norway. This proposal caused a disagreement among the British Chiefs of Staff. The First Sea Lord
took the view that heavy warships, supported by aircraft carriers and
destroyers, could guarantee the safe transport of the expedition
across the North Sea, and secure its lines of sea communications.
The Chief of the Air Staff argued that the essential prerequisite
for the success of any sea or land operation—a sufficient degree of
air superiority—was unattainable in the circumstances. The Expeditionary Force, though it might be safely landed, would have to
operate in a theater of war in which all the strategic advantages
were held by an enemy who also possessed undisputed air superiority.
The air resources available for use in Norway were very limited.
Only one wing of fighters could be spared and, owing to the distance
from Britain, they would have to be sent by sea and operate from
improvised bases in Norway. There could be no question of basing any
bomber forces in Norway, since the resources of Bomber Command
at that time were very small, and it had been agreed with the French
that the whole strength of Bomber Command would be available
to delay a German advance in the event of an attack on the Western
front. Coastal Command was working to the limit of its capacity in
escorting convoys and carrying out routine sea reconnaissances. The
Norwegian air force had been quickly overwhelmed during the first
few days, and could not be counted on to give any assistance.

Nor was it possible for Bomber Command to operate effectively from bases in Britain. The Whitleys, from their bases in Yorkshire, would have to fly a total distance of 820 miles to Stavanger and back, over 1,000 miles to Oslo, and nearly 1,500 to reach Trondhjem.

This meant that only small bomb loads could be carried and that the time available for locating and attacking targets would be very limited.

The Air Staff believed that the task of establishing bases in Norway for the fighter and army cooperation squadrons, against the massive opposition of the German air forces based in Denmark and southern Norway, would be formidable if not impossible. Even if the Expeditionary Force could be transported to Norway and safely disembarked, it would have very inadequate air support and its ports and supply depots in Norway would have no fighter protection, apart from any that could be provided from aircraft carriers, until air bases could be established. The Air Staff therefore concluded that the Expeditionary Force would have little chance of carrying out its task successfully, and that there was a grave risk that its communications might be seriously hampered or even interrupted.

Taking all these factors into consideration, the Air Ministry took the view that the operation had very little prospect of success. These divergences of view were considered by the British Government. The crux of the matter was the ability of fleets and armies to perform their tasks successfully against the opposition of a powerful land-based air force. The government decided to take the risk and dispatch the expedition. In taking this decision the British were as much influenced by political considerations—the desire to help Norway if at all possible—as by purely military factors.

The first essential was to secure an adequate base port. Trondhjem offered the best facilities and was also considered essential as a seat of government by the Norwegians. It was planned to recapture it by making landings at the small ports of Namsos to the north and Andalsnes to the south, followed by a simultaneous advance on Trondhjem by the two forces.

Andalsnes lay at the extreme effective radius of action of bombers based in Britain, while Namsos and Trondhjem were beyond their range, and the whole of Norway and the eastern half of the North Sea were beyond the reach of British-based fighters. The expedition therefore had to rely on carrier-borne air protection and support, until airfields could be established in Norway and air forces transferred there. It was, however, realized that the German air forces at Sola near Stavanger and at Trondhjem could not be ignored. Bomber Command was given the task of bombing the airfield at Sola, while that at Trondhjem was allocated to the Fleet Air Arm. These air bombardments were to be followed by a bombardment of Sola from the sea, carried out by the cruiser *Suffolk*. These attacks were not very successful and did little damage to the German air force. The *Suffolk* limped back to Scapa Flow on the morning of April 18 "with the sea lapping over her quarter-deck; she had bombarded Sola airfield, Stavanger, and so far from putting it out of action had suffered seven hours' counter-attack from the air."[1] Several other British warships operating in the Namsos area were also damaged by German air attack.

Several thousand infantry were put ashore at Namsos and at Andalsnes, but they were almost without artillery, motor transport, or A. A. defenses, and had no armored forces. Their orders were to push on quickly, make contact with Norwegian troops still resisting the German forces, which occupied at that time only a few key points in Norway, and capture the port of Trondhjem. This strategic concept was quite unrealistic. Within a few days German air attacks seriously damaged both base ports. Quays and warehouses were destroyed, water and electricity supplies cut off, and the railway damaged and rolling stock demolished. The local inhabitants fled, taking with them every vehicle that could move. There were no means of repairing the ports, which in full working order barely had the capacity to support the forces based on them. In these circumstances the British troops, attacked by German forces supported by tanks, artillery, and aircraft, had to withdraw.

An attempt was made to base a British fighter squadron on a frozen lake at Lesjaskog. The squadron was ferried over in the aircraft carrier *Glorious*, and on the evening of April 24 was flown off at sea led by two aircraft of the Fleet Air Arm. At Lesjaskog there were no facilities of any kind; it was just a bare expanse of ice. The weather was very cold and there was little shelter. By a tremendous effort the squadron flew forty sorties on April 25, shooting down at least six enemy aircraft. The Germans then began seriously to bomb Lesjaskog. The aircraft were shot up and bombed while they were

[1] *British History of the Second World War: The Campaign in Norway;* p. 74.

AIR MINISTRY OFFICIAL PHOTOGRAPH

Marshal of the R. A. F.
Viscount Trenchard—
"The Father of the Royal
Air Force."

IMPERIAL WAR MUS

A bomber of the First World War—BE-2C.

A bomber of 1918, used by the Independent Air Force—The DH-9A with Liberty engines.

IMPERIAL WAR MU

AIR MINISTRY OFFICIAL PHOTOGRAPH

Intended for the bombing of Berlin—a giant bomber: the Handley-Page V-1500.

BY COURTESY OF COLONEL ZUCCONI

A prophet of air power—
General Giulio Douhet of
the Italian air force.

U. S. AIR FORCE OFFICIAL PHOTOGRAPH

Sacrificed a career for air
power, Brigadier General
"Billy" Mitchell.

IMPERIAL WAR MUSEUM

A German Zeppelin Airship of the kind used in air attacks on Britain.

A huge bomb that was never dropped—The 1,650 lb. bomb designed to be carried by the four-engined Handley-Page V-1500

AIR MINISTRY OFFICIAL PHOTOGRA

PHOTOGRAPHIC NEWS AGENCIES LTD.

A great bomber commander, Marshal of the R. A. F. Sir Arthur Harris.

U. S. AIR FORCE OFFICIAL PHOTO

First Commander of the U. S. Eighth Air Force, Lieutenant-General Ira C. Eaker.

being fueled and rearmed. The ice surface of the lake was broken up, and by nightfall of April 26 only four aircraft were serviceable. Twenty-four hours later only one aircraft was left.

The British forces at Andalsnes and Namsos, faced by an enemy enjoying complete air superiority, were unable to hold on. Their position was becoming precarious and on April 27 the decision was taken to evacuate central Norway. The only direct air support at Andalsnes was provided by long-range Blenheim night-fighters operating from a base in the Orkneys. Owing to the distance, each sortie could patrol for one hour only over the base. Namsos was completely out of range. Attacks were made by Bomber Command from bases in Britain against German airfields at Stavanger, Fornebu near Oslo, and Aalborg in North Jutland. These attacks had some effect, and substantially reduced the scale of German air activity during the re-embarkation of the troops. Further north, the British had fared somewhat better. Two fighter squadrons were successfully established at Bardufoss, which was about fifty miles northeast of Narvik. After a naval bombardment a force was landed, and Narvik was captured on May 28.

This relative success was due to the remoteness of Narvik from the German air bases, but it was clear that this advantage was only temporary. The Germans were moving their air forces into more northerly bases, and the British had only one and a half divisions in Norway against eleven German divisions. Although the German forces included a good many second-line units, composed of older men and reservists, the disparity in numbers was too great, and the British inferiority in the air was decisive. No reinforcements could be sent to Norway, as the Germans had attacked the Western front on May 10, carrying all before them. The British armies were being evacuated from Dunkirk and Calais; the fall of France seemed to be imminent, and Britain would need every ship, every airplane, and every man in the coming trial of strength with Germany.

It was decided to destroy the railway, the ore-loading machinery, and other port installations, and withdraw from Narvik. The evacuation began on June 4, and like those at Namsos and Andalsnes, was carried out with great skill.

But the final blow was yet to come. The aircraft-carrier *Glorious* and her escort of two destroyers, carrying all the evacuated R. A. F. units, were intercepted by the *Scharnhorst* and *Gneisenau* and sunk with the loss of more than 1,500 lives.

So ended one of the most ill-conceived campaigns of the Second World War. It was of secondary importance, for its strategic consequences had no vital effect on the conduct of the war. But it was a test case—a milestone in the history of air power—and it had a profound influence on future military policy. It marked, with unmistakable clarity, the end of an era; the era of the supremacy of British sea power in the waters of the North Sea and English Channel. After this sharp lesson the Admiralty was forced to recognize that command of the air over the sea was as important as command of the sea itself. And the British army no longer had any illusions about the paramount importance of achieving and maintaining air superiority in the battle zone, over the base areas, and along the lines of communication.

The British people were shocked and dismayed by this ignominious failure. Centuries of reliance on sea power had made it difficult for them to realize that times had changed, and that the Royal Navy could be challenged and even defeated by land-based air power. The Prime Minister, Mr. Neville Chamberlain, was made the scapegoat for this fiasco and was forced to resign. Indeed Mr. Chamberlain, who had rendered great services during the period of rearmament and whose intervention at the time of the Munich crisis had given the Allies the breathing space needed to avert disaster, was not the man to lead the British people in war.

On May 10, by another coincidence the day on which Hitler attacked in the West, Mr. Winston Churchill, the First Lord of the Admiralty, was invited to form a new government.

It is easy to be wise after the event. But in this campaign the Air Staff had been wise before it, but their counsel was not heeded. They had pointed out that there was no way open to the British of countering the devastating effect of German air superiority, which predestined the campaign to failure. The *British Official History*, after noting this fact, sums up in these words:

This was the obvious lesson of the campaign—or in a sense no lesson at all, since the Air Staff, knowing the insignificant size of the air support which would be available for any Scandinavian expedition, had correctly appreciated in advance the peril to which our lines of communication would inevitably be exposed. An Air Ministry historian is even able to say, *"It is very rare in war that dangers that have been anticipated correspond so exactly to the dangers that eventuate."*[2]

[2] *The Campaign in Norway*, p. 234.

9 Disaster in Western Europe

One of the first acts of Mr. Winston Churchill's new government was to set up a Ministry of Aircraft Production, which at once took over from the Air Ministry the responsibility for producing aircraft, engines, spare parts, and all ancillary air force equipment. Lord Beaverbrook was appointed Minister, and he was especially charged with doing everything possible to increase the rate of production of fighters and all equipment needed for the coming battle with the German air force. He was a man of boundless energy, whose administrative methods were fluid and improvised rather than orderly, and he set about his task with immense zeal. He spared no effort to make the people of Britain realize the importance of fighter production. He even asked all householders to give his Ministry every aluminum cooking pot and pan that they could spare, and many did so in the belief that these would be turned, in the twinkling of an eye, into Hurricanes and Spitfires.

There were in fact only three ways in which an increase could be made in the planned production of fighters during the next few months:

1. By bringing home to the aircraft industry and the trade unions the vital need to increase output.

2. By ensuring that all priorities were concentrated on air defense, at the expense if necessary of the air offensive.

3. By cutting down on the production of spare parts and using

the capacity thus released to build airplanes instead.

Lord Beaverbrook used all three methods. The first one did much to remove, temporarily at least, restrictive practices in offices and at the workbench. The second had some effect, though at a cost to Britain's subsequent war effort which it is difficult to assess but which was certainly substantial. The third produced the most obvious result, but it was largely illusory, as the lack of spares compelled the squadrons to "cannibalize"; that is, to rob unserviceable aircraft of spare parts to keep the others going.

Although the Minister was unable, owing to shortage of time, to achieve very much in the way of material results, his iconoclastic activities had a salutary moral effect, both on the Royal Air Force and on the general public.

The defense systems upon which the Dutch, the Belgians, and the French relied were massive and imposing, but unfortunately they were not well adapted to deal with the system of mobile warfare which had been developed by the German army and air force. They were related to the two-dimensional theory of warfare, and depended upon obstacles, inundations, fortresses, and static lines of defense. The gravest weakness of the French defense system—the fact that the Maginot Line did not cover an advance through Belgium—has already been referred to.

On the eve of the German attack the Advanced Air Striking Force (A. A. S. F.) based in France, consisted of eight squadrons of Battles, an obsolescent single-engined light bomber; two of Blenheims, a more modern twin-engined light bomber; and three of Hurricane fighters. There was, in addition, the Air Component of the Field Force (A. C. F. F.) with four squadrons of Blenheims; four of Lysanders, for army cooperation duties; and six squadrons of Hurricanes.

The first indication of Hitler's intention to attack in the west was a flood of warnings in the German press and wireless, in early May, that the Allies were about to occupy the Low Countries as a preliminary to an Anglo-French invasion of the Ruhr and Rhineland. On May 10, 1940, German forces simultaneously invaded Holland, Belgium, and Luxembourg.

Three main tasks were allotted to the Royal Air Force during the first week of the campaign. The first was to delay the advance of German armored forces through Luxembourg and in the Maastricht area, which was allocated to the A. A. S. F. The second was the support of the Allied advance to the assistance of Belgium, for which the A. C. F. F. and the A. A. S. F. were responsible. The third was the attack of railway centers and supply depots in the Ruhr and the Rhineland, which was the duty of the night bombers of Bomber Command. In addition, a considerable number of Hurricanes of No. 11 Group, Fighter Command, was employed in operations in the battle areas, refueling in France, and returning each night to their home stations in Britain.

The main weight of the German attack fell upon Holland, which was quickly overwhelmed. The Germans made three main thrusts; into Friesland and northern Holland; a central attack on the main Dutch defenses; and a southern advance into Limburg and Brabant. The northern attack failed, and in the flooded central area the Dutch maintained a stubborn resistance and for three days they held up a vastly superior force. The Germans made a considerable use of parachute and airborne troops in this early phase. They were employed to capture airfields, bridges, and centers of communication; to spread confusion and cause panic; and to force the Dutch to disperse their reserves. These airborne penetrations behind their defense lines were largely responsible for the final collapse of the courageous Dutch resistance.

Three difficulties confronted the Royal Air Force in its attempts to help the Dutch. In the first place, its major responsibility was to support the British Expeditionary Force, which had been ordered to advance to the assistance of the Belgians, and it could spare only limited resources for use in Holland. Secondly, fighter aircraft based in Britain could not operate effectively over Holland, since Rotterdam was at the extreme limit of their range. Thirdly, air operations were hampered by a lack of precise information as to the military situation, which was confused and subject to rapid changes.

The task of the Advanced Air Striking Force was even more formidable. On May 10 and 11 repeated attacks were made on German armored and motorized columns in Luxembourg. A very heavy price was paid for these attempts to stop this advance, for the German mobile antiaircraft defenses were extremely effective, and the Battles, when carrying out low-flying attacks, were very vulnerable. In the first attack, on May 10, 12 aircraft out of 32 were lost in an attack on a German column. Most of these casualties were due to light

A. A. fire. In the German organization all A. A. units were an integral part of the German air force, and the Air Ministry under Goering had seen to it that they were numerous and efficient. In France and Britain the antiaircraft weapons were under Army control and had tended to be neglected. Certainly the effectiveness of the German A. A. fire came as an unpleasant shock to the Allied air forces.

In spite of severe losses the Battles of the A. A. S. F. continued to press home their attacks with great gallantry. On May 12 a concentrated attack was made on a number of bridges over the Albert Canal west of Maastricht, across which German troops were pouring. The Blenheims destroyed two road bridges and a railway bridge at Maastricht and attacked troops on the roads. The Battles destroyed an important road bridge over the Albert Canal. Strong fighter opposition and heavy A. A. fire were encountered and losses were heavy.

But these sacrifices did not stop the German advance into Belgium, and by May 14 they had crossed the Meuse in three places. The A. A. S. F. attacked bridges near Sedan, and destroyed several of them, but although the German advance was slowed, it could not be stopped. The R. A. F. carried out a total of 87 sorties against the bridges over the Meuse, and 40 aircraft were lost. Eight bridges were destroyed. In all, between May 10 and 15 the Battles and Blenheims made some 200 sorties in attempts to halt the German advance, and from these 73 aircraft failed to return.

Meanwhile Bomber Command had made little progress with its task of bombing supply depots and railway centers in the Ruhr and Rhineland. This was mainly due to the opposition of the French, who were obsessed by the fear of German retaliation. The French General Staff had consistently opposed the bombing of these or any other targets in Germany, and advocated the employment of the British long-range bombers in direct support of the land forces.

On May 15 the government of the Netherlands was transferred to Britain and the Dutch forces laid down their arms. The morale of the French and Belgian forces on the Meuse, harassed by incessant dive-bombing attacks by the German air force, was showing signs of collapsing. On May 16 the Germans began a drive westward which resulted, within a week, in the loss of the main Channel ports, forcing a rapid withdrawal of the British Expeditionary Force, and culminating in the complete defeat of the French armies. The Royal Air Force in France was kept on the move and this seriously reduced its operational efficiency. In these circumstances French objections were over-ruled, and Bomber Command carried out vigorous attacks against road and rail centers in the hope of hampering the German advance. There is evidence that these operations caused some damage and confusion.

At about this time the German air force, which had been employed in close support of the land forces, was switched to the attack of strategic targets. After the German break-through it concentrated on the attack of road and rail centers with the object of paralyzing the movement of the Allied reserves. In this it would probably have been successful had there been any Allied reserves assembled and ready to move.

German air attacks were also made against Allied supply and ammunition depots, ports, and oil installations.

On May 19 it was clear that nothing could avert the fall of France, and it was decided to bring the A. A. S. F. and the A. C. F. F. back to Britain while there was yet time to do so. The British Expeditionary Force was fighting its way northward and westward in the hope of evacuation from the Dunkirk area. By May 24 all the flying units had been withdrawn, and the rear party arrived in Britain on May 27.

On May 26 the Belgian Government suddenly capitulated, leaving a 20-mile gap on the flank of the British Expeditionary Force. Every effort was made by the Royal Air Force, operating from bases in southeast England, to support the withdrawal. A very large number of sorties were flown by units of Fighter Command. Intensive attacks were carried out by the light bombers of No. 2 Group, Bomber Command, against the advancing German columns and road and rail bottlenecks. During the week commencing May 17 the long-range bombers flew by night 193 sorties against targets in the Rhineland; 260 sorties in attacks on communications in the Namur-Mezieres area; and 72 against enemy positions in the forward area.

Between the evening of May 26 and June 4, under the protection of Fighter Command and using every suitable warship, merchant vessel, fishing boat, and yacht that could be found, 309,682 Allied troops were evacuated to Britain from the port and beaches of Dunkirk. In addition, 6,981 sick and wounded men were brought back in hospital ships. Of this number 186,587 were British and the rest were French, many of whom elected to fight on with the Free French forces. It was rightly called by Mr. Winston Churchill a miracle of deliverance. He added "There was a victory inside this deliverance which should be noted. It was gained by the Royal Air Force."[1] During the evacuation the bombers had not been idle. Between May 30 and June 4 some 250 sorties were made by the Blenheims against enemy troops and positions in the Dunkirk area, and many of these attacks were successful. On May 30 it was decided that the attempts to interfere with German communications by the long-range bombers were no longer worth while and, as it was believed at that time that Germany's oil resources were very small, Bomber Command was ordered to devote a larger proportion of its effort to the attack of German synthetic oil plants. Between the nights of May 30 and June 4, 63 per cent of the Command's effort was directed against the synthetic oil industry, 26 per cent against objectives in the battle zone, and only 11 per cent against German communications.

On June 5 the Germans began a new advance, with the object of forcing the crossing of the river Somme, and completing the destruction of the Allied forces. There were two British divisions—one infantry and one armored—on the Somme, and some hastily regrouped formations of the French Army. The Germans prepared the way for their advance by an air offensive against railway centers, airfields, and ports. Tanks and dive-bombers were used in great numbers in the battle area, and by the evening German forces had crossed the Somme and were advancing toward the Seine. Air support was given to the Allied forces by Battles and Blenheims, based in Britain, using advanced landing grounds in the southern Champagne area, and later in the district around Vendome. They were mainly employed in attacking bridges and armored columns. The night bombers, while still continuing their attacks against German oil resources, concentrated a good deal of their effort against the Seine bridges, and road and rail junctions north and east of Paris.

During the whole of this campaign the French air force had done very little. Their fighters were obsolescent and were no match for the German Messerschmitt 109's and 110's. Most of the rest of their air force was equipped and trained for reconnaissance and the control of artillery fire in static warfare. In a war of movement, against the massive opposition of the German fighter forces and A. A. fire, the French air force was almost helpless. The aircrews were not lacking in gallantry and determination, and, with good leadership and more

[1] House of Commons, June 5, 1940.

suitable equipment, they would have given a better account of themselves.

On June 13 Chalons fell and two British brigades and 20,000 French troops were captured, and on June 14 the Germans entered Paris. Organized French resistance then collapsed and on June 16 the government opened negotiations with the Germans for an armistice.

Toward the end the June the British Government took stock of its position. Most of the men of the Expeditionary Force had been saved but practically all their weapons, transport, and equipment had been lost. If the Germans could succeed in landing a substantial force in Britain, there would be little with which to oppose them. The Prime Minister, indeed, suggested equipping the Home Guard—a force mainly composed of elderly veterans of the First World War—with pikes. The Royal Navy was still stronger than the German navy, but all its heavy ships were based at Scapa Flow, and the Admiralty was unwilling to station anything more than a few light cruisers and destroyers in the English Channel and southern North Sea. The issue clearly turned on whether or not the Germans could gain air control over the waters of the Channel.

After the German break-through on the Meuse the policy of the British Government had been dominated by the need to keep in being an air force capable of preventing the Germans from gaining that control. The Battle of France was seen as a prelude to the coming Battle of Britain. In some respects the war on the Continent, and especially the operations at Dunkirk, had placed a greater strain on Fighter Command than did the ensuing Battle of Britain. It was fought under immense pressure, both political and military, and presented problems for which Fighter Command, equipped and trained for the defense of Britain, was not very well adapted.

At the end of the battle both Fighter and Bomber Commands were temporarily left in a dangerously weakened condition. Had the Germans followed up the evacuation from Dunkirk by an immediate air attack on Britain, the results would have been serious. But, fortunately, the German air force was also in need of a breathing spell. The Germans now possessed a great number of airfields, from northern Norway through Denmark, Holland, Belgium, and France to the Brest Peninsula. This brought the whole of the British Isles within range of their bombers. Time was needed to re-deploy their squadrons, to build up stocks of fuel, bombs, ammunition, and spare parts on the captured airfields, and to give their aircrews a much needed rest.

The operations in May and June had revealed some defects in the British equipment and organization, and steps were immediately taken to remedy them. But, broadly speaking, the battle experiences of the Royal Air Force had been encouraging. They had given confidence to the Air Staff in the soundness of their equipment and training, and to the aircrews in the quality of their aircraft, the effectiveness of their tactics, and the skill of their leaders. Although greatly outnumbered, the British Hurricane pilots had quickly acquired a marked moral ascendancy over the German fighters. This was partly due to material success—the losses inflicted on the enemy being far greater than those sustained by the Hurricanes—but also largely due to the determined fighting spirit of the British pilots and the courage with which they attacked superior numbers without hesitation. This was a marked characteristic of the fighter pilots of the Royal Flying Corps in the First World War, and it had become a tradition of the Royal Air Force.

The Battle of Britain began on August 8, 1940, with a heavy air attack on British shipping in the Channel. Much has been written about the conduct of the battle from the fighter point of view, but the contribution of the bombers to the victory is less well known. For Bomber Command the battle to defeat Hitler's plans for the invasion of Britain—operation "Sealion"—began as soon as France surrendered. In July the British bombers mainly attacked German ports and shipping and laid sea mines, though a proportion of their effort was directed against oil plants and communications. The Blenheims of No. 2 Group were allotted the task of attacking German airfields in daylight. Although some of these attacks were very successful, it is doubtful whether they were worth while. The Germans had over three hundred airfields at their disposal, and it is unlikely that the British attacks would have sufficed to cause the Germans any difficulties over air bases, or have done serious damage to their air forces dispersed over so wide an area.

During August the main objectives of the German bombers were the airfields of Fighter Command. They concentrated against the sector stations of No. 11 Group, where the main British Fighter strength was accommodated. These attacks by the whole weight of the German bomber force against some 20 vital airfields did a great deal of damage to the ground organization of Fighter Command. In addition, the number of Hurricanes and Spitfires destroyed on the ground so greatly exceeded the intake from production that it was estimated toward the end of August that three more weeks of such operations would have exhausted the British reserves of fighter aircraft.

In these circumstances the Prime Minister decided to play a bold card. On the night of August 24 a number of German bombs were dropped on London—the first since 1918—and the government ordered a heavy raid on Berlin as a reprisal. On the night of August 25, 81 aircraft of Bomber Command carried out a successful attack on the German capital, although the night was scarcely long enough to allow the aircraft to go and return in darkness. The German High Command reacted sharply, and within a few days their main air attack had been switched to London and other towns and cities. The pressure against Fighter Command's airfields, which was imperiling the British defense system, was relieved. Although this meant that the civilian population had to suffer, it was a turning point in the battle, and greatly improved the British chances of victory.

Early in September air reconnaissance showed large numbers of huge barges moving toward the sea along the South Beveland and Terneuzen-Ghent canals. Soon there were hundreds of these barges in Ostend and Flushing, and many more in Dunkirk and Calais. Convoys of these barges moved westward every day close to the coast, and vast quantities of military stores were being accumulated at the Channel ports.

There could be no doubt that operation "Sealion" was imminent. On September 7 the British Government issued a warning that invasion was probable within the next few days. That night the whole strength of Bomber Command was concentrated against the barges and military stores in the Channel ports. Large numbers of barges were sunk, stores were destroyed and set on fire, and large ammunition dumps exploded. Night after night the British bombers pounded the invasion ports and on September 11 the date of "Sealion" was postponed until September 24.

The British bombers made an especially successful attack on the night of September 13, doing tremendous damage and sinking over 80 barges in the port of Ostend alone. But Goering had an exaggerated idea of what the German air force had achieved. He assured Hitler that "given four or five more days of good weather, the results would be decisive." On September 15, however, the German air force suffered a severe defeat at the hands of the British fighters. This day is generally regarded as the climax of the battle.

On September 17 Hitler decided to postpone operation "Sealion" indefinitely. He could no longer maintain his concentrations of barges, troops, and stores in the Channel ports in the face of Bomber Command's attacks. He gave orders that the remaining barges and stores should be widely dispersed, and the troops moved away from the danger areas of the ports.

On September 23 air reconnaissance confirmed that the German concentrations were melting away and, although the British bombers continued to attack barges and invasion stores wherever they could be found, it was clear that the danger of immediate invasion had passed. On October 12 the Germans postponed operation "Sealion" until the spring of 1941, but in reality the plan was dead. As the winter closed in the German air force concentrated on the night bombing of London and other industrial and administrative centers.

Although Fighter Command must be given the chief credit for the victory known as the Battle of Britain, that victory would not have been so decisive and the price in lives would have been higher, had it not been for the successful operations of Bomber Command. Its attacks on shipping and its mine-laying hampered the German preparations for invasion, and the daring attack on Berlin caused the German air force to switch from its damaging concentration on the British fighter airfields to the less dangerous bombing of London and other cities. Later, the bombers did tremendous damage to the loaded barges, the accumulations of stores and ammunition, and other military equipment in the Channel ports. So successful were these attacks that the Germans were compelled to order a dispersal.

The Battle of Britain deserves to rank as one of the decisive battles of the world. In it the British defeated the much larger German air force, wrecked Hitler's plans for operation "Sealion," and forced

him to rely on the dubious policy of attempting to bring about the
reduction of Britain by means of his night bombers.

But it was, as Mr. Winston Churchill told the House of Commons,
"not the beginning of the end, but the end of the beginning."

10 Britain Stands Alone

The Royal Air Force had won its battle, and Britain had survived the opening defensive phase of the war, but the cost of Western unpreparedness had been high. Britain now stood alone, with only 20 miles of sea separating it from the victorious Nazi armies.

The strategic concept with which the Allies had begun the war lay in ruins all about them. The Royal Navy had been roughly handled in the Norwegian campaign and elsewhere, and had begun to realize that warships could not operate on the surface of the sea, within striking distance of enemy land-based air forces, unless they were under the protection of superior land-based air power. The A S D I C echo-sounding system, on which the Admirality had relied for the location of submerged submarines had proved to be relatively unsuccessful, and the losses of British merchant shipping, already serious, threatened to rise to a dangerous level.

The British army had suffered one of the most catastrophic reverses of its long history. Although it had proved possible, by a great combined sea and air effort, to bring back most of the troops from the Continent, almost the whole of their equipment had been lost. In Britain itself it was still scarcely possible to muster a single division fit for battle. It would clearly take many months to re-equip the Army with up-to-date weapons and train it to use them. Only in North Africa had Britain any substantial land forces in fighting order.

The Royal Air Force, though in better shape than either of the other Services, had suffered severely. But, although its losses had been great, it had won most of its battles, its equipment was good and improving all the time, and its morale was high. Its doctrines had proved to be generally sound and the Air Force was, on the whole, trained and equipped along the right lines. Alone among the three Services it was not compelled to rethink the whole of its policy and recast its training. In 1943 the Prime Minister, speaking in the House of Commons, said: "As between the different Services, while avoiding invidious comparisons, I should certainly say that the outlook of the Royal Air Force upon this war was more closely attuned to the circumstances and conditions as they emerged by painful experience than those of either of the two other Services." If Mr. Winston Churchill's language on this occasion was not quite as clear and forceful as usual, this was no doubt because he wished to avoid hurting feelings, but the meaning is perfectly plain.

The relative success of the Air Staff in foreseeing the nature of operations in the Second World War was mainly due to two things. In the first place, the Royal Air Force had the great advantage of a fresh start in 1919. The newly formed Air Staff and the commanders of Royal Air Force formations had inherited no traditional or classical doctrines, the truth of which it was impious to doubt. They had therefore been able to think out their problems in an objective manner. Secondly, the Air Ministry had—especially in the decade before the war—enlisted the aid of a number of distinguished scientists, sitting together with senior serving officers on joint committees. Chief among these were the Air Defence Committee and the Committee for the Scientific Survey of the Air Offensive. Many leading scientists freely gave their valuable services in this way, and the names of Sir Henry Tizard and Sir Robert Watson-Watt, in particular, will always be remembered with gratitude by the Royal Air Force. This close integration of responsible military and scientific thinking—by means of which the methods of scientific research were applied to the preparations for, and the conduct of, warlike operations—produced extremely valuable results.

In the late autumn of 1940, when it became clear that the Battle of Britain by day had been won, the War Cabinet was faced by four major problems. Three of them were defensive in character; the fourth was offensive.

The German air force was making heavy bombing attacks by night

on London and other cities and towns, and it was a matter of great
urgency to solve the problems of night air defense. The war in North
Africa, the object of which was to protect the Suez Canal and British
access to Middle Eastern oilfields, was causing some anxiety. The
main difficulty lay not so much in the strength of the Italian military
threat, as in the impossibility, in the face of German and Italian
land-based air power, of using the Mediterranean sea route. This
meant that the line of communications to North Africa, only some
2,500 miles via the Straits of Gibraltar, had to go through submarine-
infested waters in the North and South Atlantic and round the Cape
of Good Hope, a total distance of more than 12,000 miles. Thirdly,
the Admiralty was perturbed by its inability to cope with the German
submarine campaign against merchant shipping and military transports, and was demanding a much greater concentration of resources
on naval affairs.

The fourth problem, though in a sense less urgent than the other
three, was by far the most important. Briefly, it was the problem of
what offensive action, if any, could be taken against Germany.

There must have been a very strong temptation at this time to
put all available resources into the solution of the three really pressing
problems; defense against German night bombing, defense in North
Africa, and defense against the German submarine campaign. But
the War Cabinet realized that even the most successful defensive
could not, in itself, bring final victory any nearer. It could stave off
defeat, and buy time, but no more.

The prospects of being able to take any worth-while offensive
action against Germany did not, at first sight, seem very hopeful. The
Navy's task was wholly defensive and it was incapable of bringing
any serious strategic pressure to bear on Germany. The only effective
land forces were committed in North Africa against the Italians, and
for this and other reasons there was no prospect of being able to
attack Germany on the ground. The only force, therefore, capable of
undertaking a strategic offensive was the Air Force.

The Prime Minister was well aware of this fact. Indeed, on September 3, 1940, on the first anniversary of the outbreak of the war,
he wrote a masterly minute for the War Cabinet. In this he said:

The Navy can lose us the war, but only the Air Force can win it.
Therefore our supreme effort must be to gain overwhelming mastery

*in the air. The Fighters are our salvation, but the Bombers alone
provide the means of victory. We must, therefore, develop the power
to carry an ever-increasing volume of explosives to Germany, so as
to pulverize the entire industry and scientific structure on which the
war effort and economic life of the enemy depend, while holding him
at arm's length from our Island. In no other way at present visible
can we hope to overcome the immense military power of Germany. . . .*

These words were written at a time when the Battle of Britain
was approaching its climax, and when most people were fully pre-
occupied with the urgent demands of that great defensive air battle.
They show a quite remarkable detachment, and a very clear grasp
of the situation.

In October 1940, the War Cabinet decided to order the heaviest
possible air offensive against Germany, to begin at the earliest
possible moment. This was certainly a correct decision and, in the
circumstances, a bold one. And it is a tribute to the confidence
inspired by the Royal Air Force that few people seemed to think it
strange that, as soon as Fighter Command had shown that defense
in the air could defeat a stronger force enjoying an excellent strategic
position, Bomber Command, small though it was, should be expected
to succeed in far less favorable strategic circumstances, and in the face
of the massive German air defenses. It is true that the policy of an
air offensive against Germany met with a good deal of opposition
in some quarters, but the chief argument advanced against it was
that it would be ineffective, not that it would be impracticable.

This decision was a challenge to the Air Ministry and especially
to Bomber Command. While they recognized that the policy was
strategically correct, and welcomed it, it was clear that several serious
difficulties would have to be faced before it could be made effective.
One of these difficulties was inherent in the strategic situation, while
the others were soluble, given time and an appropriate re-allocation
of priorities.

The first difficulty was inescapable and, although its effects could
be reduced by various measures, it was not removed until the Allied
armies had liberated western Europe from German occupation. All
British prewar planning had, by direction of the government, been
based on the assumption that the British bomber forces would be
able to operate from advanced bases in France, and probably in the

Low Countries also. This meant that the necessary penetration over defended territory, in order to reach many important targets in western Germany, such as the Ruhr, would be relatively short. It also meant that practically the whole of Germany would be within the range of night bombers, even during the short summer nights. It was no doubt politically impossible, before the outbreak of war, to plan on any other assumption, but it meant that the Air Staff had never been allowed to make overt preparations for a situation in which Europe up to the Pyrenees was in enemy occupation. Although it is true that many members of the Air Staff had no great confidence in the government's assumption, and took such steps as were open to them to prepare for the situation created by the fall of France, it is also true that, broadly speaking, British aircraft and equipment were not designed to cope with the situation with which they were now faced.

Next, the British and French failure before the war to create offensive air forces sufficiently powerful to carry the air war into the enemy's skies, inevitably meant that the main emphasis had to be put on preparations for the air defensive. From 1935 onward priorities in scientific air development, and especially in radar, had been increasingly concentrated on defensive problems. If the new air offensive were to have any chance of succeeding, however, it would require top priorities in research, development, and production.

Finally, Bomber Command was much too small for the task it had been set. It had suffered severely in gallant but futile attempts to stem the westward advance of the German armies in the early summer of 1940, and to avert the fall of France. In October 1940, when the air offensive against Germany began, it could muster a daily average of no more than about 250 light and medium bombers serviceable and fit for operations. A large expansion of the Command was essential.

The object of the air offensive against Germany was not clearly defined until the Allied Conference at Casablanca in January 1943, when it was set out in the following words: "Your primary object will be the progressive destruction of the German military, industrial and economic system, and the undermining of the morale of the German people to a point where their armed resistance is fatally weakened."[1]

[1] Directive by Combined Chiefs of Staff, Jan. 21, 1943.

Although not clearly defined, the idea in 1940 was much the same; though their experiences of being bombed had inclined the British to put rather too much emphasis on the moral effect among the civil population of heavy air attacks. Insufficient allowance was made for the degree of control over the population exerted by the authorities and the police in a totalitarian state.

The bomber offensive got off to a rather slow start, but by the end of 1940 a considerable number of attacks had been carried out against military targets, especially oil and benzole plants, in the Ruhr and the Rhineland. Meanwhile Bomber Command watched anxiously for the shift of priorities without which it would be impossible for it to carry out its colossal task. But as the year 1941 went on, it became clear that nothing of the sort was going to happen. Hurricanes and Spitfires were being produced in larger numbers than could be used, while the production of medium bombers was barely adequate to replace wastage and support a modest expansion. The heavy bombers, from which effort had been diverted in May 1940 to speed up the production of fighters, seemed as far off as ever. Nor was there much prospect of obtaining suitable aircraft from the United States under the provisions of Lend-Lease, because all the American long-range heavy bombers were designed for high-altitude daylight operations, and for various reasons were unsuitable for night work. The Command's light bomber force, No. 2 Group, which was chiefly employed on attacks against enemy shipping in daylight, was gradually re-equipped with excellent types of American light bomber, but this did not, of course, strengthen the strategic air attack on Germany.

What was even more serious, however, was the fact that no real effort had been made to allocate scientific manpower to the development of radar devices to assist the air offensive. Although requirements for radar navigation and blind-bombing devices had been issued by the Air Staff before the outbreak of the war, the need to concentrate on the air defensive had meant that almost no progress had been made in the solution of these problems.

A production drive acquires in time a momentum of its own, because the many thousands of people engaged in organizing and controlling it get a fixed idea that certain things are vitally needed, without knowing why, and striving to produce them becomes a habit. In addition, the Ministry of Aircraft Production, anxious to maintain a high numerical output, did not wish to forgo the production of a large quantity of fighters, three of which could be built for the same number of man-hours as one medium bomber. Nor was it particularly sympathetic to the idea of a bomber offensive. The truth is, of course, that to shift priorities on a national scale, when they have been directed with great emphasis and for a considerable time in certain well-known directions, requires firm and resolute handling at the highest level.

Not only did the air offensive suffer from lack of the required priorities, but it was further emasculated by the insistent demands of the antisubmarine war and the operations in North Africa. Both of these were defensive in character and, although they were important, the extent to which they were allowed to encroach on the resources available for the offensive should have been closely watched.

The Admiralty, obsessed by the danger to our sea communications, insisted on a powerful increase in the strength of Coastal Command. On March 6, 1941, the Prime Minister yielded to this pressure, and issued a directive giving absolute priority to the Battle of the Atlantic. Additional squadrons of long-range aircraft for antisubmarine duties could be found from only one source, and during 1941–1942 no less than 17 squadrons (204 long-range aircraft with crews) were transferred from Bomber to Coastal command. Some of these were supposed to be on loan, but none of them ever returned. Since Coastal Command had at that time no facilities for operational training, all replacement crews were drawn from Bomber Command Operational Training Units, creating a further serious drain on its resources. In addition, the Admiralty consistently pressed for the bombing of submarine bases, many of them in occupied territory, and for the attack of any German warships that happened to come within range. The two battlecruisers, *Scharnhorst* and *Gneisenau*, after one foray in the Atlantic in the spring of 1941, during which they sank about 115,000 tons of British shipping, came into Brest to refuel. There they were continually bombed and kept in an unserviceable state, but they could not be sunk because they were berthed in dry docks. After they came into Brest neither of them ever sank another British ship. But an enormous effort, and many thousands of tons of bombs, were diverted from Germany to the attack of these ships. In this sense, and in this sense alone, did these ships perform a valuable service to Germany. In February 1942 they were patched up sufficiently to make a dash through the Channel to get home to Germany, an episode that will be dealt with more fully in its proper place.

The war in North Africa was rather a different matter. Britain could have been defeated if she had been unable to maintain her sea communications, but the war could neither be lost nor won in North Africa. The immediate object of the campaign, the defense of Egypt and the Suez Canal, was not a vital British interest. The Suez Canal, in any event, was unusable as a main sea route because the Mediterranean was closed by enemy air power. The oil fields in Iraq and Persia, and the huge refinery at Abadan, were certainly of great importance, but there were alternative sources of oil available. And they could have been successfully defended with smaller forces by taking up a position further to the east. But the War Office, having no other land campaign, continually pressed for a strong reinforcement of this theater, and for an offensive policy to clear the enemy out of North Africa. In support of this plan, further considerable numbers of aircraft and crews were sent from Bomber Command to the Middle East.

As a result of these diversions Bomber Command, which succeeded in forming approximately 18 new squadrons during 1941, lost to Coastal Command and the Middle East a force of almost equivalent size. Thus the Command ended a year of great effort but little stronger numerically than at the beginning of it, and indeed temporarily weakened as a result of the dilution caused by its successful efforts to expand.

These difficulties and diversions impeded the development of the air offensive against Germany. Although it succeeded in pinning down a substantial part of the enemy resources in the defense of their homeland, it had but little effect, during 1941, on German productive capacity. An even more fundamental reason for this lack of success, however, was to be found in the absence of radar aids to navigation and bombing at night, which will be dealt with in some detail in the next chapter.

For the air offensive, therefore, the year 1941 was one of hope deferred. The War Cabinet, in the late autumn of 1940, had made the correct decision, but it had failed to insure the consequential re-deployment of the national effort on which the success of the air offensive depended.

It had willed the end, but it had neglected to will the means.

11 Air Bombardment Faces Difficulties

Toward the end of 1941 the Air Staff at Headquarters, Bomber Command, prepared an appreciation of the situation. This included a review of progress to date, and a consideration of future policy and requirements.

The British Government still adhered to the view that air bombardment should be confined to strictly military targets, such as railway centers, bridges, synthetic oil plants, and similar installations. It is true that some attacks on German towns and cities, including Berlin, had been ordered, but these were justified as reprisals for the German bombing of London, Birmingham, Manchester, Liverpool, Glasgow, Coventry, Portsmouth, Southampton, and other ports and industrial areas.

Air reconnaissance photographs of these small military targets, some of which had been attacked several times, showed very little damage. It was argued in some quarters that many kinds of damage would not be revealed by such photographs, and British experience of German air bombardment gave some support to this view. There had been many instances where production had been seriously interrupted as a result of damage to some relatively small key point, which probably could not have been detected by aerial photography.

This optimistic view was not accepted by Bomber Command Headquarters. There was reason to believe that these small targets had seldom been hit. A study of raid reports by aircrews showed that

108

they often had great difficulty in finding their aiming points, even in good weather. In conditions of bad visibility, with a rigorous German black-out in force, amid the distractions caused by A. A. fire, searchlight glare, and enemy decoy lighting and fires, it was almost impossible for them to do so. At the end of 1940 Bomber Command had urged that every bomber aircraft should be equipped to take a night photograph of the ground beneath it at the moment when it released its bombs. Tests had shown that this could be done by carrying a suitable camera, and releasing a flash bomb at the same time as the rest of the bomb load. But the Ministry of Aircraft Production was not anxious to find the industrial capacity to provide the large number of cameras and flash bombs involved, nor was the Air Ministry fully convinced of the need for them.

A small number of cameras and flash bombs became available early in 1941, but squadron commanders tended to give them only to their best crews, and the proportion of photographs showing that the aircraft was at or near the aiming point at the moment of releasing its bombs was therefore higher than the general average. It was, nevertheless, disturbingly low. Bomber Command continued to press for the supply of these cameras and flash bombs, and as the number in use increased it became painfully clear that the majority of photographs did not show the aiming point, and that a substantial number indicated that the aircraft were miles away from it when their bombs were released. It was also plain that by far the best results were obtained on clear nights with bright moonlight, and on occasions when the identification of the target was made easier by the existence of unmistakable leading marks, such as a large lake or the estuary of a river.

During most of the period under review the German defenses had been relatively ineffective, and it was common practice for aircrews to spend as much as half an hour cruising around trying to identify their targets. By the end of 1941 this was becoming too dangerous, especially on clear moonlit nights.

The conclusion from all this was that the attack by night of small military targets by aircrews using visual methods was ineffective, and would probably become impracticable in the near future.

The ultimate solution of these problems was the provision of efficient radar aids to night navigation, and radar devices to make accurate blind bombing possible. Such radar equipment had been

an Air Staff requirement since 1939, but—as has been explained—
the concentration of scientific resources on air defense problems had
made it impossible to make much progress in the development of
radar devices to assist the air offensive. At this stage Bomber Command did not know whether such devices were a possibility or not,
but it was clear that renewed pressure ought to be brought to bear
on the Ministry of Aircraft Production to devote much greater resources to the investigation of these problems.

This ultimate solution, even if practicable, was obviously not
attainable in the near future. But things could not go on as they were,
and some interim solution had to be found. After a very careful study
of the relevant factors, Bomber Command put forward the following
proposals.

It was suggested that the policy of attempting to attack small
military targets should be abandoned in favor of attacks on industrial
areas. British experience had shown that this form of attack had been
very effective in reducing the production of war materials. This was
mainly due to the cutting off of gas, electricity, and water supplies,
the blocking of roads, and the destruction of the workers' dwelling
houses. An analysis of the results of German bombing showed that,
weight for weight, the incendiary bomb was a more powerful destructive agent than the high-explosive bomb. Whereas the effects produced by an H. E. bomb are the direct result of the explosive force
carried in the bomb itself, the effects of the incendiary are relatively
unlimited. The incendiary bomb can take advantage of the com-
bustibility of a target and, by releasing this energy, can produce
results wholly out of proportion to the weight of the bomb. One
bomb might, for example, set fire to a huge building and thus bring
about its total destruction. The British had discovered that in an
industrial area surprisingly few objects were resistant to incendiary
attack. The most unpromising things would burn, and they did not
forget that the famous Crystal Palace, apparently constructed of
wrought iron and glass, had before the war given London its most
spectacular fire of the 20th century.

Bomber Command therefore proposed that concentrated attacks
should be made on German industrial cities and towns, using a large
proportion of incendiary bombs. It was objected in some quarters
that this so-called "area bombing" would degenerate into scattered
attacks, the aircrews releasing their bombs more or less at random

over an industrial area without attempting to make use of a precise aiming-point. There was in fact no danger of this happening. At that stage the most concentrated attack that the British bombers could make, using every aid to navigation and target identification available to them and all trying to bomb the same aiming point, was too scattered to be contained within the largest industrial area. The adoption of area attacks would in no way reduce the demand for radar aids to night navigation and accurate bombing by night. An analysis of the German night bombing of London had been made, plotting the fall of every bomb in an area of 225 square miles around Charing Cross. It was found that the density over this large area was very constant. Approximately the same number of bombs fell in a square mile in the outer suburbs as in the docks or the center of the city. This distribution was characteristic of night bombing by individual aircraft using normal navigation methods and visual target identification. The Air Staff of Bomber Command had little doubt that an analysis of British attacks in the Ruhr, supposed to be aimed at small military targets such as synthetic oil plants, would show a very similar pattern of distribution.

The failure of Bomber Command to expand during 1941 emphasized the importance of improving the accuracy of its bombing. If the bombing error could be halved, it would be roughly equivalent to doubling the size of the force. A study of raid reports showed that fires were frequently used as aiming points, mainly because they were easily visible, but also because the aircrews hoped, and perhaps believed, that such fires were caused by bombs from earlier aircraft hitting and igniting the target. It would therefore help to concentrate the bombing if the most able and experienced crews, who were most likely to be able to find and hit the target, were to lead the attack using a large proportion of incendiary bombs.

Bomber Command decided to arrange that the best crews should be the first to attack the target in the hope that they would start fires in the right place, and that thereafter the remainder of the force would bomb the fires. If, and when, radar aids to night navigation and bombing became available, it was proposed that they should be given to the best crews to assist them in marking the aiming point in this way. Thus the idea of using "pathfinders" to find and mark the aiming point came into existence.

Plans for the attack of several targets in Germany, known to be vulnerable to incendiary attack, were drawn up and it was proposed that a number of experimental attacks should be made to test the effectiveness of this technique.

These conclusions and proposals were put to the Air Ministry as a basis for the formulation of future bombing policy. They met with a mixed reception. There were some senior officers, with little or no practical experience of night bombing, who thought that Bomber Command was being unduly pessimistic about the possibilities of attacking small targets. And the British Government was reluctant to authorize the attack of industrial cities and towns, and to abandon its policy of confining air bombardment to precise military targets. But it was unmistakably clear that Bomber Command, with its present equipment, was incapable of destroying small targets, except in very good weather conditions and when the target had particularly obvious leading marks which could be identified with certainty. The photographs taken by aircrews at the moment of bomb release provided incontrovertible evidence of that fact. It was hypocritical to order the bombers to attack small military tragets when it was known that the bombs would in fact fall in a wide pattern all around the aiming point. It was even more hypocritical to take credit for such a policy, which bore little relation to what was happening in practice.

After a considerable discussion the Air Ministry agreed to the experimental attacks on selected German industrial towns, and it was decided that the definition of future bombing policy would be postponed until the result of these tests had been evaluated.

Bomber Command further pointed out that since the end of the Battle of Britain in October 1940, radar research had been largely concentrated on the evolution of instruments for air-to-air interception (A.I.) and for air-to-ship detection (A.S.V.). The night bombing of Britain had almost ceased after Hitler's attack on Soviet Russia in June 1941, because most of the German bombers had been sent to the Eastern front. There was now no pressing need for radar priorities to be concentrated on the solution of the problems of air defense by night. And by the end of 1941 the A. S. V. had reached the stage at which its practical usefulness was assured. The way seemed to be open at last for the air offensive to receive full priority in the development of radar aids to night navigation and blind bombing. The Air Ministry agreed in principle, and Bomber Command hoped that the time had come when effective steps would be taken to solve its pressing problems.

At the beginning of 1942 Bomber Command had made all the necessary preparations for trying out the new policy, but before it could do so an incident occurred which had an effect far greater than its military importance warranted. It has been mentioned that the two German battle cruisers, *Scharnhorst* and *Gneisenau*, came into Brest to refuel. They arrived there on March 28, 1941, after a successful foray in the Atlantic in the course of which they sank about 115,000 tons of Allied shipping. The British Admiralty were extremely anxious that these ships should not make another sortie into the Atlantic. The Navy could not deal with them while they were at Brest, as no surface ships or submarines could attack them and aircraft carriers could not—without unacceptable risk—approach close enough to the French coast to launch a strike. The responsibility for dealing with them was therefore passed to the Air Ministry. Bomber Command was ordered to attack the ships with the object of sinking them or, if that proved to be impracticable, of damaging them sufficiently to prevent them from leaving harbor and making further attacks on Allied shipping.

The Command carried out attacks by night at frequent intervals on the two ships. During these operations a radar aid to night bombing was tried out for the first time. Though not very effective, it showed considerable promise and raised hopes that, with further development, it would be of great value. In spite of the difficulties caused by searchlight dazzle and very powerful A. A. defenses, the attacks were successful and both ships were damaged. The Germans then moved the two battle cruisers into drydocks and covered them with camouflage netting. In addition, a smoke screen was operated to assist in making it difficult for the aircrews to locate the ships. On June 4 the eight-inch gun cruiser *Prinz Eugen*, which had accompanied the *Bismarck* into the Atlantic, took refuge in Brest after the sinking of the great German battleship. She was added to the target list, and all three ships were hit and damaged.

One of the battle cruisers sailed from Brest by night and went to La Pallice, where she was discovered by air reconnaissance. As the air defenses there were less formidable than at Brest, she was attacked in daylight by Bomber Command and hit near the stern. Next day she was seen back in the dry dock at Brest under camouflage netting.

In addition to the routine night bombing occasional daylight attacks with fighter escort were undertaken against the ships at Brest. Month after month these attacks continued and there is no doubt that all three ships received further damage. They remained inactive in harbor until the end of 1941.

A British raid on the Norwegian island of Vaagso in December gave Hitler the idea that an invasion of Norway was being planned. The German Intelligence must have known that the British had not the resources available to carry out such an invasion, but they were unable to shake his conviction. He therefore decided that the three warships at Brest must be brought back into German waters. It is also possible that he realized, more clearly than did the German naval staff, that the ships were wasting their time at Brest and could not be made fit for operations in the face of Bomber Command's attacks.

The plan for bringing the ships back was Hitler's own. Against the advice of his naval staff, he decided that the ships should make a dash through the Channel, leaving Brest by night and, hugging the French shore, should pass through the Straits of Dover in daylight. The German air force was ordered to give the ships the strongest possible fighter protection during the hours of daylight.

The British had long foreseen that the Germans would not be content to leave the ships in Brest indefinitely. After considering the various possible alternatives the Admiralty took the view that the safest and most probable course would be for the ships to make a dash through the Channel. It was, however, expected that they would sail from Brest in daylight and make the passage of the Straits of Dover during the hours of darkness.

As early as April 1941, nine months before the actual occurrence, the Admiralty and the Air Ministry had concerted a plan for dealing with it. Bomber Command issued an operation order on May 1, 1941, to give effect to this plan. Coastal Command issued on September 8 an operation instruction laying on attacks by torpedo-bombers. Arrangements were also made by Bomber Command to lay mines ahead of the ships during the hours of darkness.

By the end of January 1942, information from many sources indicated that it was probable that the ships would leave Brest in the near future. On February 8 the Commander-in-Chief, Coastal Command, advised Bomber and Fighter Commands that the ships were likely to leave Brest and pass through the Channel at any time, but that the most likely date, taking into account the state of the moon and the tides, would be February 10.

Bomber Command had been keeping some 300 aircraft bombed-up and ready since February 3, but when February 10 came and went and nothing happened, Bomber Command was partially released to resume the bombing of targets in Germany. An air photograph taken on the afternoon of February 11 showed the ships still in harbor with torpedo-nets in position. They looked quite static, but in fact they were about to sail. An air attack that evening delayed their departure for several hours, but about midnight the three ships left Brest accompanied by an escort of seven destroyers. The night was dark and the weather calm, and by daybreak they were off Cherbourg, where their escort was reinforced by 15 "E" class torpedo boats and a strong cover of German fighter aircraft.

Coastal Command had three patrol lines of aircraft, equipped with A. S. V., astride their probable course. At that time this instrument was not very reliable, and for one reason or another all three patrols failed to detect the ships. At 8:30 A. M. several British radar stations reported a concentration of German aircraft off the French coast, but as it seemed to be milling round and round, the controller at No. 11 Fighter Group Headquarters came to the conclusion that it was an air-sea rescue operation. The controller should have had the matter investigated, and this error was to have unfortunate consequences.

By chance it happened that two British fighter aircraft were on patrol over the French coast, and at 10:45 A. M. they ran into the German fighter escort and caught sight of the German battle cruisers. Owing to an order enforcing wireless silence, they were not able to report it, but they returned at once to their base, and by 11:30 A. M. all concerned knew that the *Scharnhorst* and *Gneisenau* were on their way back to Germany through the Channel. But there were only five hours of daylight left and the most energetic action was needed to deal with the situation.

Next to time, the most important factor was the weather. West of Cherbourg there was broken cloud and fair visibility, while eastward the cloud was almost unbroken at 2,000 ft. lowering to 700 ft. in squally showers. A warm front was moving southward and the weather was likely to get worse during the afternoon.

The Admiralty decided that the Fleet Air Arm Swordfish torpedo aircraft should attack as soon as possible. The weather was deteriorating and they took off without waiting for their fighter escort. None of them returned and no hits were scored. Owing to the weather conditions the fighters would have been largely ineffective, and their absence probably made no difference to the result. The naval torpedo boats from Dover and Ramsgate were unable to penetrate the screen of destroyers and "E" boats, and fired torpedoes from long range without any success. The Beaufort torpedo-bombers of Coastal Command made three attacks. The visibility was very poor and no hits were obtained on the ships. Four of these aircraft failed to return. The six destroyers held at readiness in the Thames estuary made contact with the German squadron off the Maas soon after three o'clock. Owing to heavy fire from the battle cruisers and their escort, the destroyers had to launch their torpedoes from long range and all of them missed. One destroyer, *Worcester*, was hit and set on fire, but succeeded in getting back to harbor.

Everything else had failed and all depended on what Bomber Command could do. There had been a fairly heavy attack on Germany the night before and many aircraft were being serviced and their crews were in bed. A force of 100 aircraft was standing by, at four hours' notice, but they were loaded with armor-piercing bombs designed to be dropped from a considerable height in order to achieve penetration.[1] It would not be possible to attack the ships before 2:30 P. M. by which time the clouds were expected to be at about 1,000 ft. with a visibility of some 2,000 yds. In such circumstances the armor-piercing bombs were useless, and it was necessary to change the load to general purpose bombs.

By a tremendous effort 242 aircraft were made available. But it was clear that bombing of the ships in such adverse weather conditions had almost no chance of success. The only hope of doing serious damage to them was to lay sea-mines ahead of them. Bomber Command suggested that this should be done on a large scale, instead of wasting effort on bombing attacks that could not possibly succeed, but the Air Ministry, after consultation with the Admiralty, took the view that the operation should be carried out as planned.

The bombing attack, which began about 3 P. M. was a complete failure. Only 39 aircraft succeeded in finding the German ships in the mist and rain; 188 failed to see anything, and 15 did not re-

[1] See Appendix A.

turn. At 2:30 P. M. the *Scharnhorst* detonated a mine, probably laid by Coastal Command some time previously. The damage was not serious, and the ship was able to keep her place in the formation.

Toward dusk Bomber Command sent some 50 bombers, mainly Whitleys which were unsuitable for the bombing attacks on the ships, to lay mines ahead of them. Later that evening both ships were seriously damaged by these mines. The *Gneisenau* put into Wilhelmshaven and beached herself in shallow water. A few days later, after repairs, she arrived at Kiel. The *Scharnhorst*, though crippled, was able to continue at slow speed and eventually reached Kiel.

Bomber Command carried out several very heavy night attacks against these ships at Kiel, and both received further serious damage. The *Gneisenau* was set on fire and gutted and was later towed stern-first to Gdynia, where her guns were removed and used for coast defenses. It took more than a year to repair the *Scharnhorst*, and the first time she put to sea she was sunk by the Royal Navy while attempting to attack a Russian-bound convoy near the North Cape.

It is surprising that the passage of these ships through the Channel in bad weather, heavily escorted and hugging the French shore, should have caused so much anger and dismay in Britain. It was thought to be in some way insulting that the Germans could do this; although every day, in all weathers, the British passed convoys, under naval and air escort, safely through the Channel close to their own shores. The government, which was well aware of the facts, could have calmed public indignation by an explanatory statement. But nothing of the sort was done, while articles and letters appeared in the press and speeches were made denouncing the incident as a gross failure of British arms, and especially of air power. Indeed, some factions eagerly seized upon it to denigrate the Royal Air Force.

So great was the outcry that the government set up a board of inquiry, presided over by a judge of the high court, with a senior naval and air force officer as assessors, to investigate the matter and report. The board, while finding that there had been some errors of judgment and failures of equipment—and no operation of this size has ever been free of some errors and failures—attached no blame to anyone. They were satisfied that everything that could have been done in the circumstances was done, and they recorded that they were "impressed by the countless acts of gallantry which have come to their notice, and by the evident determination of all our forces to press home their attacks."[2]

In fact, Bomber Command had succeeded in carrying out the task allotted to it. After their arrival at Brest in March 1941 the *Scharnhorst* and *Gneisenau*, and later the *Prinz Eugen*, were immobilized for more than ten months. When they attempted to escape from Brest through the Channel, Bomber Command succeeded in seriously damaging both the battle cruisers, in circumstances in which all the other forms of attack had completely failed and success of any kind could hardly be expected. The ships were again damaged at Kiel, with the result that the *Gneisenau* was destroyed as a fighting ship, and the *Scharnhorst* put out of action for a further year. But the facts were not made public until 1946, and at the time an impression was created that the Command had not acquitted itself well.

A few days after this incident Air Marshal A. T. Harris became Commander-in-Chief of Bomber Command. He at once realized that he was faced by a very serious situation. It was clear that with their existing equipment his bombers were unable to inflict sufficient damage on German industry to fulfill their task. And the escape of the *Scharnhorst* and *Gneisenau* through the Channel was being used by those who had no faith in the air offensive to injure the reputation of the Command.

It was a time for clear thinking and resolute action.

[2] British White Paper (Command 6775) March 1946.

12 Operation "Millennium"

The fall of France had profoundly shocked the government and people of the United States. The eventual entry of America into the war was seen as possible, even probable, and the American people were determined to have the best armed forces, and especially the best air force, that money could buy. When General Arnold went before Congress in June 1940, he was told that any funds he needed would be provided. The War Department asked for 18,000 airplanes by April 1942, and a productive capacity of 18,000 a year by that date. An immense expansion of the aircraft and engine industry was put in hand; the training facilities of the Army Air Corps were greatly augmented, and many new airfields were constructed. Large increases in the Naval Air Service were also authorized.

In June 1940, conversations had begun in Washington with the object of investigating all ways of giving aid to Britain short of war. Under the provisions of Lend-Lease—as unselfish an act as any in history—a considerable number of aircraft, mainly light bombers and reconnaissance types, were made available to the Royal Air Force and the air forces of the Commonwealth. No less than 6,756 airplanes had been delivered in this way between July 1940 and December 1941. The framework of an Anglo-American military alliance had also been worked out, though no political commitments were undertaken at that stage. A joint strategic concept was formulated, in which it was agreed that the Atlantic and European area was to be

119

regarded as the decisive theater of war. Cooperation was furthered by
the existence of a British Joint Staff Mission in Washington, and
a group of American military observers in London.

On December 7, 1941, the Japanese launched a heavy attack by
carrier-borne torpedo-bombers against the American Pacific Fleet
and its base at Pearl Harbor. This treacherous attack took place
early on a Sunday morning and, although the Japanese formations
were seen on the radar early warning system, by an unlucky chance
they were not reported to the responsible authorities. The attack
came, therefore, as a complete surprise, and it sank or crippled all
the major units of the Pacific Fleet, with the exception of three
aircraft carriers which happened to be at sea at the time. Over 250
of the 400 aircraft stationed there were destroyed, most of them on
the ground, and serious damage was caused to the main installations
of the base. If anyone still doubted whether aircraft were able to
sink or cripple capital ships, this attack on the Pacific Fleet finally
settled the matter.

The disaster to their forces at Pearl Harbor and strong national
resentment against the behavior of the Japanese might well have led
the government of the United States to give priority to the war in the
Pacific. But although large forces had to be diverted to that theater
of war, it was decided not to alter the basic strategic concept that the
war in Europe and the defeat of Germany still came first in order of
priority. This is one of the honorable examples, rare in military history, in which national feelings and strong popular emotions were
not allowed to overrule correct strategic principles.

At his headquarters hidden among the beech woods of the Chiltern
hills, Air Marshal Harris carefully studied Bomber Command's appreciation and its proposals for a future bombing policy. He was
fully in agreement with them. Being a practical airman of great
ability and resource, who had served in day and night bombing
squadrons, he understood the position very well. He began at once
to represent to the Air Ministry the urgent need to hasten the
production of the four-engined heavy bombers and the development
of radar navigation and blind-bombing devices. He also reminded
those concerned that, if the new policy were to be adopted, a large
increase in the production of incendiary bombs would be necessary.

The new Commander-in-Chief had been in command of No. 5

Bomber Group at the outbreak of the war and he was therefore no stranger to the problems of Bomber Command. But he had been away in Washington for nearly a year with the British military mission, and he was not fully conversant with the latest developments in the Command. He was surprised and disappointed to find how little progress had been made in its expansion and re-equipment.

At the beginning of the war, after ten squadrons had been transferred to the Advanced Air Striking Force in France, and the withdrawal of ten more to act as operational training units, the Command had a daily average of 315 aircraft serviceable with crews. In February 1942, two and a half years later, the daily average was 374.

But if progress in building up the air offensive had been disappointing, Britain no longer stood alone. The United States was now fully engaged in the war against Germany and Italy as well as against Japan, and Harris knew that arrangements had been made to send a large force of American heavy bombers to bases in eastern England. Toward the end of February 1942, Brigadier General Ira C. Eaker arrived and took command of the advanced echelon of the U. S. Eighth Air Force. Harris and Eaker were firm friends, and they at once laid the foundations of a cooperation between the two long-range bombardment forces that was both admirable and enduring.

Eaker hoped to start his daylight bombing campaign against Germany in about four months' time, but owing to various developments, which will be dealt with later in this book, this estimate proved to be too optimistic.

By the beginning of 1942 the British four-engined heavy bombers were just coming into service. When the Air Staff had issued requirements for a long-range heavy bomber in 1936, three designs had been provisionally accepted.[1]

The normal procedure would be to build prototypes of each design and, after thorough tests and comparative trials, to select one for production in quantity. This process is the best safeguard against a failure, but it takes time. Had it been adopted for the heavy bombers it would have been at least seven years before they could have been available in any numbers. But the Air Ministry could not contemplate waiting until 1943 for these bombers, and it was therefore

[1] Actually two specifications were issued, B. 12/36 and P. 13/36, but there was little difference between them in practice.

decided to omit the comparative trials of the prototypes, and to give orders for the production of all three aircraft before any of them had flown. In this way it was hoped to save two or three years, and to get them into service in 1940–1941. It was then intended, as soon as possible after the delivery of the bombers to squadrons, to decide on the best of the three and concentrate on building it, giving no further production orders for the other two. Although it was realized that this "ordering off the drawing-board," as it was called, involved some risk, it was considered that in the circumstances it was acceptable.

A number of things combined to prevent this plan from working out as intended. The first was the decision of the Minister of Aircraft Production, in May 1940, to give the production of the heavy bombers a lower priority in order to concentrate the maximum resources on fighter production. This decision was no doubt inevitable at the time, but the priorities were not restored to bomber production as early as they should have been. The result was that the date at which deliveries would begin was postponed from the autumn of 1940 to the autumn of 1941.

The three heavy bombers were the Stirling (B. 12/36); and the Manchester and Halifax (P. 13/36). The Stirling had Bristol Hercules engines, but the other two were originally designed to take four Rolls-Royce Merlins—the engine which powered the Hurricane and the Spitfire. In 1938 it became clear that there would not be enough Merlin engines to go round. As the fighters had to have priority, it was necessary to find some other engine for one of these two heavy bombers. In the circumstances the Rolls-Royce firm suggested that the Manchester, which had the smallest unladen weight of the three, should be powered by two Vulture engines. This was done, but it was found that its performance was inadequate, and in 1941, it was decided, as sufficient Merlin engines were becoming available, to revert to the original design. This proved most successful and the redesigned aircraft, named the Lancaster, was the outstanding British long-range bomber of the war. Although the final result was excellent, the need for a partial redesign delayed it by about six months.

In the meantime the production of the Stirling and Halifax had become well-established. The Stirling was the least promising of the three. Its speed and altitude with full load were both relatively inferior, and the Air Ministry notified the Ministry of Aircraft Production that no more Stirlings would be required. Unfortunately it was not practicable, for various reasons, to cease producing the Stirling immediately, and a good many more were built than were needed by Bomber Command. As their rate of loss made them unsuitable for long-range bombardment, they were used in operational training units and for towing gliders.

The Halifax was a sound aircraft, better than the Manchester but not as good as the Lancaster. The Air Ministry continued the production orders for it, as a reinsurance.

In February 1942, the daily average in Bomber Command of 374 aircraft serviceable with crews made up of 55 light, 275 medium, and 44 heavy bombers.

The substance of Bomber Command's appreciation and future proposals had become fairly widely known in high official circles. It provided an opportunity for those who had never approved of the policy of the strategic bombing of Germany to return to the attack. The photographic evidence of the crew's inability to find and hit small targets was exaggerated to support an assertion that they could not hit any target. The War Office contended that most of the heavy bombers should be sent to North Africa, and used to disrupt German and Italian communications across the Mediterranean. The Admiralty argued that all the heavy bombers should be employed in the anti-submarine campaign—escorting convoys, seeking out and destroying U-boats at sea, and bombing their bases. A most elaborate paper, supporting this proposal with a wealth of statistics, was presented to the War Cabinet by the First Sea Lord. And a considerable number of eminent people, who knew little or nothing about the matter, put forward various proposals for the employment of the long-range bombers. Most of their suggestions involved using the bombers for purposes for which they were not designed, and for which the crews were not trained.

A critical point had been reached in Britain's war policy. It will be remembered that in 1940 the Prime Minister had written:

The Navy can lose us the war, but only the Air Force can win it. . . . We must, therefore, develop the power to carry an ever-increasing number of explosives to Germany, so as to pulverize the entire industry and scientific structure on which the war effort and economic life of the enemy depend, while holding him at arm's length from our

*Island. In no other way at present visible, can we hope to overcome
the immense power of Germany.*

He fully realized the importance of maintaining an air offensive,
but in March 1941, the mounting losses of British merchant shipping
and the insistent demands of the Admiralty for more air support
had compelled him to give first priority to the defense of British
sea communications. A large number of bomber aircraft and crews
had been transferred to Coastal Command. At the time it was
thought that this arrangement would be a temporary one, to tide
over a crisis, and most of the bombers were supposed to be on loan.
But the Admiralty now sought to make their transfer permanent, and
to demand many more, not because the situation at sea had become
worse, but because, in their view, the bombers would be better employed hunting U-boats than scattering their bombs all over the
German countryside.

The proposals put forward by the War Office and Admiralty offended against the basic strategic principle that wars can be won
only by offensive action against the main elements of the enemy's
strength. Since the war could not be won or lost in North Africa,
too large a reinforcement of this theater would weaken British offensive action against the military powers of Germany. It was true that a
successful campaign there might open up a chance of clearing the
Axis forces out of North Africa, and invading the continent of
Europe by way of Sicily and Italy. But such things were as yet far off
and, if considered at all, could be regarded only as remote possibilities.

If there was some hope that the campaign in North Africa might
conceivably lead to eventual offensive action in the main theater of
war, the same could not be said of the Admiralty's proposals. The
safeguarding of Britain's sea communications was unquestionably
of vital importance. As the Prime Minister had said, failure to safeguard them could have lost the war. But the converse was not true;
success in safeguarding them could do nothing, in itself, toward
winning the war. It could do no more than maintain the existing
situation. The Admiralty's plan would have misused the most powerful offensive force at Britain's disposal—and the only one capable
of striking directly at Germany—in a purely defensive role.

At no time during the war did the British Admiralty appear to recognize the strategically defensive character of the Navy's task. Nor did they appreciate that, if the war was to be won, the minimium force should be diverted to defensive measures, no matter how essential such measures might be. What that minimum force should be was a matter of judgment, and open to argument. The transfer of the heavy bombers from Bomber Command to Coastal Command during 1941 could be justified as a necessary minimum allocation to the defensive. But the Admiralty's proposal to divert the whole of Britain's long-range bombardment force to a purely defensive role was a very different matter.

The War Cabinet did not accept the War Office or Admiralty proposals but agreed that an effort should be made to re-equip some squadrons in North Africa with the Liberator (B-24), an American long-range heavy bomber. It was also decided that the squadrons lent by Bomber Command to Coastal Command during 1941 should be permanently transferred. In addition, Bomber Command detached an operational training unit to St. Eval, in Cornwall, which combined training in navigation with submarine hunting with considerable success.

The Admiralty and the War Office were far from being satisfied with these decisions. It was clear that the whole policy of attempting to reduce the German military strength by air bombardment was under very heavy attack. Harris realized that unless Bomber Command could, in the near future, produce convincing evidence of its power to hit and destroy important targets, it would inevitably be diverted to secondary or defensive tasks. And, as any student of three-dimensional war could hardly fail to understand, unless Britain could by air bombardment achieve the progressive destruction of the German military, industrial, and economic system, there could be no progress toward victory and the war might even be lost. The Prime Minister knew this very well, and had frequently pressed for improvements in the equipment of Bomber Command. But few, if any, of his colleagues in the British War Cabinet had much understanding of strategic principles, and the pressure from the Admiralty and War Office was very great. He might, at any time, find himself unable to carry his colleagues with him.

Bomber Command decided that the time had come when it must prove that it could, in the right circumstances, carry out its task. It could not afford to wait for the development of radar aids to navigation and blind-bombing. By the time these became available, irrevocable decisions might have been taken, and it would then be too late.

For some time a concentrated attack on the Renault engine factory, in the suburbs of Paris, had been planned. This important plant was building and repairing engines for German aircraft, tanks, and motor transport. As it was in an area heavily populated by French people, it was most important that all the bombs should fall in the target area. For this reason it was decided to order the attack only in clear weather with bright moonlight. The whole affair was very carefully planned. It took place early in March, and was a great success. The factory was very extensively damaged—indeed much of it was almost obliterated—and hardly a single bomb fell outside the target.

This was encouraging, but Bomber Command knew very well that the weather conditions had been perfect, and the defenses, caught unawares, had not been very effective. What was needed was some way of carrying out attacks of similar accuracy, in poor visibility, deep in the heart of Germany. Fortunately, at this time the first effective radar aid to the air offensive became available. This was "Gee," which was a navigational device of great value and importance.[2] It enabled an aircraft to fix its position with a high degree of accuracy at a range of up to 300 miles from its home base. It could, however, only be carried in aircraft modified to take it, and this modification was incorporated in aircraft on the production line. It could not be done retrospectively. All new aircraft were therefore sent to the squadrons, to replace unmodified aircraft which were transeferred to operational training units. But the earliest date at which the whole Command could be equipped with Gee was the end of May.

Preliminary trials of Gee took place in late February, but the results were not as good as had been expected. This was due to poor organization of the ground equipment, and lack of telephone communication between the monitor station and the transmitting stations. Bomber Command suspended all further Gee trials, while the Air Ministry reorganized the ground stations and installed adequate communications. The first operational use of Gee occurred in early March, and on March 13 a really successful attack was made on an important industrial area in Cologne. This was followed a fort-

[2] See Appendix D.

night later by an outstanding attack on Cologne when 120 bombers dropped their bombs on one aiming-point in twenty minutes, without the loss of a single aircraft. Subsequent photographs showed that heavy damage had been caused, and that this was confined to an area close to the aiming-point. Bomber Command was feeling its way toward greater concentration in time and space.

On the night of March 28/29, the long-planned incendiary attack on the town of Lübeck took place. Very large fires were caused and more than 200 acres of the built-up area were destroyed. Three weeks later the port of Rostock was attacked on four successive nights with a large proportion of incendiary bombs. The destruction was very great; a large proportion of the built-up area was burned out and the Heinkel aircraft factory severely damaged. In all these operations Gee had proved to be a first-class navigational aid, but they had been undertaken in good weather conditions in bright moonlight, and the Command still lacked any device for blind-bombing or target location.

The results of these attacks had been encouraging, but they did not suffice to check the criticism of Britain's bombing policy, which had by now become widespread. Harris was convinced that if the Command could dispatch a great force of bombers, even if once or twice only, against an important industrial target, it would give the British Government, and the world, a demonstration of what a properly expanded and equipped bomber force could do. Gradually this idea began to take shape. It was planned to make the heaviest possible attack, with the greatest number of aircraft that could be made available, against an industrial city such as Hamburg or Cologne. Since the success of the operation would largely depend on Gee, the earliest date at which it could be mounted would be the full-moon of May, by which time it was hoped to have almost all the squadrons of the Command equipped with this device.

The Commander-in-Chief set a target figure of 1,000 bombers for this attack. The daily average of aircraft serviceable with crews in May was 416, consisting of 70 light, 210 medium, and 136 heavy bombers. If 100 per cent serviceability in squadrons could be reached, this figure would be increased to about 550. Several hundred heavy and medium bombers, manned by instructors and senior pupil crews, could be raised from the operational training units. The use of the training organization in this way was, however, risky, because serious losses, especially of instructors, would prejudice the future expansion of the Command. It was therefore decided to explore the prospects of obtaining as many aircraft as possible from other commands. Coastal Command had a large number of suitable aircraft and crews, most of which had originally been in Bomber Command. There were a number of medium and light bombers in Army Cooperation Command which were unemployed operationally, and a few in Flying Training Command.

At first the prospects seemed good and Bomber Command was promised a substantial force, but as soon as the War Office and the Admiralty realized the probable consequences of a successful attack on this scale, they raised objections to the use of any aircraft from Army Cooperation and Coastal Commands. In the end only a few light bombers from Flying Training Command were made available. Harris, undaunted, went ahead with his plans, and raised more than a thousand bombers from the squadrons and operational training units of his own Command.

When the time came everything was ready. Though few realized until the last moment the full scope of the plan, everyone in the Command knew that something big was going to happen. The enthusiasm raised was tremendous, and all worked with a will. The reserve aircraft were fully manned by volunteers from Station, Group, and Command staffs, and hundreds of crews from the Operational and Heavy Conversion Units were standing by. The returns showed that 1,048 aircraft with crews were available and ready.

The object of this great operation, which was given the code name of "Millennium," was threefold. First, it was hoped to show that it was a practical proposition to attack a single target with more than a thousand bombers in a short period of time. Secondly, it was expected to demonstrate that a heavy concentrated attack would saturate the defenses and thus reduce the loss rate, and at the same time overload the fire-fighting services and thus cause large uncontrollable areas of fire. Thirdly, Bomber Command believed that such an attack, if successful, would capture the imagination of the British public and impress the government, and thus enable it to obtain the priorities it so desperately needed.

Harris believed that only in this way could the Command attract the support, official and unofficial, without which it would never be able to carry out its task successfully. On the other hand, he was fully aware of the penalties of failure. He realized that if the operation failed there would have been no worth-while expansion of Bomber Command and no hope of gaining the priorities essential to its success. Those who opposed the policy of the air offensive against Germany would receive a powerful reinforcement. There was a danger that if the British Government decided to abandon its air bombardment policy, the United States might not feel inclined to "go it alone" against Germany in the air, and might transfer its long-range bomber force to the Pacific theater. The war in Europe—if it had not been lost—would certainly not have been won in 1945.

Harris planned to put the thousand bombers over a large German industrial city in an hour and a half. This concentration, about eleven per minute, was far higher than any which the Command had previously attempted. There was some anxiety over the risks of collision and of one aircraft dropping its bombs on another in the stream. This question was referred to the Operations Research Section at Command Headquarters, which studied the matter and reported that the probability of loss from these causes would be one aircraft per hour. It was decided to choose two aiming-points, and to divide the force into two parallel streams. In this way it was hoped to eliminate any risks from collision and the bombing of one aircraft by another.

Now all depended on the weather, which was not good. The night of May 30/31 was the last night on which the conditions of moonlight would be suitable. The weather looked rather better on the morning of May 30, and the forecast was awaited with more than the usual interest. It promised good weather for the home bases—an important point since so many inexperienced crews would be taking part—but conditions over western Germany were dubious. Harris laid on the 1,000-bomber plan, with Hamburg or Cologne as the target. At the meteorological conference at 4 P. M. the morning forecast was confirmed. The weather over Germany was more promising in the south than in the north, with a 50 per cent chance of clear weather over Cologne. Harris was faced with a difficult decision. If he cancelled the operation, he would have to postpone it till the June full-moon period. He realized that the position of Bomber Command was bad, and was still deteriorating. If he postponed the operation until late June he might never be able to carry it out at all, or if he did, it might be too late to save the situation. He decided to go ahead with the plan, with Cologne as the target.

As soon as the first few returned crews had been interrogated it was clear that the operation had not failed. There had been banks of cloud up to 15,000 ft. on the route, but 20 miles from the target they had vanished, leaving clear air and good visibility. The reports of the crews were wildly enthusiastic, and the last to leave the target area spoke of enormous fires and huge palls of smoke. No photographs could be taken next morning owing to the smoke in which the stricken city was enveloped. But there was no doubt as to the success of operation "Millennium." When reconnaissance photographs were at length available they showed damage on a wholly unprecedented scale.

The news, when released, resounded throughout the world. Bomber Command had achieved its threefold object. The losses were 44 out of a total of 1,046 aircraft dispatched, which, in spite of the employment of many inexperienced crews, was less than the normal loss rate over Cologne in bright moonlight. The attack, on a single objective by a force of 1,000 bombers, had been shown to be a practical proposition. The fires had clearly got out of hand and the damage was, by any previous standards, colossal. The imagination of the British and American publics was captured, and the Prime Minister was greatly impressed. He sent the following message to the Commander-in-Chief:

I congratulate you and the whole of Bomber Command upon the remarkable feat of organization which enabled you to dispatch over a thousand bombers to the Cologne area in a single night, and without confusion to concentrate their action over the target in so short a time as one hour and a half. This proof of the growing power of the British Bomber Force is also the herald of what Germany will receive, city by city, from now on.

The last sentence of this message showed that the government was firmly committed to the policy of reducing German military and industrial strength by means of air bombardment. And steps were taken at long last to insure that a concentration of scientific and productive effort, comparable to that which had enabled Britain to survive the opening defensive phase, was applied to the expansion of the air offensive and to the solution of its problems. Bomber Command still had to struggle against apathy and obstruction, but it had justified the confidence shown in it by the Prime Minister, and his powerful support thereafter never wavered.

The opponents of the policy of the air bombardment of Germany were silenced, and enthusiasm for it was rekindled in many quarters in which it had become lukewarm.

The crisis which threatened to destroy the sound strategic policy adopted by the British Government at the end of 1940 had passed, and in operation "Millennium" can be discerned the beginning of the end.

13 Final Preparations

Before the forces assembled for the thousand-bomber raid on Cologne were dispersed and returned to their normal occupations, it was decided to stage an attack in similar strength against Essen in the Ruhr, in the hope of causing severe damage to the vast Krupp Works in that town. Essen was one of the most difficult targets to find and identify, situated as it was in a large and murky industrial area, obscured by the smoke of countless factory chimneys, with the sky above it a blaze of searchlights and A. A. fire. The attack took place on the night of June 1/2, but the weather was not as good as had been expected. The fading moon was in its last quarter, and there were several layers of broken cloud and much haze. Few crews positively identified Essen and most of them bombed various industrial areas. Essen escaped relatively lightly, but severe damage was done and large fires were started in Duisburg, Oberhausen, Mülheim and Hamborn. Just over a thousand aircraft were dispatched, and of these 31 failed to return. This was a rate loss substantially lower than that usual in attacks on the well defended area of the Ruhr.

The failure to achieve concentration in this attack showed that mere numbers were not enough, and that radar methods of night navigation and blind-bombing were an absolute necessity.

Although the damage and destruction caused by the thousand-bomber raids were very great, their influence on the war policies of Germany and Britain was far more important. They emphasized the fact that Germany had lost the initiative in the air, at least in the Western theater of war, and they accelerated the process of turning the German air force onto the defensive. In Britain, the dramatic accounts of these great operations which appeared in the press stimulated public morale and encouraged the offensive spirit. But their most important result was their success in consolidating the policy of reducing German military and industrial strength by means of air bombardment, and in persuading the Prime Minister and the British War Cabinet of the need to back up this policy with the necessary resources. It is no exaggeration to say that, up to this point, almost everything had enjoyed priority over the bomber force, which had to make do with what was left when other demands had been satisfied.

After the thousand-bomber raids all was changed. The Prime Minister made it clear that no effort should be spared to develop as quickly as possible those radar aids to the air offensive which had been Air Staff requirements since 1939, but which had made hardly any progress during the last three years. Perhaps nothing illustrates the changed atmosphere more clearly than a minute from the Prime Minister dated June 15, 1942. At this time there was some idea of repeating the thousand-bomber raids during the June full-moon period. The Prime Minister wrote to the Chief of the Air Staff:

I hope you will approve of this, unless there is some very serious reason to the contrary. Meanwhile I have asked the Admiralty to make sure that they do not prevent Coastal Command from playing its part. I understand Joubert[1] had 250 machines ready,[2] but that the Admiralty stopped their use.

In the end, however, it was decided that further thousand-bomber raids should not be undertaken, owing to the disruptive effect on the training organization.

Within the next few months two radar devices, under development at the Telecommunications Research Establishment, received much attention, and reached the stage at which they became practical propositions. The first of these, which was given the code name of "Oboe," was a method of directing the accurate bombing of a given point from two radar stations on the ground, situated about a hundred miles apart. The point in the air at which the bombs should be

---

[1] Air Marshal Sir Philip Joubert, Commander-in-Chief, Coastal Command.
[2] For the 1000-bomber raid, on May 30/31.

released was worked out. The bomber then flew at a constant distance from the first ground station, traveling along the circumference of a circle which would take it to the calculated release point. When it reached this point is was given by the second station a signal to drop its bombs.[3]

There were three tactical limitations to the use of this method. It would require an aircraft to approach the target flying for all practical purposes straight and level for a considerable distance, which would present ideal conditions to the A.A. guns. Secondly, the range was proportional to the height at which the aircraft could fly; the greater the altitude, the longer the range. But the heavily loaded bombers could not fly much above twenty thousand feet, and this would mean that targets even in western Germany would be out of range. And thirdly, a pair of ground stations could handle only one bomber at a time, and could with good organization deal with one aircraft every six minutes.

It was clear that these limitations would make it impossible to use the method for controlling the bombing of the main force. It would enable the Command to carry out an accurate small-scale attack on a precise target, or it could be used to start fires or place marker bombs at the aiming-point as a guide to the main force. With the conception of marking the aiming-point with some sort of pyrotechnic bomb, the idea of a Pathfinder element in Bomber Command was carried one stage further. The Air Ministry was asked to provide, as a matter of urgency, marker bombs possessing the same ballistic characteristics as the normal high-explosive bombs used by the Command. These marker bombs should produce an easily identified and unmistakable pyrotechnic display on the ground, available in red, white, and green, which should persist for at least two minutes.[4] In addition, the Command asked that the small incendiary bombs in general use, which were very effective but had unsatisfactory ballistics, should be made into clusters enclosed in streamlined cases having ballistic characteristics similar to those of the H.E. bomb. The idea was that a time or aerostatic fuse should open the case at a height of about a thousand feet above the ground, releasing the small bombs and allowing them to scatter sufficiently to produce the maximum incendiary effect.

But there still remained the problem of finding a suitable airplane, able to operate at a height great enough to extend the range of Oboe

[3] See Appendix D.
[4] See Appendix B.

to the Ruhr and the Rhineland, and to reduce to an acceptable point the risks from A.A. fire. This problem was solved by the timely arrival of the Mosquito bomber, now just coming into service. The Mosquito was a very high-speed, high-altitude two-seater bomber, of wooden construction, powered by two Merlin engines, originally made by the de Havilland firm as a private venture. It could carry a load of about a thousand pounds of bombs with a radius of action of some six hundred miles. It had no defensive armament. It was offered to the Air Ministry in 1940 as a high-speed unarmed bomber, but it was not accepted. But it was realized that it would make an excellent night fighter, to replace the Beaufighter,[5] which would soon become obsolete. A little later it became apparent that a bomber version of it would be the ideal aircraft for marking aiming-points using the Oboe system, and that it would make a very good photographic reconnaissance aircraft to replace the single-seater Spitfire, which had limited navigational facilities. The Mosquito was unique in that it was the only British aircraft used by the Royal Air Force during the war which was not built to Air Staff requirements, and also in that it was employed with great success for almost every purpose except that for which it was designed.

The preliminary trials of Oboe were very encouraging. They showed that a Mosquito flying at an altitude of thirty thousand feet, at a distance of some three hundred miles from the ground stations, could be expected to drop its bombs within four hundred yards of the aiming-point. This was a degree of accuracy far greater than anything that could be achieved by visual methods at night, except from a low altitude in ideal weather conditions, against slight defenses.

It was decided to build three pairs of ground stations, so situated in southern and eastern England as to give the maximum Oboe coverage of western Germany. With accurate timing, to which the system lent itself, it should be possible for a force of Mosquitoes to drop one bomb load at the aiming-point every two minutes.

The other device, called H 2 S, was a radar set carried in the aircraft, which showed a sort of picture of the ground underneath and in front of the aircraft. This set transmitted high-frequency radar waves and the reflections back from the ground were received and recorded on a screen. These reflections differed according to the nature of the earth's surface beneath the aircraft; water produced hardly any

[5] A conversion of the Beaufort sea reconnaissance aircraft.

reflection and showed as a dark area, open country returned a medium reflection, while built-up areas gave a brilliant response. Thus towns and even large isolated factories could be seen, and their characteristic shapes were reproduced on the screen so that it was possible to recognize them. The navigator would therefore have a continuously moving and recognizable picture of the surface beneath him, and because the apparatus was carried in the aircraft it was not subject to ground control or to limitations of distance from the home base.[6]

At first the picture was not very clear, and some considerable training was needed to make the best use of the device. It was, however, soon discovered that the higher the frequency the clearer the picture. The production of these very high-frequency waves depended upon a valve known as the magnetron, which was an entirely British invention. Because it was believed that the Germans had not discovered the principles on which the magnetron valve worked, the proposal to carry it in aircraft operating over Germany was very strongly opposed. It was argued that as soon as examples of it fell into German hands they would be able to copy it and produce such excellent defensive equipment that the British bomber offensive would be brought to a standstill. But Sir Robert Watson-Watt took the view that even if the Germans obtained examples of the magnetron valve, and thereby discovered the principles of its construction, it would take them at least twelve and probably eighteen months to develop it for operational use in sufficient numbers. After studying the matter, Lord Cherwell, scientific adviser to the Prime Minister, strongly supported this view. Harris pointed out that H 2 S would be almost useless without the magnetron, and of great value with it. He therefore argued that if the magnetron could not be used, a most valuable aid would be denied to the bomber offensive, with a strong probability that the Germans would discover it and would be the first to use it. A meeting was held at the Air Ministry on July 15, 1942, with the Secretary of State in the chair, attended by Lord Cherwell, Sir Robert Watson-Watt, and Air Marshal Harris. It was decided that the development and production of H 2 S, using the magnetron valve, should proceed, and should be given the highest priority. This decision was endorsed by the War Cabinet.

The way was now clear for the development and quantity production of Oboe and H 2 S. Oboe was to be used to direct Mosquito

[6] See Appendix D.

bombers, armed with marker or incendiary bombs, to mark the aim-ing-point for the main force. H 2 S was to be used in the main force, at first to equip the best crews so that they could find and mark the aiming-points that lay beyond the range of Oboe.

The prospects for Bomber Command were thus much improved, but at the beginning of August there was a temporary setback. The Germans had begun effectively to jam Gee. This was serious, as the Command had come to rely on it as a navigational aid and could not afford to be deprived of its use. The radar staff at Bomber Command Headquarters reacted to this emergency with great energy and skill, and within five days had devised a modification to overcome the jam-ming which proved completely effective. The Ministry of Aircraft Production estimated that it would take approximately four weeks to modify the five or six hundred sets of Gee involved. The Command radar staff were horrified at the idea of so long a delay and undertook, if given the necessary components, to complete the task in forty-eight hours. The components were supplied, and the job was done with four hours to spare. This example of energetic self-help on the part of the Command drew attention to the apathy and lack of any sense of urgency too often displayed by the Ministry of Aircraft Production, and did, indeed, bring about some improvement in their attitude to such problems.

A very close cooperation was established between Bomber Com-mand and the Telecommunications Research Establishment, which did much to save time and avoid misunderstandings during the de-velopment of radar devices for the air offensive. One of the first fruits of this liaison was the production of Gee Mk. II, which possessed a wide band of frequencies, to guard against further efforts at jamming by the Germans. Constant vigilance and ingenuity succeeded in pre-serving the full use of Gee for the remainder of the war.

By the summer of 1942 the idea of using Oboe and, at first, the best heavy bomber crews equipped with H 2 S to mark the aiming-point as a guide to the main force, had become generally accepted. The way in which this should be organized, however, was the occasion for a divergence of views between the Air Ministry and Bomber Command. Such target marking as had been undertaken to date had been done by selected crews or squadrons. The Air Ministry, however, favored the creation of a separate Pathfinder force, manned by transferring to its squadrons the best crews from the main force groups. It was proposed that this force should have a monopoly of Oboe and even of H 2 S equipment, and should be responsible for all target marking. Harris opposed this, as he did not like the idea of the creation of a *corps d'élite* within the Command. He foresaw the difficulties that would occur when the main force squadrons were ordered to select and transfer their best crews to another formation. He preferred to allow each group to select its own pathfinding squadrons, and he believed that this would create a healthy competitive spirit between the groups and even within them, and that this system would be more efficient and flexible than the monopolization of pathfinding duties by a specialized force. He also foresaw that, as the groups increased in size and as bombing became more accurate, the time would come when they would be required to operate independently, with the groups attacking simultaneously a number of targets. This might be difficult, or even impossible, to organize with a centralized Pathfinder force.

The Air Ministry, however, did not accept these views, and on August 15, 1942, the Pathfinder force was formed. It rapidly increased in size and on January 25, 1943, it was re-formed as No. 8 Group. Although there were some initial advantages in centralization, and the Pathfinder Group was undoubtedly efficient, relations between it and some of the main force groups were not always very cordial and, later, when the groups were required to operate independently, a partial decentralization of pathfinding duties to other groups became necessary.

Since the spring of 1942 the United States long-range bomber force, equipped with the B-17, the Flying Fortress, had been steadily building up at bases in East Anglia. A headquarters had been formed at High Wycombe, within a few miles of Bomber Command Headquarters in the Chiltern Hills. General Eaker, the Commander of the U.S. Eighth Air Force, was looking forward to the opening of his daylight bombing campaign against Germany.

Under the pressure of Communist propaganda for a "second front now," there had been some vague idea of a large-scale Allied invasion across the Channel in the late summer of 1942. Considerable numbers of American troops had been allocated to this project, and had begun to arrive in Britain. There were also several British divisions available for this operation. But a more detailed study of the project —given the code name "Round-up"—made it quite clear that it could not possibly be undertaken before the summer of 1943. It would not be practicable, however, to keep large land forces unemployed for a year in Britain, while the war against the Japanese in the Pacific and in Burma was crying out for reinforcements. It was obvious that some worth-while employment for them must be found.

Meanwhile a reconnaissance in force against Dieppe on August 19, 1942, which failed with heavy losses in killed and missing, fully confirmed the hopelessness of attempting an invasion of Europe that year, and even raised doubts about the possibility of doing so in 1943. It was therefore decided to send a joint expedition to northwest Africa—operation "Torch"—in the late autumn of 1942. The idea was to make surprise landings at Algiers, Oran, and other ports, and secure the whole of French north African territory as far east as Tunisia. It was hoped that the offensive planned by the 8th Army would drive the Germans and Italians westward into Tunisia, where they would be trapped and finally defeated. After much detailed argument the plans for this operation were agreed, and the date fixed for early November. Operation "Torch" naturally had the first claim on American attention and resources in the European theater, and the building up of the Eighth Air Force was slowed down.

On August 17, the first American bombing attack took place, with fighter cover provided by No. 11 Group, Fighter Command, against the railway marshaling yards at Rouen in occupied France. The weather was good and the bombing was very accurate. This was followed by a number of attacks on targets in France and the Low Countries. But attacks on targets in Germany had not been undertaken by the time the year ended. There were several reasons for this. It was necessary to train the crews in formation flying, and to give the air gunners practice, under operational conditions. The British had little faith in the ability of the Flying Fortress to carry out deep penetrations of the German defenses, and this lack of confidence was beginning to affect the morale of the U.S. Eighth Air Force. The Prime Minister and the Chief of the Air Staff had expressed their doubts about it, and re-affirmed their belief in the superiority of night bombing. But it was not possible for the Americans at this stage to change their policy; the bombers were designed and equipped, and the crews trained, for daylight operations. British opposition to their policy could not change it, but it might undermine American confidence in it.

In January 1943, Eaker requested to see Mr. Churchill, who admitted that he was skeptical of the success of daylight bombing. Eaker explained the position and argued the case for the Flying Fortress with great force and clarity. The Prime Minister remarked that America had been in the war for more than a year, and so far had made only one attack on a target in Germany. Eaker agreed that this was true, but pointed out that many things had combined to delay the start of his offensive. He could not attempt the penetration of the German defenses in daylight until he had large formations available, well drilled in formation flying and air gunnery. But he now had nearly five hundred B-17 bombers available, and he was ready to begin it. The Prime Minister realized that British opposition to the policy of daylight bombing could serve no useful purpose, and he decided to back the American policy fully. This decision greatly eased the situation, and before long the B-17's began to attack targets in Germany. How they fared, and how they overcame their difficulties will be dealt with in the next chapter.

By the end of 1942 Bomber Command was nearly ready for the great offensive. The first operational use of Oboe occurred on the night of December 20-21 and was very successful. H 2 S was first employed operationally on the night of January 30/31, against Hamburg. The Command had expanded considerably since the spring of 1942, and the Lancasters and Halifaxes were at last being delivered to the squadrons in substantial numbers. Since the load of the heavy bomber was at least double that of the mediums, the weight of bombs that could be carried was greatly increased.

The daily average of aircraft serviceable with crews in January 1943, was 514; composed of 53 light, 148 medium, and 313 heavy bombers. By March, when the offensive really began, it had risen to a total of 663 of all types—37 light, 213 medium, and 413 heavy bombers.

The Command was by this time equipped with bombsights of improved design, combining a high degree of accuracy with considerable tactical freedom of approach to the aiming-point.[7]

[7] See Appendix C.

Thus, by March 1943, the Allied long-range bombers were equipped and ready at last to start the air offensive against Germany. Although Bomber Command, since the beginning of the war, had dropped over 100,000 tons of bombs and done much damage to many important objectives, all that had gone before was merely the overture to the main work. And the U.S. Eighth Air Force was also ready and eager to play its part. For the next year Germany was to endure a sustained bombardment of her industrial areas, her ports, and centers of communication, by day and by night, which was wholly unprecedented in the history of warfare.

It had taken the British three and a half years of war to reach this position. The Americans had achieved it in sixteen months of war, but they had been making intensive preparations for it since the fall of France in June 1940. The Allies now had the initiative in the air, and they were determined to exploit it to the fullest possible extent.

The years of preparation were over, and the period of fulfillment was at hand.

Part IV

THE SECOND WORLD WAR: FULFILLMENT

14 The Allied Air Offensive: March 1943–March 1944

Much space has been devoted to describing the efforts made to improve the technique of bombing and to expand the bomber forces. But little has been said about the very difficult problems of deciding what should be bombed. This had been a highly controversial subject from the beginning of the war, and it remained so for a very long time.

At the Casablanca Conference in January 1943, the Combined Chiefs of Staff had clearly laid down, as we have already noted, the object of the Allied air offensive against Germany. This directive is so important that it is worth restating here:

Your primary object will be the progressive destruction of the German military, industrial, and economic system, and the undermining of the morale of the German people to a point where their armed resistance is fatally weakened.

It will be noted that the definition is very wide; the destruction of almost anything in Germany could be justified as coming within its terms. And it will also be noted that the reference to the fatal weakening of the German armed resistance suggests that the ultimate object of the air offensive was the softening up of Germany to permit Allied forces to re-enter the continent of Europe and administer the *coup de grâce*.

Eaker and Harris interpreted the directive in this way, but Eaker decided to concentrate on the attack of German aircraft and engine factories, while Harris continued to attack large industrial areas and ports, and devoted considerable effort to sea-mining. Eaker's preliminary object was to reduce the strength of the German fighter force, in order to give his bombers more tactical freedom and to reduce his losses. This object was strategically defensive, though it could be justified as a prelude to his main offensive operations. Harris intended to strike as hard as he could at the German industrial system, believing that this would offer the best prospect of reducing German military and economic strength, and also of undermining the morale of the German people.

When due allowance is made for the differing tactical requirements and abilities of day and night bombing, these decisions appear to be sound. The day bombers flying in a close formation could, in favorable circumstances, identify and attack an individual factory and put down a very dense pattern of bombs on and around the aiming-point. And, since they had to face and defeat the German fighters in battle, it was important to reduce the strength of the defending air forces. But the night bombers relied chiefly on their powers of evasion for their safety. They tried to do everything possible to outwit the defenses by feints at other targets, indirect routing, and by concentration in time and space. It was not so important for them to reduce the strength of the German defense forces as to evade them, and they had not yet developed sufficiently accurate methods of night bombing to permit the identification and destruction of aircraft factories. Their best policy, therefore, was to make a direct attack on the main sources of Germany's industrial and military strength.

There was, however, an influential school of thought which believed that there must be, in the German industrial system, some key points and bottlenecks which, if they could be verified, located, and destroyed, would produce a result wholly out of proportion to the small effort involved. The British Ministry of Economic Warfare devoted much thought and inquiry to this subject and frequently recommended the attack of some target the existence of which was said to be vital to the continuance of Germany's war effort. On several occasions such targets were in fact completely destroyed, without any apparent effect on Germany's ability to conduct the war. On investigation, it was always found that the supposedly vital nature of the target was a myth, based on incorrect or out-of-date information. Repeated disappointments of this kind never deterred the enthusiasts, and as soon as one project failed they were ready with another one. Bomber Command had little faith in them, and Harris called them "panacea" targets, as they were supposed to produce far-reaching and almost magical results. The Command found it difficult to believe that key points, the destruction of which would have disastrous consequences, could still be in existence after more than three years of war in the industrial organization of a nation such as Germany.

Both the U.S. Eighth Air Force and Bomber Command were constantly troubled by numerous and sometimes conflicting demands for the attack of special targets. Some of these were operationally impracticable, and some were even out of range. In October 1944, in order to protect the two long-range bomber commands from these pressures, a body known as the Combined Strategic Targets Committee was set up. It included representatives of the Air Ministry, the War Office, the Ministry of Economic Warfare, the American and British bomber commands, and other interested organizations. Its task was to examine the various possibilities and recommend priorities, to keep the current problems under constant study, and to evaluate the merits of any specific proposals that might be submitted to it. The work of this committee, which proved extremely valuable, will be more fully dealt with later.

In March 1943, the U.S. Eighth Air Force got off to a good start, and carried out some very successful attacks against important German aircraft and engine factories. But before long two serious difficulties began to hamper its operations. One was a direct, and the other an indirect, result of the weather conditions in northwest Europe. Since the aircrews could not take off and assemble in formation in the dark, and were not trained in night landings, in the short days of spring it was possible to attack targets in Germany only during a brief period midway between dawn and dusk. This period normally coincided with the maximum cloud development, and thus hampered the visual identification of the target. Secondly, this concentration of the daylight attacks within a brief midday period enabled the Germans to calculate the probable time of the attack and to concentrate their defending fighters. They needed to be on the alert only from about three hours after sunrise to three hours before sunset. The B-17's met with increasingly severe opposition from the German fighters and their casualties rose to a serious level. As the days lengthened the period during which attack was possible was extended, and before the days closed in again in the autumn steps had been taken to train the aircrews to take off, assemble, and land in the dark. This tactical disadvantage became less acute, but the difficulty caused by the diurnal building up of cloud remained. On the other hand, Bomber Command was frequently able to take advantage of the adiabatic clearance of the sky which tended to occur toward sunset, and on the whole the nights in northwest Europe are less cloudy than the days.

The German fighters, realizing that the B-17's had no nose-turrets and were relatively defenseless against attacks from ahead, developed a technique of frontal attack which was very effective. Such U.S. fighters as were available were used for escort duties, but their range was short, and they could accompany the bombers only for some two hundred miles.

In May 1943, the Combined Chiefs of Staff issued a new directive for the Allied bombing offensive against Germany. The objectives of the Eighth Air Force were widened to include the German aircraft, ball-bearing, and oil industries. The R.A.F. Bomber Command was to give priority to the attack of industrial areas containing factories and plants engaged in the manufacture of these products. In June it was decided to create a force of long-range fighters for escort duties, by modifying the P-38 and P-47 fighters.

Before these became available, however, the B-17's were ordered to carry out heavy attacks against the Messerschmitt aircraft factory at Regensburg, which produced about half Germany's single-engined fighters, and the large plants at Schweinfurt, which were believed to produce half the German output of ball-bearings. The economic experts firmly believed that if these targets could be destroyed, or even seriously damaged, Germany's capacity to wage war would be very adversely affected.

The plan for these attacks was a bold one. The formation attacking Regensburg, which involved a penetration of over three hundred miles into Germany, was to fly on and land at bases in Algeria, now, as a result of operation "Torch," in Allied hands. The Schweinfurt

AIR MINISTRY OFFICIAL PHOTOGRAPH

The best British heavy bomber of the Second World War—The Avro Lancaster

The famous Flying Fortress—The B-17.

U. S. AIR FORCE OFFICIAL PHOTOGRAPH

AIR MINISTRY OFFICIAL PHOTOG

Used for every purpose except that for which it was designed—the De Havilland Mosquito.

An excellent long-range escort fighter—Mustangs in formation (P-51's).

U. S. AIR FORCE OFFICIAL PHOTOG

The Mohne Dam breached by Bomber Command.

IMPERIAL WAR MUSEUM

IMPERIAL WAR MUSE

Krupp's great works in Essen, showing destruction after air bombardment.

Devastation among oil installations at Hamburg docks.

IMPERIAL WAR MUSE

U. S. AIR FORCE OFFICIAL PHOTOGRAPH

The Daimler-Benz works in Berlin bombed by B-17's.

AIR MINISTRY OFFICIAL PHOT

Leader of the British air forces in the Mediterranean theater, and later Deputy Supreme Commander for the invasion of Europe, Marshal of the R. A. F. Lord Tedder.

IMPERIAL WAR MUSEUM

Bielefeld railway viaduct after attack by 12,000 lb. and 22,000 lb. penetrating bombs.

German V-1 flying bomb immediately after launching.

IMPERIAL WAR MUSEUM

Preparing a German V-2 rocket for firing.

IMPERIAL WAR M

attack was timed to follow shortly afterward, and it was hoped that the earlier attack would have drawn off most of the German fighters to the southward, where they would have to land for refueling and rearming. In addition, arrangements were made for Bomber Command to attack Schweinfurt the same night, and, if possible, for several subsequent nights. It was hoped that the American attack would have started fires which might still be burning, and thus indicate the target to the night bombers.

The Regensburg force, consisting of 146 bombers, was fiercely attacked as soon as its fighter escort turned back near the German frontier. Fortunately the attacks became less intense as the bombers approached the target, and the aiming was excellent. Very severe damage was done to every important building in the Messerschmitt works. The formation then flew on unopposed to North Africa, but twenty-four B-17's had been destroyed.

The Schweinfurt attack was delayed for several hours by bad weather, and so the advantage which it was hoped to obtain from the preceding attack on Regensburg was not realized. The German fighter force had ample time to refuel and rearm, and the B-17's were attacked without respite for nearly two hours. Thirty-six were lost and many more damaged. The bombing, however, was good and a number of direct hits were obtained on the two main plants producing ball-bearings.

The attacks were successful, but the cost was very high. Of the total of 376 bombers dispatched, 60 (16 per cent) had been destroyed and over 100 damaged, some of them seriously.

A second attack against Schweinfurt some weeks later, on October 14, succeeded in doing very serious damage to the ball-bearing factories, but the losses were even more severe. Sixty B-17's (20.6 per cent) were destroyed out of the 291 dispatched.

Two important lessons were learned from these operations. First, it was now clear that unescorted B-17's could not undertake deep penetrations into Germany in daylight. The provision of long-range fighters was an urgent necessity. The difficulty was to find a fighter which combined long-range with sufficient performance to meet the short-range defending fighters on favorable terms. At first the P-38 and P-47 fighters were used for this duty, equipped with additional fuel tanks that could be jettisoned when empty, but they had insufficient range to accompany the bombers to their full radius of action. For some months after the Schweinfurt attacks the B-17's seldom undertook missions over Germany beyond the range of their fighter escorts. But every effort was being made to provide a suitable long-range escort fighter. The answer to this problem was found in the P-51, the Mustang, an aircraft of remarkable qualities which proved to be almost ideal for this purpose. By the end of 1943, when deep penetrations were resumed, the escort fighters soon took a tremendous toll of the German defending fighters. Now at last the B-17's were able to range over Germany at will. A number of very heavy and successful attacks were carried out against important objectives, culminating in two attacks on Berlin on March 6 and 8, 1944, when more than a thousand B-17's, escorted by hundreds of fighters, bombed objectives in the German capital.

The second lesson concerned the supposed importance of key targets. It caused surprise in some quarters that the effects of the massive and successful day and night attacks on the ball-bearing factories at Schweinfurt were not more noticeable. Although there is no doubt that the production of these factories was seriously affected, the Germans had already taken energetic steps to disperse their ball-bearing industry, and the program was considerably hastened as the result of the first attack. The German Minister of War Production, Albert Speer, was an exceptionally able man, and he well understood the danger of relying on the output of one small industrial area for a product of vital importance. In addition, the Germans were able to buy large quantities of ball-bearings from Sweden and Switzerland. Schweinfurt, though important, was not therefore the vital key point that the economic experts had supposed.

During the first three months of 1944 the U.S. Eighth Air Force, now greatly expanded and adequately escorted, carried out an intensive and successful campaign against numerous important objectives. The Germans were forced to turn over almost the whole of their aircraft industry to the production of defensive fighters. But even this did not avail them, and their day-fighter losses were very high. It is now known that during February and March 1944, the Germans lost over 800 fighters, and they became short of well-trained pilots. Thereafter their effectiveness rapidly declined. The B-17's, aided by their fighter escorts, had won their battle and had established air superiority. This marked a turning point in the war, second in importance only to the Battle of Britain.

In March 1943, Bomber Command, expanded and largely equipped with Lancasters and Halifaxes, began a sustained offensive against the main industrial centers of the Ruhr Valley. Using the Oboe system, Mosquitoes of the Pathfinder force were able to mark the aiming-points with great accuracy. The town of Essen, and the great Krupp Works, were repeatedly attacked, and enormous damage was done. In addition, many successful attacks were made against Cologne and the towns of Aachen, Bochum, Duisburg, Wuppertal, Dusseldorf, and Dortmund. Attacks were also made against other great industrial cities and towns such as Kassel, Mannheim, Hannover, Frankfurt-am-Main, and the ports of Hamburg, Bremen, Wilhelmshaven, and Kiel, with Lancasters of the Pathfinder force marking the targets by the H 2 S technique. Although H 2 S was a tremendous help, it was never quite as accurate and reliable as Oboe. But only Cologne and the Ruhr area lay within Oboe range.

Before the war, when the Plans Directorate of the Air Staff at the Air Ministry was studying the possibilities of air attack on the Ruhr, the importance of the Möhne, Eder, and Sorpe dams was observed. These three dams impounded a vast acreage of water, on which the Ruhr area largely depended for industrial and domestic supplies. Their destruction, it was thought, would have a serious effect on the productive capacity of the area. But there was in existence no weapon which could destroy such massive structures of earth and concrete. It would not be possible to drop torpedoes against them, as they were protected by strong nets, nor would any known type of bomb be capable of even seriously damaging them. In 1938 the Air Staff issued requirements for a weapon capable of destroying large dams, but no one was able to think of anything which had a chance of success. In 1942 Dr. Barnes Wallis, of the Vickers Aircraft Company, hit on an idea which seemed very promising. A scale model of the Möhne Dam was built in Wales, and preliminary trials showed that the project was worth pursuing. The weapon, after some setbacks and disappointments, was finally perfected by a team headed by Dr. Wallis. A special squadron, No. 617, was formed in No. 5 Group to carry out the operation. After intensive training, 19 Lancasters attacked the three dams on the night of May 16/17, 1943. The Möhne and Eder dams were destroyed, but the Sorpe, which was a very massive earth dam, withstood the attack. Eight of the aircraft failed to return. The destruction of the two dams caused severe damage by flooding and considerably reduced the water supply to the Ruhr, which added to the difficulties caused by fire and high-explosive bombing.

Between the nights of July 24/25 and August 2/3, Hamburg was very heavily attacked on four nights, during which 8,623 tons of bombs were dropped. The effects were catastrophic; huge areas of fire became quite uncontrollable, and the resulting convection currents caused a fire-storm. Winds of 60 m.p.h. and more raged through the streets, raising the temperature among the blazing buildings to a terrifying level. No city had ever been so extensively damaged before, except by an earthquake. Major-General Kehrl, the police president and air protection leader of the city, reported that "the damage was gigantic." He estimated that 40,385 dwellings and 275,000 apartments, representing 61 per cent of the living accommodation in the city, had been destroyed or rendered uninhabitable. A total of 580 industrial plants, including many producing armaments, were out of action. Goebbels referred to this in his diary as "a catastrophe, the extent of which simply staggers the imagination."

It is now known that the loss of production in Hamburg as a result of these attacks was roughly equivalent to three months' output.

During this attack "Window" was used for the first time by the bombers with excellent results. "Window" was the code name of a device for destroying the effectiveness of the German radar control of searchlights and guns, and of the A.I. sets carried in their night fighters. It consisted of metalized paper strips, cut to the correct length, which were scattered in very large numbers by the bombers, and which produced so great a response on the German radar screens as to blot out everything else. After this "Window" was used on all occasions, but the Germans gradually developed countermeasures to overcome it with a fair amount of success.

During August and September heavy attacks were made against Hannover, Stuttgart, Münster, Osnabrück, Würzburg, Munich, Nuremburg, and other industrial cities. The nights were growing longer, and in August 1943, the Battle of Berlin began. Using H 2 S the Pathfinder force marked carefully selected aiming-points in the German capital. The weather was on the whole bad, and sky markers[1] often had to be used. The prevalence of cloud also prevented the photographic reconnaissance from obtaining evidence of the effectiveness of the attack. The battle went on, the bombers attacking on every suitable occasion, until the night of March 24/25, 1944, when the last attack was made. During this battle Bomber Command made 16 major and several minor attacks, involving more than 10,000 sorties. The heaviest attack occurred during the night of February 15/16, when 2,643 tons of bombs were dropped.

When the weather improved, and it became possible to take air photographs, the battle was nearly over. It was not easy to assess the damage done by this sustained operation but it was clear that, especially in the industrial areas, it was immense. A very large number of important factories had been severely damaged or burned out. The area destroyed, including the effects of the American daylight bombing, was 6,427 acres. This was slightly larger than that in Hamburg, but Berlin is a very large city.

It was estimated that 30 per cent of the industrial plants in the city had ceased work as a direct result of the damage caused by the bombing, and a further 10 per cent through shortage of labor and raw materials. Some 60 per cent of the commercial establishments, including retail businesses, had been forced to close down. This estimate was later proved to have been conservative.

There could be no doubt that the target marking by the Pathfinder force had been carried out with great skill, and that the operations of the night bombers had been highly successful.

Before the war the Royal Aircraft Establishment at Farnborough had designed a magnetic mine to be laid by aircraft. When it was sufficiently advanced for its success to be beyond reasonable doubt, the Air Ministry informed the Admiralty and invited their cooperation. The Admiralty was reluctant to have anything to do with it, and pointed out that British dependence on sea-borne supplies made them far more vulnerable to the effects of such a weapon than Germany could ever be. They therefore proposed that all work on the project should cease at once, and every effort be made to suppress any hint of its existence. The Air Ministry argued that it was improbable that the Germans had overlooked such an obvious line of development, and that if work on it were stopped, it was not unlikely that the Germans would produce and use it, while the British would

[1] See Appendix B.

be without it. The Admiralty did not agree, and the matter was referred to the British Government, which decided that no further work
on these mines should be undertaken. Thus it came about that,
when the war broke out a year or two later, the Germans had a
magnetic mine, while the British had none. But the development
work done by the R.A.E. had two great advantages. The British study
of the magnetic mine had revealed the countermeasures necessary to
defeat it, and they were able to put in hand at once an effective
system of protecting ships against it. In addition, they were able, in
a comparatively short time, to produce magnetic mines of their own.

Most of the important German sea routes were in the Baltic or
close to the German coasts, and it was not possible for minelaying
vessels to reach them. Almost all the mines, therefore, had to be laid
by aircraft. At first, it had been the duty of Coastal Command to lay
these mines, but it was soon clear that the Command was more than
fully occupied with the antisubmarine campaign and had no aircraft
to spare for mine-laying. It therefore became one of the duties of
Bomber Command. By the end of 1942, 11,391 mines had been laid,
and in 1943 the total rose to 25,225.

This mine-laying campaign produced excellent results, which will
be more fully dealt with in Chapter 21.

In March 1944, it was judged that the air bombardment of Germany, and the decline in the effectiveness of the German Air Force,
together with the effects of attrition on the Eastern front, had produced the conditions needed for a successful invasion of Europe by
the Allies in the summer of 1944.

The Allied bomber offensive had played its part in weakening the
German armed resistance, and had broken the power of Hitler's
air force. It had thus performed the task laid upon it by the Combined Chiefs of Staff in the Casablanca directive of January 1943.
For the next three months it was to be mainly employed in destroying German defenses and communications in preparation for the
landing of Allied troops on the northern coast of France.

15 Air Bombardment in the Mediterranean Theater

We have seen how, in the First World War, the British sent military forces to the Middle East in order to protect the Suez Canal and the Anglo-Persian oil fields and refineries. We have noted the way in which the original defensive purpose was forgotten and a vigorous offensive policy adopted, leading to the eventual diversion of more than a million men to this secondary theater. And we have seen how this diversion so weakened the Allied armies in the decisive theater of war on the Western front that Ludendorff's final desperate attack in March 1918 very nearly succeeded.

During the years of peace a number of military writers had pointed out the folly of allowing Germany's ally, Turkey, to pin down so vast a force in a subsidiary campaign. But the lesson was not learned, because the Middle East had long exercised a fatal fascination for the British Government.

On June 10, 1940, Italy declared war on France and Britain. There could be no doubt that Mussolini thought that the war was all but over, and that Germany had won it. The declaration of war did not inspire much enthusiasm in Italy. In spite of the strong feelings aroused by the Abyssinian war the Italians had no great sympathy for the Germans, and had always been friendly with the people of Britain.

Soon after the declaration of war, Italy suffered a heavy loss in the death of General Italo Balbo. He was killed in an airplane accident in Libya on June 29. Balbo was one of those airmen, who, between the two world wars, made a marked contribution to the development of military aviation. He was a man of colorful personality and the Regia Aeronautica owed much to him, for he had done more than anyone else to create it and build it up.

Germany now had an ally in the Mediterranean theater, and thus possessed the means of tempting Britain, which at this time stood alone and was handicapped by shortages of military equipment of every kind, to divert forces to the Middle East. The British Government was not able to resist the temptation. It was decided to endeavor to hold Malta, and to build up land forces for the defense of Egypt and the Suez Canal. It was also resolved to take the offensive against the Italians in Abyssinia[1] and Eritrea.

If there was some justification for the policy of defending the Suez Canal against military attack in the First World War, there was none in 1940. The Mediterranean Fleet was stronger than the Italian navy, but, even if the British could hold Malta, they could not guarantee the safe passage of their shipping through the central narrows of the Mediterranean Sea. That route was closed to them, not by Italian sea power, but by the air forces of Italy, backed by Germany. Even the convoys to Malta, to deliver the minimum supplies and equipment needed for the defense of that island, were operations of great difficulty and danger.

In the Second World War, therefore, the Suez Canal was not even the by-pass route to the Persian oil fields, or to India and the Far East. From a strategic point of view, it was almost valueless. All supplies for Egypt and the Middle East had to be routed far out into the Atlantic, round the Cape, and up the east coast of Africa, a total of at least 12,000 miles. It was the decision to fight a large-scale war in the Middle East, at the end of a very long and dangerous line of sea communications, that was the main, if not the only cause, of the chronic shortage of British shipping during the first three years of the war.

On strategic grounds the British decision to build up large forces in the Middle East could not be justified. But for political, moral, or sentimental reasons it is often very difficult to apply correct strategic

[1] Now Ethiopia.

principles to any given situation in war. Coming so soon after the fall of France, a policy of withdrawal in the Middle East to positions covering the oil supplies, involving the abandonment of Malta, might have depressed and demoralized the British people. It was a critical time, and the fact that Britain could take the offensive somewhere, even though in a subsidiary theater, was welcome evidence that the initiative in military affairs had not been wholly lost. In addition, the troops and tactical air forces acquired a battle-worthiness that proved of great value later in operation "Overlord."

The Italian forces were expelled from Abyssinia and Eritrea in a series of well-conducted operations, in the course of which the R.A.F. gave exemplary support to the British land forces. These successes heartened the people of Britain and correspondingly discouraged the Italians.

The British then advanced rapidly westward from Egypt, and might have succeeded in driving the Italians out of Libya if it had not been for Mussolini's attack on Greece, which began on October 28, 1940. The Greek forces resisted stoutly, and would probably have been able to defend themselves successfully, but the British felt morally bound to come to their aid. General Wavell, commanding in North Africa, was ordered by the British Government to hold what he had gained with the minimum force, and to send as large an army and air force as possible to the assistance of Greece.

From a strategic point of view, this was a blunder of the first magnitude. British intervention caused Mussolini to demand German aid, which Hitler could scarcely refuse, though it is improbable that he would have spared German troops to help the Italians as long as they were fighting only the Greeks. The British forces were too small to be effective on two fronts. Supplies and communications were difficult to organize in Greece and airfield accommodation was poor. It eventually became clear that the British forces must be evacuated if they were to escape annihilation. Some 43,000 of the 58,000 men sent to Greece were re-embarked in April 1941, of which 27,000 were sent to Crete.

In May the Germans began a heavy air attack on Crete. The three airfields on the island were the main target for this attack, and many British aircraft were destroyed on the ground. The remaining aircraft were evacuated to Egypt to avoid destruction. It was known that the Germans intended to capture Crete by means of an airborne invasion, but the British navy did not believe that this had any chance of success.

The assault opened with a heavy attack on the Maleme airfield on May 20. Thousands of paratroops were dropped and nearly a hundred gliders, filled with troops and equipment, landed nearby. By sunset that day, over 7,000 airborne troops had been landed. On May 21, further large numbers arrived. Crete was too far from Egypt for effective air support, and the German air force dominated the skies over the island. German air attack virtually cut all communications with Crete by sea. Several British warships were sunk, including the cruiser *Gloucester*, and many more were badly damaged. On the nights of May 30 and 31, 14,580 men were evacuated from Crete, leaving behind 12,970, most of whom were dead, wounded, or missing.

The fate of Crete, an island far from the British air forces based in Egypt and close to the German air forces based in Greece, was inevitable. It could never have been held against a determined assault. But, until the loss of Crete drove home the lesson, the British army and naval commands did not fully realize that the days of two-dimensional warfare had gone for ever.

Meanwhile the situation in North Africa had deteriorated. The Germans had sent to Libya the Afrika Corps, a fine, well-trained formation under the command of Lieutenant-General Erwin Rommel, to reinforce the Italian army. The depleted British forces, at the end of a long line of communications, were soon hard pressed. On March 31, the Axis offensive began, with very strong air support, and the British were forced to retreat. Except for a garrison at Tobruk, which was besieged but which managed to hold out, the British lost almost the whole of Cyrenaica. The R.A.F., sadly depleted by its losses in Greece and Crete, and by the difficulty of obtaining new aircraft to replace wastage by the long sea route via the Cape, or by the long air route across equatorial Africa from Freetown, was almost overwhelmed by the powerful air forces at Rommel's disposal.

The truth was that the British had attempted far too much. With 12,000 miles of submarine-infested waters between them and their home bases, their inadequate forces had endeavored to drive the Italians out of Abyssinia, Eritrea, Cyrenaica, and Libya; had tried to give the greatest possible military aid to Greece, and to hold on to Crete and Malta. They had divided their forces and been defeated in detail.

If Malta had not suffered the fate of Crete it was simply because no attempt had been made to capture it. The Italians had not the means of organizing an airborne assault on the island, and the Germans were not interested in doing so. They thought it unnecessary, as they did not believe that the British garrison in Malta was capable of doing them any serious harm. Malta had suffered a good deal from air attack, but, although the defenses were weak, the island possessed many natural air raid shelters. Gradually the defenses were improved, and the time was to come when the air forces in Malta would take the offensive against the Axis line of communications across the Mediterranean.

The British army suffered a number of vicissitudes—advances alternating with retreats—in Cyrenaica, until in August 1942, General Montgomery[2] assumed command of the 8th Army. The British were then holding a short defensive line in western Egypt, stretching from El Alamein on the coast to the Qattara Depression. On August 31 Rommel attacked the El Alamein position in full strength. This was the battle that was expected to put an end to all British resistance in North Africa, and Mussolini had come from Italy to lead the victory parade in Cairo mounted on a white horse. The 8th Army held on to its defensive positions grimly, causing heavy losses in Rommel's forces, while the R.A.F., now reinforced, joined battle with the German and Italian air forces, and relentlessly attacked their airfields. The British bombers pounded the Axis communications by rail, road, and sea with great success. The four-engined Halifax and Liberator bombers lent new weight to their blows, and Rommel began to run short of supplies. His attack faltered and came to a standstill. He had relied on capturing British fuel dumps, and his failure to do so left him in danger of immobilization. By September 5 it was clear that his attack had failed. British supplies were now coming forward in quantity, while the R.A.F. did everything possible to cut Rommel's communications. By the third week in October, the 8th Army was ready to counterattack, and on October 23 the Battle of El Alamein began. It was successful and by November 3 the Axis forces were in full retreat. The bombers were now switched from the attack of communications to harassing the retreating armies, littering the roads and

[2] Now Field Marshal Viscount Montgomery of Alamein.

deserts with broken and burned-out tanks and transport vehicles. By day and night the fighters and bombers kept up the pursuit, and Rommel's sea communications were forced westward to Tripoli. Now Malta was able to take the offensive, and Axis shipping and Tripoli itself were attacked by British aircraft operating from that base.

Meanwhile the combined Anglo-American expedition—operation "Torch"—had begun. Large forces were landed in Algeria and the Axis forces, making a last stand in Tunisia, were attacked from east and west. By May 13, 1943, all enemy resistance had ceased.

The Allied air forces had gained complete air superiority and no evacuation from Tunisia was possible. In all, the Axis forces in North Africa lost some 50,000 men killed, and nearly 300,000 were taken prisoner.

It will be remembered that during the First World War the effectiveness of British air power on the Western front was seriously vitiated by its decentralized organization. The air forces were under the command of Army General Headquarters, but they were split up into relatively small formations controlled by subordinate military commanders. This unsatisfactory state of affairs was one of the main reasons for the unification of all air forces in the Royal Air Force. During the years of peace, whenever exercises were carried out with the Army, there was the same tendency to break up the Air Force and allocate portions of it to corps, divisions, and even brigades. For this reason the Air Ministry was most unwilling to allow air forces operating in support of land operations to be placed under the command of the Army. Their view was that the Air Force should be centralized into one formation, under an air commander who would work with, but not under, the military commander. The Air Ministry was especially anxious to insure that the strength of the bombers was not dissipated, as it had been in the First World War, in the attack on a multitude of minor objectives.

The Army did not like this arrangement, because they felt they could not be certain that the air forces would do exactly what they wanted them to do. The Air Ministry tried to meet this objection by undertaking that the air commander would be instructed to use his force, in the best way possible—of which he was to be the judge— to achieve the object as defined by the army commander. But by the time the Second World War broke out there was no mutually agreed system of organization for air forces engaged in the support of armies.

It was the Germans who first demonstrated the way in which air forces should be used to further the course of land operations. Although the German air force was a third separate Service and even had control of all antiaircraft weapons, it was designed, equipped, and trained for the support of the German army. Indeed, when Hitler's victorious campaign put an end to land warfare in western Europe, and his air force had to be used in an independent role to create the conditions needed for the invasion of Britain, it proved to be unsuited to its task. It was defeated by a much smaller force in the Battle of Britain, and failed to achieve its object.

But the effective handling of the German air force in support of their armies showed what could be done. When the campaign began in North Africa it was decided to have a centralized air force, working with but not under the Army. Before long the Army began to appreciate the valuable help that concentrated air power could contribute, and became reconciled to the position. Under General Montgomery and Air Marshal A. W. Tedder,[3] the system was perfected, and by the time the war in North Africa had ended it had become accepted as the model organization.

Montgomery fully understood the importance of air power in land operations. On December 27, 1943, referring to the North African campaign, he said "First of all you must win the battle of the air. That must come before you start a single sea or land engagement. If you examine the conduct of my campaigns, you will find that we never fought a land battle until the air battle was won." And Montgomery knew very well that the air battle could be won only by a centralized air force operating under its own commander. In a lecture to the Royal United Service Institution in October 1954 he said "The greatest asset of air power is its flexibility. If you split it up into compartments you merely pull it to pieces and destroy its greatest asset—its flexibility." And in another lecture a year later in the same place, he said "The war in the air is essentially one battle against a single enemy. If it is planned and conducted as a series of separate battles, we lose flexibility and the ability to concentrate."

The original object of the campaign in North Africa was the defense of the Suez Canal and the Anglo-Persian oil fields. Later it was

[3] Now Marshal of the R.A.F. Lord Tedder.

widened to include the defeat of the Axis forces in North Africa and
the capture of the whole southern shore of the Mediterranean Sea.
That had now been accomplished, and the Allies had in Tunisia
large land and air forces, well-trained and battle-tested. The question
of their future employment now had to be settled. There was no
prospect of invading France across the English Channel in 1943, and
they would either have to follow up their success by invading Sicily
and Italy, or the bulk would be transferred to Burma and the Southwest Pacific theater, leaving defensive garrisons in North Africa. The
object of an invasion of Sicily and Italy would be to eliminate the
Italians from the war, and possibly to advance into Austria and beyond, in the hope of liberating Jugoslavia, Hungary, and Czechoslovakia.

It was decided to adopt this course, and it was also intended to
bring the heavy bombers of the U.S. Fifteenth Air Force within range
of targets in southeast Germany.

The air battle over Sicily began even before the fighting in Tunisia
had ended. The train ferries from Italy across the Straits of Messina
and their terminal ports were heavily attacked with considerable success. Then the bombers turned their attention to the Sicilian airfields,
and a large number of aircraft were destroyed on the ground. In early
July the sea-borne assault took place, assisted by airborne troops, and
by the middle of August all Axis resistance on the island had ceased.
The Allied long-range bombers at once began a strategic bombing
campaign against the railways in the north of Italy, paying particular
attention to the Simplon, St. Gothard, and Brenner passes.

These events caused a political crisis in Italy. Mussolini resigned
on July 25, and a new government was formed under Marshal
Badoglio, who at once began negotiations for an armistice. On September 8, 1943, it was announced that Italy had unconditionally surrendered to the Allies. After his resignation, Mussolini had been im-
prisoned by the Italians. He was rescued on September 12 by a
German Commando force and went to live in Salo, by the shores of
Lake Garda. He was finally recaptured by Italian partisans on April
29, 1944, and executed a few days later.

But Hitler, who was by now showing signs of the irrational and
even lunatic obstinacy that added so much to the sufferings of the
German people, decided to fight on in Italy and ordered his forces
to yield no ground. The Allies fought their way stubbornly from the

heel of Italy to the fall of Rome on June 4, 1944. The struggle northward, through a terrain admirably suited to defense, was long and arduous. The Allied air forces bombed without ceasing German communications, railway bridges, airfields, and supply depots. Hardly ever before in history had any army attempted to conquer Italy from the south. Even the Carthaginian general, Hannibal, in the Punic Wars, had preferred to cross the Alps, with his elephants, in order to enjoy the advantage of an approach to Rome from the north.

On November 2, 1943, the heavy bombers of the U.S. Fifteenth Air Force, based in Tunisia, carried out their first attack. As soon as possible they moved northward to new airfields at Foggia. This brought the heavy bombers within range of many targets in southeast Europe, which had hitherto been beyond the reach of Bomber Command and the U.S. Eighth Air Force based in Britain. It took a considerable time, however, to provide at Foggia all the stores and facilities needed for the successful operation of a heavy bomber force, and the weather, especially over the high ground in northern Italy, was generally bad. The Fifteenth Air Force was able, nevertheless, to carry out a number of successful attacks against important objectives. These were, in so far as weather and other conditions allowed, co-ordinated with the attacks made by the Allied heavy bombers operating from British airfields.

The decision had now been taken to invade France across the English Channel during the summer of 1944. This commitment—operation "Overlord"—had already begun to affect the conduct of the war in Italy. On December 24, 1943, General Eisenhower, the Supreme Commander in the Mediterranean theater, was appointed to command the invasion from the west, and he proceeded to Britain to take over his new command. With him went his air commanders; Tedder, Commander of the Mediterranean Allied Air Force, and Coningham, Commander of the 1st Tactical Air Force. Seven experienced divisions were taken away from the Italian theater. The advance northward slowed down, and the chances of liberating any of the countries of southeastern Europe inevitably began to fade and eventually disappeared.

16   *Allied Bombers and the Invasion of Europe*

When Hitler decided to stand on the defensive in the west and attack Russia in June 1941, he ordered the Todt organization[1] to fortify the coasts of the Low Countries and northwestern France against an attempted invasion by the Allies. By the spring of 1944 this work had been completed, and German propaganda frequently stressed the impregnable nature of the Fortress of Europe, guarded by Hitler's Atlantic Wall. But the Germans forgot that the Fortress of Europe had no roof. Hitler's action was not unlike that of the old farmer on the Devon coast, who built a wall eighteen feet high round his land to keep out the sea gulls. While the strength of Germany's armed forces was draining away on the Eastern front, the steadily growing might of the Allied bombers struck at the heart of their industrial and military strength. Hundreds of war factories were rebuilt only to be destroyed again, while whole industrial areas and centers of administration had been methodically reduced to ashes and rubble.

The Atlantic Wall had not prevented the bombers from harrying Germany, nor could it stop them from effectively carrying out the preparations needed before a successful invasion could be undertaken.

The problems of the invasion, though numerous and immensely varied, all turned on the ability of the Allies to do three things. First,

[1] The German civilian engineering and construction corps.

164

they had to transport their armies across the Channel and land them on the coast of France. This would require unchallenged air and naval superiority in the selected area. Next, they had to establish themselves firmly ashore and enlarge their beach-heads, which meant that they must be able to build up their forces and supplies more rapidly over their sea communications than the Germans could move their reserves, by rail and road, to the threatened points. To succeed in this they must be able to secure their own communications while destroying those of the enemy. Their own communications could be safeguarded by air and sea power in cooperation, but the destruction of the German communications was a task that could be undertaken only by air power. Thirdly, they had to build up enough force to break out of their beach-heads and assume the offensive, driving back the Germans and capturing sufficient port accommodation to insure their own supply lines. For this the Allied armies would need close air support.

A new organization, the Allied Expeditionary Force Bombing Committee, was set up to consider the best way of dealing with these problems. The Allied Supreme Headquarters ruled that the success of the invasion would be jeopardized unless the whole railway system from the Rhine to the assault area was so paralyzed as to deny to the Germans the possibility of moving major reinforcements by rail.

This railway system is composed of an especially dense network of lines, with many alternative routes available in all directions. Interruptions caused by bombing could be avoided with comparative ease. All railway systems have highly organized repair facilities to deal with breaks in the line. The efficient working of an elaborate railway system, however, is peculiarly dependent on its traffic control centers. If these could be destroyed, confusion and chaos would be bound to follow. And, of course, no railway can continue to function if its motive power has been destroyed or immobilized.

It is true that, given time, control centers can be improvised and locomotives repaired, but the standard of maintenance on the French, Dutch, and Belgian railways had, after four years of war, sunk to a low level. The combined effects of air attack, sabotage, and the removal of locomotives and rolling stock in large numbers for use in Germany and the Eastern front, had seriously affected their capacity. But although there was a real shortage of rolling stock, and repair facilities were overstrained, the existing capacity of the railways was more than ample for the military needs of the Germans.

Locomotive running and repair sheds, control centers, and marshaling yards where trains are sorted and made up, are often found together in one large complex. It was decided, in consultation with transportation experts, to select as aiming-points the locomotive running sheds and repair depots. A list of eighty of the most important railway centers was drawn up. Of these thirty-seven were allocated to Bomber Command, and the remaining forty-three were divided between the U.S. Eighth Air Force and the Allied Expeditionary Air Force. The latter was, as its name implied, a combined force consisting of the U.S. Ninth Air Force, which was a tactical formation, the British Second Tactical Air Force, and a fighter formation oddly named the Air Defense of Great Britain, which was really Fighter Command under another name. The object of the plan was to reduce the capacity of the railway system to the greatest possible extent by a sustained air bombardment, and then on and after D Day[2] to attack, mainly with tactical air forces, the rail and road bridges, trains in motion, and any traffic bottlenecks. It was hoped, by these means, to paralyze almost all movement by rail or road at the critical time. In addition, a number of railway targets in southern France and Germany were allocated to the U.S. Fifteenth Air Force, based at Foggia in Italy.

An experimental attack was made by Bomber Command on the night of March 6/7 against the railway center at Trappes. This was one of the important depots and marshaling yards near Paris. Guided by marker bombs dropped by Mosquitoes of the Pathfinder force using the Oboe technique, 263 heavy bombers dropped 1,258 tons of bombs with great accuracy. The result was very encouraging, and the center was so severely damaged that it was out of action for nearly five weeks.

There was some opposition to this plan for attacking the railways on the grounds that it would cause heavy casualties among French civilians at a time when their help and good will would be urgently needed. But every possible effort was made to reduce civilian casualties to the minimum. Main force crews were instructed not to drop their bombs unless the markers were clearly visible. On some occasions they were not allowed to bomb until the position of the markers had been checked by a "Master Bomber," who would give

[2] The actual date fixed for the invasion.

permission for the attack to proceed only when he was satisfied that the markers were on or very near the aiming point.

By D Day, as a result of the combined efforts of the three bomber forces, almost all the targets on the list were assessed as damaged so severely that no further attacks were necessary until repairs had been effected. Air reconnaissance photographs showed that repairs were on a small scale, due no doubt to the widespread nature and severity of the damage. And this was the more remarkable because soon after the start of this operation the Germans had drafted 50,000 railway-men into France in order to keep the system working in the face of the bombing attacks and of sabotage on the part of the French, Dutch, and Belgian workers. By June 2nd Bomber Command had made 8,800 sorties against transportation targets and dropped 42,000 tons of bombs. The Eighth Air Force had dropped a total of 24,500 tons. And both Commands had continued to attack Germany, though less intensively. During the period Bomber Command made thirteen major assaults on strategic targets in Germany, while the B-17's carried out a similar number of daylight attacks.

The railway targets allotted to the night bombers did not require a concentrated attack by the whole Command, and for most of them the effort of one main force group was sufficient. Consequently several targets were sometimes attacked simultaneously, and the Oboe Mosquitoes of the centralized Pathfinder force were unable to mark so many targets at one time. This led to experiments with visual target marking from a low level, which was developed to a high degree of accuracy and reliability in No. 5 Group. It was first employed as a means of carrying out relatively small but very accurate attacks against important factories. The first of these attacks was against a radar factory near Friedrichshafen, which was close to the Swiss frontier. Sixty Lancasters of No. 5 Group were employed, and the attack was a great success. The leader or Master Bomber laid or assessed the position of the markers, and then gave bombing directions by radio telephony to the rest of the force. Group Captain Leonard Cheshire pioneered the development of these methods. He showed great courage, and became an exceptionally reliable and experienced Master Bomber. In the course of the next few weeks eleven small but important targets in France were bombed, and all were very severely damaged. Four of them, indeed, were damaged beyond any hope of repair. In these small attacks the new 12,000 lb.

bombs were frequently used,[3] and they proved to be very effective. On one occasion four out of five of these heavy bombs scored direct hits on an important factory, completely wrecking it.

On the night before D Day, June 4/5, a very heavy attack was made by Bomber Command on the coastal batteries in the assault area. No less than 1,136 heavy bombers took part, dropping a total of 5,315 tons of high-explosive bombs. Next morning only one battery was able to offer any resistance to the armada of ships approaching the French coast.

Almost complete air superiority was achieved over the Channel and the French coast, and the Allied armies were safely transported and put ashore on the beaches. The effectiveness of the three months' offensive against the railways was demonstrated by the fact that the main German reinforcements arrived in the battle zone too late to prevent the firm establishment of the Allied armies on the Normandy beach-heads. And when they did arrive they found themselves operating under very disadvantageous conditions. They were fighting under the threat of overwhelming Allied air superiority against which the German air force was utterly powerless, and they were attempting to hold a front behind which the railway system was almost completely paralyzed.

After the landing the main task of the heavy bombers was to prevent supplies and reinforcements from reaching the battle zones. Every morning a conference was held at Supreme Headquarters, at which priorities were decided and suitable targets allocated to the various commands.

The U.S. Eighth Air Force and Bomber Command carried out heavy attacks against the principal railway centers in the Nantes-Angers-Saumur-Tours-Orleans area to cut rail traffic from southern France; in the Paris area, to cut rail traffic from northeastern and eastern France; and in the Rennes-Pontaubault area, to cut rail traffic from the Brest Peninsula. One of the most remarkable of this series of attacks occurred on the night of June 8/9, when 16 Lancasters, armed with 12,000 lb. bombs, attacked the southern entrance of the Saumur Tunnel. One bomb penetrated the roof of the tunnel near the entrance and others scored direct hits on the track. The tunnel was completely blocked, and remained so until it was captured by the Allied armies many weeks later.

[3] See Appendix A.

So thoroughly had the work of preparation been done that bad weather, threatening to interrupt his sea communications, was the chief cause of anxiety to the Supreme Commander.

With the armies safely ashore and well-established, Bomber Command turned its attention to the German light warships based at Le Havre and Boulogne, which it was feared might attack the streams of shipping bringing supplies of all kinds to the beach-heads. Very heavy and accurate attacks were made on both ports. At Le Havre 14 "E" boats, 3 "R" boats, 3 torpedo boats, and 16 other vessels, totaling some 15,000 tons, were sunk. At Boulogne 7 "R" boats, 6 mine-sweepers, and 9 other vessels were destroyed. After these attacks attempts by German naval forces to interfere with the Allied sea communications almost ceased.

The partial collapse of the German air force led to a revival of large-scale daylight attacks by Bomber Command, with fighter cover provided by No. 11 (Fighter) Group. It was decided to waste no time in training the pilots to fly in formation, and the bombers operated by day in concentrated streams in the same way as by night. For the time being, however, these daylight attacks were confined to short-range operations in France and the Low Countries.

When the time came for the Allied armies to take the offensive, the British 2nd and Canadian 1st armies were held up at Caen by strong German defenses. A tremendous attack by some 1,500 heavy bombers of the U.S. Eighth Air Force, and more than 900 light bombers and fighters of the Ninth Air Force, had opened the way for a break out southward of the American armies. The armored forces of the Third U.S. Army poured through the gap, and pushed ahead in the hope of outflanking the main German forces. But the holdup of the British and Canadian armies on the left flank was becoming serious, and Bomber Command was called in to deal with the situation. On July 7, in daylight, 457 heavy bombers dropped 2,350 tons of high-explosive bombs on the German defensive positions in 38 minutes. Bewildered and dazed by the violence of this concentrated attack, the German troops, who were still suffering from the effects of concussion for several hours afterward, were able to offer but slight resistance to the advance of Montgomery's armored forces. They broke through without difficulty east of Caen, and within an hour had reached Cagny. At last the way was open, and the German forces were in full retreat.

These were the first occasions on which the heavy bombers had been used for the close support of troops in battle, but they were not the last. Within the next two months Bomber Command alone made six more such attacks, involving a total of 4,076 sorties, and dropping some 16,000 tons of bombs. The targets, in this type of bombing, were very close to the Allied troops, since it was important to follow up the bombing attack by an advance with the least possible delay. It was therefore essential that the bombing should be very accurate and that no bombs should fall on positions held by Allied troops. Strict precautions were taken to avoid the risk of such accidents, including the use of a timed run from some clearly identifiable landmark, such as the coast line. Two incidents did occur, one British and one American, when Allied troops were accidentally bombed, but in neither case were the results serious. The precautions then taken avoided any repetition of such incidents, and, in fact, as their confidence increased, the Allied troops approached so close to the target areas that they caused some anxiety in the bomber forces.

The port of Cherbourg was captured before the end of June, but the Allies were badly in need of further port capacity. When the Germans retreated they left garrisons in the ports of Boulogne, Calais, and Le Havre, which were ordered by Hitler himself to resist to the last, thereby denying to the Allies the use of these valuable harbors for as long as possible. It was decided to call in the heavy bombers to deal with the situation. Boulogne was heavily attacked and with a few days the garrison of 8,000 men surrendered. The defenders of Calais did not surrender until six attacks had been made, during which over 8,000 tons of bombs were dropped. The most remarkable result, however, was achieved at Le Havre. In just under a week seven attacks were made, a total of 9,790 tons being dropped. The town was then taken by assault with the loss of 50 Allied troops. The entire garrison of 11,000 German soldiers was captured. These spectacular results showed the effectiveness of heavy and concentrated bombing in reducing strong defensive positions. In the diary of a German officer, captured at Boulogne, the following words were found: "Can anyone survive after a carpet of bombs has fallen? Sometimes one could despair of everything if one is at the mercy of the R.A.F. without protection. It seems as if all fighting is useless and all sacrifices are in vain." It is impossible not to feel some sympathy for those who had to endure these concentrated, intense, and accurate bombardments.

It was inevitable that in many of these attacks on objectives in occupied territory there should have been casualties among friendly civilians. Everything possible was done to reduce these to a minimum and this was understood and appreciated. The unavoidable loss of life and destruction of property were bravely accepted and patiently endured.

On the night of August 14/15 the invasion of southern France, known as operation "Anvil," began. This project had aroused much controversy. Those who opposed it argued that it was unnecessary; that preparatory air attacks to facilitate it would do further damage to French property, and cause loss of life; that it would not draw off German resources from northern France; and that it would so weaken the Allied forces in Italy that any prospects of liberating the countries of southeast Europe would be destroyed. Those who were in favor of it contended that nothing should be left undone that could contribute to the success of "Overlord," and that the Allies should concentrate on the liberation of France. The case in favor of operation "Anvil" was not a strong one; but it was powerfully urged by the Russians, who were interested in diverting Allied forces away from southeast Europe. They wished to do so because they wanted the Red Army to "liberate" Rumania and Hungary—and indeed as much of Europe as possible—with the intention of bringing these areas within the Communist orbit. In the end it was Stalin's insistence that persuaded the Allies to carry out operation "Anvil."

The Allied attack, which was in considerable force with powerful air support, met with little resistance. The land forces moved quickly northward, almost unopposed, and joined with General Patton's army on the southern flank of the northern invasion.

Meanwhile the Allied forces in Italy, depleted and robbed of much of their air support, came to a halt on the "Gothic" line, the strong German defensive position across the Italian peninsula north of Florence. The line was eventually breached, and the advance continued more slowly until the Allied forces reached the valley of the river Po. By the time this was crossed the end of the war was at hand.

17   Allied Bombers Defeat the German "V" Weapons

When the growing severity of the Allied air bombardment compelled the Germans to turn almost the whole of their aircraft industry over to the production of defensive fighters, they knew very well that unless they could resume the offensive in the air they had no hope of winning the war. Since they had not the capacity to build bombers as well as the fighters they so desperately needed, they cast about for other means of conducting an air offensive. Their scientists and engineers did not fail them, and two weapons were designed for this purpose; a flying bomb, known as the V-1, and a long-range ballistic missile, the V-2.

Since the end of 1942 a number of reports had reached Washington and London from various sources which suggested that the Germans were developing a new kind of aerial weapon. Some reports referred to a form of pilotless aircraft carrying a bomb, while others related to some kind of rocket-propelled missile. It was known that even before the war the Germans had been experimenting with rocket propulsion for aircraft. On April 12, 1943, a committee was formed under the chairmanship of Mr. Duncan Sandys, at that time Parliamentary Under-Secretary to the Ministry of Supply, to look into the evidence and report.

As time went on suspicion began to center on an experimental station at Peenemünde on the Baltic coast, and it was kept under close

172

observation. Air photographs, taken on June 12 and 23, showed two large objects, about forty feet long and six feet in diameter, which might have been rockets. A later inspection showed a very small aircraft, with a wing span of about twenty feet, of an unfamiliar shape. Photographs were also taken of four very large unfinished concrete works, the purpose of which was unknown. These were at Watten, Mimoyecques, Siracourt, and Wizernes, all in northern France. The strange thing about these four works was that although they were all massive and obviously important, they were quite different in design. Gradually the scraps of evidence were pieced together like the bits of a jigsaw puzzle, and it was concluded that the Germans were proposing to use two new weapons. One was a small pilotless aircraft, driven by a simple ram-jet engine, with an explosive charge in the nose. This was the V-1, the flying bomb. The other was a huge rocket, the V-2, obviously driven by some very powerful propellant, about which little was known. There were unconfirmed reports that the Germans were developing a rocket missile capable of carrying five to ten tons of explosive, with a range of two to three hundred miles. This seemed so fantastic that Lord Cherwell, scientific adviser to the Prime Minister, was inclined to believe that it was a cover story, designed to conceal a secret weapon of quite a different kind.

While much was unknown, it was quite clear that these new weapons presented a very serious threat. It was feared that the Germans intended to use them to shatter the preparations for invasion, which involved the concentration along the south coasts of Britain, and particularly near the ports of embarkation, of large numbers of troops and vast accumulations of vehicles, equipment, and supplies.

As a first step, it was decided to carry out the heaviest possible attack against Peenemünde. As it was about six hundred miles from the bombers' bases, there would not be sufficient hours of darkness until the middle of August. The attack was planned with great care. Peenemünde consisted of a large area with numbers of rather isolated groups of buildings, the relative importance of which was not known. It was decided that the Lancasters of the Pathfinder force should identify and mark three aiming-points. The markers were to be visually checked, and the attack controlled by Group Captain J. H. Searby, a Master Bomber of notable skill and experience. Each aiming-point was to be attacked for forty-five minutes, and arrangements were made for re-marking them at frequent intervals. The full-moon period was chosen in order to provide the best possible visibility. It was realized that this and the long duration of the attack might lead to considerable losses, but the importance attached to the accurate and heavy bombing of this objective justified the taking of risks. And Bomber Command had learned, by this time, that the greatest losses were caused by failures at the first attempt, with the consequent need to make repeated attacks after the defenses had been alerted.

Since it was believed that the Germans had smoke screens in position at Pennemünde, every effort was made to achieve surprise in order to identify the aiming-points before they were obscured. It was also hoped to postpone the concentration of German fighters over the target, and to catch the air raid precautions and fire-fighting services off their guard. To assist in this, previous raids on Berlin were routed near to or over Peenemünde in the hope that the approach of the bombers, on the night of the attack, would be regarded as another assault on the German capital. In addition, a harassing attack on Berlin, including the dropping of marker bombs, was carried out by Mosquitoes of the Pathfinder force a few minutes before the attack on Peenemünde was due to begin. These measures achieved their object, and the attack was a complete surprise. It was carried out with great skill and determination, and was controlled with marked ability by the Master Bomber. Before very long, however, the German night fighters began to arrive and, with the aid of clear weather and bright moonlight, made numerous attacks on the bombers. Out of a total of 597 heavy bombers dispatched, 41 failed to return.

The attack was a great success. The Master Bomber reported that when he left the target area at the end of the attack, it was impossible to distinguish individual buildings owing to the tremendous fires that were sweeping the area. The main administrative block, the Senior Officers' Mess, and the drawing offices were destroyed, scores of other buildings were demolished or severely damaged, and a large hutted camp was burned out. Owing to the surprise, casualties were heavy. Dr. Thiel, the scientific officer in charge of the development of "V" weapons, and another important scientist, were killed. In all, nearly 800 persons lost their lives, though many of these unfortunately were impressed foreign workers. It was noticeable that after this attack German threats of retaliation against Britain by means of secret weapons became considerably more vague about dates.

There was reason to believe that the rocket propellant was being developed at the I. G. Farben factories at Leuna, Oppau, and Ludwigshaven, and these were attacked with some success during September. At this time, also, attacks were made on the mysterious concrete structures in northern France. Watten was attacked by 185 B-17's, which scored nineteen direct hits on the buildings.

In October 1943, a new discovery was made. An air photograph showed a site, in a wood not far from Abbeville, with quite novel features. It consisted of two small buildings, a concrete platform, and a long ramp with a curved end that looked like one of a pair of skis. This was the first of the "ski sites," as they were called. The axis of the ski was found to point directly at London. The whole of northern France was carefully reconnoitered, and by the end of November no less than seventy-nine similar sites, in various stages of construction, were identified. Further air reconnaissance showed exactly similar installations on the airfields at Peenemünde and Zempin. On November 28 a photograph showed a small aircraft on the ski site at Zempin. The connection was now clear, and it was obvious that the ski sites were the launching ramps for the V-1 flying bombs. By the end of 1943 eighty-eight ski sites had been pinpointed, and fifty works, suspected to be ski sites in the early stages of construction, were kept under observation.

There is no doubt that the Germans intended to use the "V" weapons, in the first instance, to disrupt and disorganize the Allied preparations for the invasion. If they were to be effective for this purpose, they would have to be ready for use, in massive quantities, not later than the beginning of May 1944. But they suffered from delays, due not only to the Allied bombing of Peenemünde and other important targets, but to various defects and difficulties encountered during the development of these novel weapons. The Allies knew nothing of this, however, and it was decided to take action at once. In November 1943, the Air Ministry formed a new directorate to collect and co-ordinate all information about the "V" weapons, and to direct the campaign against them, which was given the code name of operation "Crossbow." It was decided to destroy as many as possible of the sites, and the task of doing this was shared out between the U.S. Eighth and Ninth Air Forces, Bomber Command, and the 2nd Tactical Air Force. The most diverse methods were used. The Eighth Air Force relied on high altitude daylight bombing, using the Norden bombsight. The Ninth Air Force and the 2nd Tactical Air Force employed light bombers and fighter-bombers in low level attacks. Bomber Command operated by day and night, using visual methods in daylight and the Oboe technique during the hours of darkness. It was estimated, in May, that no more than ten ski sites were capable of launching a flying bomb. The Germans gave up the idea of using these sites, probably as early as March, and in April a new and much simpler form of launching ramp, easily transported and assembled, was seen. These were known as the modified sites; many of them were camouflaged to look like farm buildings and other innocent structures. Although these sites were much more difficult for the bombers to discover and destroy, their capacity for launching flying bombs was very much smaller than that of the ski sites. Instead of the hundreds a day which the ski sites were designed to operate, the modified sites, with an energetic and well-trained crew, could expect to launch one flying bomb every half hour.

The four large concrete sites in northern France, which were thought to be centers for the assembly, preparation, and launching of the rocket missiles, were also heavily attacked. They had received some attention from the U.S. Ninth Air Force and had been considerably damaged. They were, however, of such massive construction that only the heaviest bombs could destroy them. They were allocated to Bomber Command, and attacked with many 1,000 lb. bombs, and a proportion of 12,000 lb. piercing bombs. After 7,459 tons of bombs had been dropped on them, they were practically destroyed. It was not until they fell into Allied hands that their intended uses were discovered. Wizernes and Watten appear to have been rocket missile sites, while at Mimoyecques an immense fifty-barreled long-range gun was found, each barrel 400 ft. in length, set into the hillside and pointed at London. With this formidable weapon the Germans had hoped to bombard London at the rate of one 6-inch shell every minute.

On June 13 the first flying bomb was fired, falling near Gravesend in the Thames estuary. It was never a very reliable weapon and a considerable proportion of those launched never crossed the English Channel. At this time the bombers were fully employed in the support of "Overlord," and it was decided not to divert them, at that stage, to the attack of launching sites. Bomber Command continued to attack factories where it was believed the flying bombs were made, and known storage sites. Some of these were in limestone caves, which proved to be vulnerable. Concentrated bombing caused falls of rock which blocked the entrances and at least in one instance, at St. Leu d'Esserent near Paris, produced an extensive collapse of the roof. Hundreds of flying bombs stored inside were effectively sealed off, and were found when the caves were eventually captured.

The total number of flying bombs launched from June 13 to September 3, when the last one was fired from a ground site, was estimated to be just over 6,000. Of these some 1,350 were technical failures, 2,965 were shot down by guns or fighter attack, and only 1,685 reached their target areas. This was but a fraction of the enormous attack that had been planned by the Germans. The Allied bombers had reduced to a serious nuisance what might have been a most dangerous threat. But they could not entirely stop the launchings, which did not cease until the advance of the Allied armies had overrun all the territory from which they could be fired.

The first rocket missile arrived on August 8, 1944, and the last on March 27, 1945. In all, 1,115 were recorded. Although their arrival was unheralded, they were even less accurate than the flying bomb, and they did not prove very successful. Whereas 1,685 flying bombs killed 6,139 and injured 17,239 people, the comparable figures for 1,115 rockets were 2,855 and 6,268 respectively. The bombers did what they could to reduce the strength of the rocket attack. Many factories believed to be building the rockets or producing the fuel were attacked by the Eighth Air Force and Bomber Command, with considerable success. The rocket launching-pads were small and easily concealed in woods, but many were found and attacked by the fighter-bombers of the two tactical air forces.

The German "V" weapon campaign was mainly directed against the civilian population of southern England, and undoubtedly caused much suffering and hardship. But it cannot be said that the "V" weapons affected the course of the war, apart from diverting a considerable proportion of the Allied air forces to the defensive task of dealing with them. They were undoubtedly a shadow of things to come, but they were developed too late, and were insufficiently reliable, to be effective. The Allied air forces, and especially the heavy bombers—then at the height of their powers—hampered their development, damaged the factories in which they were built, destroyed their storage depots, and smashed their launching sites. And the gun and fighter defences destroyed nearly two-thirds of the flying bombs which crossed the coast of Britain.

The defeat of the "V" weapons must have been a bitter blow to the Germans, and above all to those among them who had the discernment to realize that their last hope of regaining the offensive in the air had vanished, and that they inevitably faced the prospect of final disaster.

18 The Air War in the Pacific

After the surprise attack on Pearl Harbor in December 1941, American sea power in the Pacific was temporarily destroyed and the Japanese flowed southwestward, overrunning the Philippines, the Dutch East Indies, Indo-China, and New Guinea, reaching the threshold of the Australasian subcontinent. Westward they flowed through Burma toward the frontier of India.

The Japanese landed on the coast of Malaya on December 8, 1941, the day after the attack on Pearl Harbor. The British had only 158 aircraft in Singapore and Malaya, mostly of obsolescent types. Severe attacks on the British airfields destroyed a large number of them, and in a few days the Japanese had gained complete air superiority. The only two British heavy warships in the East, the *Prince of Wales* and the *Repulse*, were sunk at sea by Japanese air attack. British land and air reinforcements were on their way from North Africa, but they did not amount to very much, and they arrived too late to be of any use. By the end of January 1942, the battle for Johore had been lost, and the Japanese occupied the whole of southern Malaya.

Although the naval base was now out of action, as it was under shellfire, an attempt was made to defend the island of Singapore, in order to deny it to the Japanese for as long as possible. But the island was indefensible from an attack from the mainland. The whole area, including the airfields, was under heavy fire, and the British air forces were almost completely destroyed. The 15-inch guns, installed at so

179

great a cost, were sited to repel a sea-borne invasion, and were useless. The water supplies were so damaged by Japanese artillery fire that on February 14 only twenty-four hours' supply remained. The following day the British garrison surrendered, and 130,000 men fell into Japanese hands.

The campaign, which had lasted seventy days, ended in disaster for the British because they were short of everything that mattered. The problems of the defense of Singapore had for a long time been bedeviled by inter-Service controversy and the activities of pacifist politicians, and latterly by the decision to put all the resources that could be spared into the Mediterranean theater. If, as Trenchard had urged, a powerful air force had been stationed at Singapore instead of the heavy guns, there would have been a very good chance of preventing the Japanese landings on the Malayan coast or at least of defeating any forces which succeeded in getting ashore.

In the southwest Pacific the bulk of the Allied forces was provided by the United States, while the British bore the main brunt of the campaign in Burma. There were, in addition, substantial Australian and New Zealand forces in both theaters of war. The sequel to the attack on Pearl Harbor was very like the bursting of a dam. The Japanese armies flowed outward till they had spent their force and gradually rumbled to a halt. The most difficult task facing the Allies was to stop the retreat. They had to get rid of the defensive attitude that was in danger of becoming a habit, and inculcate an offensive spirit. Before he could do it the Supreme Commander in the southwest Pacific, General MacArthur, had to make some changes in his team. The most notable of these, and the one with the most far-reaching results, occurred when General George C. Kenney arrived to take over the command of the Fifth Air Force. Kenney was a forceful personality, who combined a sound practical knowledge of the capabilities of air power with an unquenchable offensive spirit. Fortunately, he took to MacArthur at once, and the Supreme Commander, after a short while, came to trust absolutely in Kenney's judgment and professional skill.

Plans for the evacuation of Port Moresby in New Guinea and a withdrawal to the Australian mainland were scrapped, and a decision made to advance beyond the Owen Stanley Mountains, with Buna as the first objective. Thus began the long advance that was to end only with the surrender of the Imperial Japanese Government. The methods used in this advance were simple in conception, but often painfully laborious and drearily repetitive in practice. Realizing the vital part which strategic air bombardment would play in the defeat of Japan, it was intended to capture the bases occupied by Japan, one by one, until the heavy bombers could be brought within range of Japan itself. The immediate task of the Air Force was to prepare the way for a series of amphibious operations.

The Japanese were stubborn fighters, and the idea of honorable surrender and survival as a prisoner of war had no place in their military code. They therefore had to be fought and destroyed almost to the last man. It was fortunate for the Allies that the military knowledge and skill of the Japanese did not match their high standards of courage and endurance, and that they were ignorant of the true meaning of air power. Their air forces were designed and trained for cooperation with their army and navy, and were mostly armed with fighters, fighter-bombers, and torpedo-bombers. Nor did their punishing experiences at the hands of American air power ever teach them to avoid disaster the next time or, with few exceptions, to use their own air forces to the best effect.

The key to the Allied advance was to be found in the control of communications. In General Kenney's words:

It mattered little whether a Japanese base occupied a small island or a shore-line position on a larger land mass. In either case, there was no effective land line of communications with other bases. For reinforcements or supplies each base was dependent upon sea or air transport, and in the latter category the Japanese never showed the daring and imagination which characterized the American usage. Isolation of any chosen area came to mean then largely an attack on shipping and convoying naval vessels.

For the attack of sea communications Kenney borrowed a method from the Royal Air Force. General Arnold has described in his book, *Global Mission*,[1] the way in which the R.A.F. used "skip-bombing" —bombing from a very low altitude so that the bombs skipped along the surface of the sea—which had proved very effective. Kenney was delighted with the idea, and modified his A-20's so as to give them more fire-power ahead and thus make them more suitable for low-

[1] *Global Mission.* New York: Harper, 1949, pp. 147-148.

flying attacks on shipping. The method was, in practiced hands, the most successful means of attacking shipping available at the time.

So, time after time, Kenney "took out" a Japanese base, isolating it by cutting its communications, and pounding its airfields till all opposition had ceased. It was the aim of the Air Force to create a situation in which the land forces could go in "with their rifles on their backs." And so they did on some occasions, and very often the actual landing met with negligible resistance, though the final stages of the operation, since the Japanese usually preferred annihilation to surrender, were sometimes protracted and difficult. This softening-up process by land-based air forces, followed by powerful land-based air cover, was uniformly successful.

The air preparations for the capture of Cape Gloucester in New Britain, and the subsequent air support of the landing, became the type of such operations. Rear-Admiral D. Barbey described the air support given to the Navy as superb. And MacArthur, writing to Arnold, said, "The Air Force here has been magnificent and is the very hub of our success." The importance of thorough preparation by land-based air forces was clearly demonstrated by the difficulties encountered during the capture of Leyte. On September 12 and 13 Admiral Halsey launched vigorous attacks from his aircraft carriers against Japanese airfields in the Philippines. The reaction was comparatively slight, and hardly any attacks were made on the carriers. He drew from this the conclusion that the morale of the Japanese air force was cracking. He also formed the opinion from Intelligence reports, later proved to be incorrect, that there were only small Japanese forces on the island of Leyte. He therefore proposed that the next stage in the plan, the capture of Mindanao, should be omitted, and that an immediate assault should be made on Leyte. As this was beyond the range of the land-based air forces, he undertook to provide the necessary air preparation and support by means of his aircraft carriers.

General Kenney was at first opposed to this plan because it relied too much on the ability of carrier-borne aircraft to support an invasion against determined opposition. But later he too became convinced that the Japanese air force was utterly demoralized, and he supported Halsey's plan. He took the view that the gamble, on the whole, was worth while, though he added that if the Japanese intended to fight and could provide air support for the defense, the attacking forces would run into serious trouble. The landing at Leyte was planned to begin on October 20, and on October 13 and 14 the Japanese air forces fiercely attacked Halsey's fleet, which was making further raids on their airfields in the Philippines. They torpedoed the heavy cruisers *Canberra* and *Houston* and ordered a naval task force to mop up the cripples. The prospect of a naval action diverted the attention of the admirals from Leyte. Halsey received instructions from Admiral Nimitz, the Commander-in-Chief, Pacific Ocean Area, making it clear that if opportunities for the destruction of major units of the Japanese fleet offered or could be created, such destruction was to be regarded as his primary task.

Hoping to bring on a fleet action, Halsey trailed his cripples as bait, but a Japanese aircraft sighted his powerful force, and their fleet withdrew before it could be engaged. Meanwhile Halsey had sent a signal to MacArthur saying that no fast carrier support could be made available to Leyte until further notice. The landing at Leyte was carried out successfully, but resistance stiffened as the troops moved inland, while serious congestion on the beaches and heavy Japanese air attacks hampered the build-up ashore. On October 24 a large force of Japanese carriers was reported by an American naval reconnaissance aircraft. The report much exaggerated the size of this force, but Halsey, although he knew that MacArthur was relying on him to provide air support over Leyte and guard the sea approaches, decided to leave that task to Admiral Kinkaid, and steamed northward in full strength. Kinkaid's fleet consisted of a squadron of escort carriers, and a miscellaneous collection of obsolete battleships, old cruisers, and mine-sweepers.

Soon after Halsey had disappeared to the north, the main Japanese battle fleet appeared, advancing toward the Gulf of Leyte. It withdrew temporarily to avoid an air attack and, having taken the measure of Kinkaid's force, returned next day. The situation was desperate; Kinkaid's old ships could not stand up against the 18-inch guns of the Japanese battleships. But, somehow, the heroic efforts of the small escort carriers managed to hold them off, and the Commander of the Japanese fleet, Admiral Kurita, impressed by the show of force, became apprehensive. He had not fully grasped the realities of the situation, and feared that if he entered the Gulf of Leyte his ships would be attacked "by very many planes, like a frog in a pond." So he withdrew and turned away, intending to attack, as he explained later, a naval force falsely reported to him off Samar.

This decision saved the Allies from disaster. Had Kurita pressed on, he could have destroyed Kinkaid's fleet, entered the Gulf of Leyte, and demolished all the military transports and supply vessels, putting the U.S. X and XXIV Corps, ashore on the island, in a hopeless plight. Halsey, failing to find the Japanese carrier force and worried by urgent calls for help from Kinkaid, steamed southward at 28 knots, but when he arrived it was all over. Kinkaid's gallant action in the most desperate circumstances had saved the situation. Ashore both sides suffered heavy losses, but eventually the American forces gained the upper hand, and Leyte was captured. But never again did the Army dispense with the solid support that Kenney's land-based air forces never failed to provide, and attempt to rely on carrier-borne air cover.

In this great and successful campaign in the southwest Pacific the influence of air power, and especially land-based air power, on an oceanic strategy can be very clearly seen. Gradually, as one Japanese base after another fell into Allied hands, the prospect of bringing the heavy bombers within range of Japan drew nearer. But the process was slow, and in the meanwhile it was decided to stage an air attack on Japan from bases in China. The aircraft which it was intended to use for this task was the B.-29—the Super-Fortress—a heavy four-engined bomber with a radius of action of some 1,600 miles. It was hoped to save time by this plan, and to begin the air bombardment of Japan without having to wait for the capture of Guam and the Mariana group of islands in the Pacific. It was intended to build a number of bases in southern China, within range of which much of Japan's industrial areas would lie. The XX Bomber Command was formed to control and operate these B-29's.

There was another reason for the decision to use bases in China for the bombing of Japan. It was felt to be necessary to encourage the Chinese, whose morale and general behavior were causing Lieutenant-General Joseph Stilwell, the American commander in the Chinese theater, some anxiety. It was hoped that the initiation of the bomber offensive, and even the measures taken in the preparation for it, would greatly stimulate Chinese morale and help to unify the Chinese people under the leadership of Chiang Kai-shek.

The weakness of this plan lay in its logistics. The only route between the United States and China lay through India, and the Japanese advance into Burma had cut the only road. All supplies and equipment had therefore to be flown from airfields in India or Assam, over an exceptionally difficult air route, the "Hump," which had to cross an extension of the Himalayas by a pass at 14,000 feet, flanked by towering peaks. The weather in the mountains, especially during the monsoon seasons, was often very bad. In addition, the problems of command and organization in the India-Burma-China theater were peculiarly complicated. The Americans, organized in two fighting services, the British, organized in three, and the Chinese, with very little perceptible organization, had somehow to be made to work together. And, apart from organization, the Allies had rather divergent war aims in this area. The Americans were chiefly interested in opening up the Ledo road from Assam to China, in freeing China from Japanese encroachments, and in obtaining viable bases for the air offensive against Japan. The British were anxious to drive the Japanese out of Burma and press on southeastward to the reconquest of Malaya and Singapore. The Chinese, if they had any war aims, concealed them, as did the Russians, under an oriental mask. General Stilwell recorded his impression that the main concern of the Chinese was to disagree on all matters of importance with both America and Britain.

The thin trickle of supplies over the Hump, which had to serve the Fourteenth Air Force under General Claire C. Chennault—responsible for air defense and army support—and the needs of the Chinese land forces, as well as those of the XX Bomber Command, made a difficult situation even worse. Each commander was inclined to think that the others were getting an unfair share of the meagre total of supplies, and the correspondence between them was regrettably acrimonious. Indeed, it is difficult to imagine a worse place in which to "shake down" a new command, equipped with a brand-new and very complicated heavy bomber, which needed large quantities of bombs, fuel, and spare parts.

On June 15, 1944, the first attack on a target in Japan was carried out by B-29's from bases in China. But the effort that the XX Bomber Command could sustain, in spite of the almost superhuman exertions of its commander, Major-General Curtis E. LeMay, amounted to very little. The B-29's were able to average only two sorties a month, and many of their missions were against targets such as Bangkok and Singapore. In all, the Command succeeded in dropping only 800 tons of bombs on targets in Japan. It soon became clear that the operations of the B-29's against Japan would never be effective until satisfactory bases could be found for them in the southwest Pacific area.

On the same day that the B-29's in China made their first attack on a Japanese target, the 2nd and 4th U.S. Marine Divisions landed at Saipan in the Marianas, and a little later Tinian and Guam were captured. The main object of these operations was to obtain bases in the Pacific for the B-29's, and it was important to begin building airfields at the earliest possible moment. But determined Japanese resistance in the Marianas caused a month's delay in starting work on Saipan and Tinian. And more serious delay on Guam was caused by Admiral Nimitz's decision to use the island as a base for the Pacific Fleet. All construction work on Guam came under naval control, working to priorities laid down by Admiral Nimitz. These were (1) harbor development; (2) headquarters for the Commander, Pacific Ocean Area; (3) supply facilities; (4) medical facilities; and (5) airfield construction. On Guam the U.S. Air Force was compelled to press continuously to get any work done at all.

On Saipan and Tinian the delays were not so serious; the first mission against Japan took off on November 24, 1944, from Isley Field, Saipan, about six weeks later than the estimated date. Airfields on Tinian were completed about ten weeks later than had been expected, but on Guam the first mission was not flown until June 26, 1945. Even by that date many of the airfield facilities had not been completed, and indeed some were still deficient when the war against Japan ended in August.

With the construction of the airfields in the Marianas, and the building up of a great force of B-29's with sound logistic support, the stage was set for the final act.

19   The Collapse of Germany

At the outbreak of the war Germany had possessed two very large, powerful and heavily armored battleships, the *Bismarck* and the *Admiral von Tirpitz*. The *Bismarck* was sunk during a foray into the Atlantic in May 1941, after a prolonged naval action in the course of which the British battle cruiser *Hood* was lost. The *Admiral von Tirpitz* had, however, never operated as a commerce raider. Apart from one ineffective raid on Spitsbergen she had achieved nothing, but she was a permanent threat to the northern convoys going to and from Russia, and the British Admiralty was always anxious lest she should make a sortie into the Atlantic and destroy Allied shipping. By her mere existence she made it necessary for British battleships to escort the northern convoys and to keep a general watch on her.

For a long time the *Tirpitz* had engaged the attention of the Allies. British naval aircraft attacked her several times and did some damage; heavy bombers of Bomber Command had attacked her at Trondhjem on two occasions in April 1942, and in July of that year a Russian submarine scored a hit on her with a torpedo, which kept her in dock for six months. When she reappeared, in Alten Fiord, she was attacked by midget submarines of the Royal Navy and the damage kept her out of action for another six months. In the autumn of 1944 Bomber Command was pressed to attack the ship, using the new 12,000 lb. piercing bombs.

At this time the *Tirpitz* was lying in Kaa Fiord moored closely against the steep side of a hill which rose almost sheer from the sea, and it was known that she was protected by a very effective smoke screen. It was thought that if an approach could be made from the north, the ship might be caught unawares and attacked before the smoke screen could be brought into action. Arrangements were therefore made to send a force of Lancasters to an advanced base near Archangel, in Soviet Russia. On September 11, 38 Lancasters of No. 5 Group, accompanied by two Liberators of Transport Command carrying spares and additional personnel, arrived at the advanced base. The attack was carried out on September 15, but the expected surprise was not achieved and the smoke screen began to operate about ten minutes before the first bombs fell. The mission was a comparative failure but some damage was done to the ship by a direct hit or near miss. After the attack the *Tirpitz* was moved south to an anchorage close to the island of Haak, four miles west of Tromsö, no doubt in order to bring her nearer to the repair facilities. But this move also brought her 200 miles closer to Bomber Command's bases, though she was still over 1,100 miles away. It was decided to make another attempt to sink her, especially as it was believed that in this position she was not yet protected by a smoke screen. The first attack on October 29 was a disappointment. There was patchy cloud which obscured the bomb-aimers' view at the critical moment.

On November 12, 36 Lancasters, each armed with a 12,000 lb. piercing bomb, took off, and found the ship in clear visibility with no clouds or smoke screen. Two or more direct hits and several near misses were obtained, and as the bombers turned for home they saw the great ship roll over and sink in shallow water. A reconnaissance aircraft two hours later was able to photograph a part of the bottom of the ship showing above water.[1]

Although the great port of Antwerp, one of the finest in Europe, had been captured almost undamaged by the Allied armies on September 4, 1944, it was not possible to use it because the Germans held the northern shore of the estuary of the Scheldt. The strongly fortified island of Walcheren guarded the approach to the estuary, and as long as it remained in German hands the port of Antwerp

[1] See also Appendix E.

could not be used. Since the facilities of the port were needed to support the further advance of the Allied armies, it was clear that the capture of Walcheren Island had become a matter of urgent importance. The Allies had a large force of airborne troops available, and it would have appeared reasonable to employ them to capture the island. They were, however, used instead on September 17 at Arnhem in an attempt to secure crossings over the Rhine. This operation was unsuccessful and led to the loss of the greater part of the British 1st Airborne Division.

Almost the whole of Walcheren lies below sea level, and it was considered that the capture of the island would be greatly facilitated if the sea wall could be breached, with the object of flooding the defending batteries and making it difficult for the Germans to move their reserves about the island. The assaulting force, embarked in amphibious vehicles, would still retain full freedom of movement.

The sea wall was a massive structure, some 200 feet wide at the base, and 60 feet wide at the top. The task of breaching this was allocated to Bomber Command and on October 3 it was attacked at a point near Westkapelle. Two hundred and forty-three Lancasters, carrying nearly twenty-five hundred 1,000 lb. bombs, attacked the wall in successive waves. The bombing was very accurate and within an hour a large breach had been made. By the following day the breach was 75 yards across and 4 square miles of the island were under water. On October 7, some 16 square miles were flooded. On that day new breaches were made on the south coast of the island near the port of Flushing, and the gun emplacements directly attacked. After several further attacks on the gun positions, the assault took place on November 1. All went well, and casualties were slight except at Westkapelle, where a battery which had survived both floods and bombing proved difficult to subdue. On November 4 mine-sweeping began in the Scheldt estuary, and by November 6 the approaches to Antwerp were opened to Allied shipping. Once again the heavy bombers had proved their effectiveness in reducing strongly defended positions.

The Allied long-range bomber forces were now removed from the control of the Supreme Commander, and returned to the attack of Germany. They were placed under the joint direction of the Deputy Chief of the Air Staff and the Commanding General, United States Strategic Air Force in Europe, though the Supreme Commander could call upon the heavy bombers whenever he considered it necessary to do so. In order to advise the D. C. A. S. and the commanding general, the Combined Strategic Targets Committee was formed on October 13, 1944. Its duties included recommendations as to the priorities of targets under the current directive, and the priorities which should be established between the different target systems. It could make recommendations for changing the current directive, and it was responsible for examining any proposals submitted by Supreme Headquarters, Allied Expeditionary Force, by the Admiralty, the War Office, or by any other interested department, which involved the employment of either the long-range bomber forces. To assist the committee in its task standing subcommittees were formed to deal with oil, the German air force, transportation, army support targets, and any other target system which might from time to time require examination.

The committee included representatives of the Air Ministry; the Ministry of Economic Warfare; the Enemy Branch, Foreign Office; the Enemy Objectives Unit of the U. S. Embassy; and Supreme Headquarters, Allied Expeditionary Force. In November, representatives of the Operations and Intelligence staffs of the British and American bomber forces were added to the committee. This was an excellent move, as it enabled the staffs of the two commands to have a direct and continuous knowledge of the background of current bombing policy, and—perhaps even more important—gave the committee the benefit of advice on operational matters. Representatives of the U. S. Fifteenth Air Force also attended when opportunity permitted.

The committee normally met once a week under the alternate chairmanship of the Director of Bomber Operations in the Air Ministry and the Director of Operations, U. S. Strategic Air Forces in Europe. A regular feature of these meetings was the presentation of a report from each of the subcommittees, which included an appreciation of the progress of the offensive against each target system, and a reappraisal, in the light of that progress, of the list of targets and their priority within each system. The recommendations of each meeting of the committee were immediately sent to both commands, and these constituted the commands' priority list for the ensuing week. The allocation of targets between the American and British Commands was agreed at command level. A weekly review of the more static target systems such as oil, aircraft and engine production, and transportation, was in practice adequate, but army support priorities could, and did, vary from day to day. Requests from the Supreme Commander were passed direct to the commands, and were given overriding priority.

With the setting up of this committee a sensible and workable scheme for the allocation of bombing priorities had at last been found. Much waste of effort would have been avoided if it had come into existence at an earlier stage.

When the Allied heavy bombers returned to the attack of Germany in the autumn of 1944, they did so under very much improved conditions. The B-17's could fly over Germany at will, since the German daylight fighter force was reduced almost to impotence. The Oboe stations had been mobilized and erected as far to the east as possible in France and Belgium, and many targets in central and southern Germany were now within its range. Although the German night-fighter force was still effective, it too was suffering from shortages of equipment and its morale was tending to decline. The vulnerability of Germany to air bombardment had also increased, especially in two important fields. The German retreat on the Eastern front had deprived them of the output of the Rumanian oil fields, and they were entirely dependent for oil fuel on their synthetic oil plants. Secondly, the German railways and canals were overstrained and far more susceptible to dislocation by bombing than at any previous time.

It is not therefore surprising that the Allied air offensive was concentrated against two target systems—oil and transportation. The attacks made on German oil plants during the last quarter of 1944 undoubtedly did much to slow down the recovery in production on which the Germans had counted when the heavy bombers were switched from targets in Germany to the preparations for "Overlord." But in the first part of that quarter bad weather had spoiled the effectiveness of the bombing attacks, and between September and November the German output of oil increased by nearly 50 per cent. The importance of this output was so great that they concentrated every effort on repairing the plants and maintaining them in working order. During December, however, the weather improved, and many heavy and successful attacks by day and night were carried out. One by one the plants in the Ruhr were destroyed, and very effective attacks by both American and British bomber forces reduced the output of the great oil plant at Leuna by no less than 98 per cent. A night attack on a similar plant at Politz reduced its output by 95 per cent, and on the night of January 16/17, 1945, the huge plant at Brux was put completely out of action.

By the end of January the German production of oil was reduced to 29 per cent of normal, and they could scarcely meet the day-to-day operational demands for fuel, while there was none available for training purposes. By the end of April this figure had fallen to 5 per cent, and for all practical purposes Germany would very soon have no oil at all.

The attack on the German railway system was equally successful. The use of heavy bombs had destroyed many bridges and viaducts, and the experience gained from the attack of railways during the preparations for "Overlord" was put to very good use. Scores of railway centers and locomotive depots were severely damaged involving the destruction of a vast amount of rolling stock. By the end of 1944, the German railway system was unable to meet the demands made upon it. Absolute priority had to be given to the movement of supplies for the armed forces, leaving very little capacity for the transport of armaments and normal food supplies.

Western Germany has always relied to a great extent on inland waterways for the transport of heavy goods. By the summer of 1944, almost 20 per cent of the freight carried in Germany was waterborne. Coal, coke, cement, and products of the heavy industries were moved from the Ruhr to all parts of Germany, and food and raw materials were brought in, by two main arteries—the Dortmund-Ems and Mittelland canals. The Dortmund-Ems Canal was breached at Ladbergen in September 1944, by Lancasters of Bomber Command, and as soon as it was repaired, it was breached again. The banks of the Mittelland Canal were completely obliterated at Gravenhorst by night attacks on January 1/2 and February 21/22, 1945. Both canals were kept out of action for the remainder of the war.

Speer, the Reichminister for Production, said on November 11, 1944:

The effects of the paralysis in coal distribution on the economic life of Germany were widespread. Coal deliveries to electric power sta-

*tions were very behindhand . . . and the coal reserves of the power
stations dropped below the ten-day limit . . . Many gasworks in West
and Central Germany had less than ten days' reserves and in many
cases the gasworks had exhausted their supplies and closed down.*

On December 16, 1944, Field Marshal von Rundstedt launched in
the Ardennes what was to prove the last offensive action of the
German armies in the west. This action met with some success.
Supported by the remnants of the German air force, and using every
tank that could be made available, von Rundstedt broke through the
Allied armies and for a time the situation was serious. But Rundstedt, like Ludenorff in March 1918, did not have the resources to
follow up his initial break-through. Bomber Command and the
U. S. Eighth Air Force were called in to help to restore the situation.
Bomber Command carried out an especially successful attack at St.
Vith in daylight on December 26, against German concentrations
of troops and armored forces. By January 16, 1945, just a month
after the launching of the attack, all was over and the operation
ended in failure.

The breakdown of von Rundstedt's offensive was due to three
things. He had not sufficient tanks and aircraft to support an operation on so large a scale, and these shortages were due, in part at least,
to the effects of the Allied bombardment of Germany. Secondly, he
was short of oil fuel, which was a direct result of the Allied bombing.
Thirdly, the German transportation system proved unable to meet
the demands made upon it. "Transport difficulties were decisive" said
Speer, "in causing the swift breakdown of the Ardennes offensive."
And for these transport difficulties, the Allied heavy bombers, and
the Allied Expeditionary Air Force, which kept the German railheads
under constant attack, were responsible.

In early 1943 the German Messerschmitt aircraft firm produced a
jet-propelled airplane, which by May of that year was sufficiently
tested to justify a production order. They had also designed a rocket-
propelled fighter, the Me 163, but technical difficulties postponed
the quantity production of this aircraft until too late. The jet-aircraft,
however, the Me 262, was extremely successful, and the leaders of
the German air force had hopes of re-equipping their air defense
force with a day fighter far superior in performance to anything pos-

sessed by the Allies. This revolutionary fighter, if the highest priority had been given to its production, might even at that late hour have wrought a fundamental change in the fortunes of the B-17's, and might have made the German Air Force a formidable factor at the time of the invasion.

Fortunately for the Allies Hitler intervened and, against the advice of his air force chiefs, he ordered that tests should be continued with the prototypes of the Me 262, and categorically forbade any preparations for mass production. Later, in December 1943, when at Insterburg he saw a demonstration of this aircraft, he asked whether it could carry any bombs. He was told that it could theoretically carry a 1,000 lb. bomb, perhaps more. Thereupon, brushing aside all further explanations, he exclaimed: "For years I have demanded from the German Air Force a speed bomber which can reach its target in spite of enemy fighter defense. In this aircraft you present to me as a fighter plane, I see the *blitz* bomber, with which I will repel the Invasion in its first and weakest phase."[2] He ordered that the Me 262 should be modified to carry bombs. This modification, however, was not as simple as he had supposed and a number of technical troubles delayed the project. Meanwhile the existing program for the production of the Me 262 as a fighter continued unchanged. Some months later Hitler was discussing the progress of the Me 262 with Field Marshal Milch, the Chief of Aircraft Production. He asked how many 262's were able to carry bombs. Milch, who had not been present when Hitler had expounded his ideas about the *blitz* bomber at Insterburg, innocently replied "None, my Fuhrer. The Me 262 is being exclusively built as a fighter aircraft." What then happened can best be described in the words of General Galland, Chief of the German fighter force. "Hitler foamed with rage. Officers who were close to him told me later that they had rarely witnessed such a fit of temper. He raved against Milch, Göring, and the German air force at large, accusing them of unreliability, disobedience, and unfaithfulness. Soon afterwards Milch was dismissed from his post."[3]

Indeed, no one at Insterburg had taken Hitler's remarks literally to mean that no Me 262's were to be built as fighters, and that all were to be modified to carry bombs. To avoid misunderstanding in future, Hitler now ordered that the whole series of the Me 262's was

[2] Adolf Galland, *The First and the Last*, pp. 337-338.
[3] *Ibid.*, p. 340.

to be modified for use as bombers, and that no one was in any circumstances to refer to the aircraft as a fighter, not even as a fighter-bomber. The effect of this muddle was to rule out the Me 262, either as a fighter or a bomber. Before the end of the war a few of them, under Galland, were used as fighters, but not in sufficient numbers to have any appreciable effect.

In the early spring of 1945 it was clear that the end of the war in Europe was near. German resistance on the Eastern front was crumbling and the Russian armies were rapidly advancing westward. The Allied armies crossed the Rhine in force at Wesel during the night of March 23/24, after a heavy attack on the German defenses by Bomber Command, which paralyzed their resistance. The Allied casualties were slight. Montgomery, in a message to the Command, said: "My grateful appreciation for the quite magnificent cooperation you have given us in the battle of the Rhine. The bombing of Wesel was a masterpiece and was a decisive factor in making possible our entry into that town before midnight."

The Allied armies continued their advance into Germany, crossing the Elbe on April 29. On April 30 Hitler committed suicide, and on May 7 the German Government surrendered unconditionally.

The final operations of Bomber Command were errands of mercy. The withdrawal of the Germans and the destruction of communications had caused chaos in western Holland, and many Dutch people were in danger of starvation. In operation "Manna," the Lancasters and Mosquitoes, in 3,156 sorties, dropped a total of 6,685 tons of food and other supplies to the civilian populations in the Hague, Rotterdam, and other towns. Finally, after the German collapse, the U. S. Air Force and Bomber Command brought back to Britain the bulk of the Allied prisoners of war in German hands, completing in two weeks a task that, after the First World War, took many weary months.

In the war in Europe the Allied long-range bombers had made a massive contribution to the final victory. Without Bomber Command, the British could not have taken the offensive against Germany after the Battle of Britain. If the Allied air offensive against Germany had not succeeded, an invasion of France in 1944 would have been unthinkable. Nor would the invasion itself have succeeded but for the thorough preparatory work of the Allied Bombers. And, after D Day, the armies could not have advanced into Germany as they did, without the powerful support of the American and British heavy bombers and the Allied Expeditionary Air Force. And in many other ways, by mine-laying, by the bombing of warships, submarines and their pens, and numerous other targets, by the defeat of the "V" weapons, and breaching dams and sea walls, the heavy bombers had done much to cripple Germany's power to wage war. But for their successful operations, the Allies would certainly not have won the war in Europe in May 1945. Indeed, it is not outside the bounds of possibility that they might never have won it at all.

20 Japan Vanquished by Air Bombardment

After the capture of Leyte, Guam, and the Mariana group of islands, a review of the strategy of the war against Japan became imperative. From the outset of the war there had been a lack of agreement between the U. S. Navy and Army, which had divergent views as to the best way of defeating Japan. General MacArthur had proposed to advance northward by way of the Philippines and the Marianas toward Japan, while Admiral Nimitz had urged the establishment of sea and air bases in Formosa and on the Chinese coast. The U. S. Joint Chiefs of Staff were unable to resolve this difference of opinion and agreed that MacArthur, commanding the southwest Pacific, and Nimitz, commanding the Pacific Ocean Area, should be allowed to go their own ways. The Chiefs of Staff observed that "for the time being there was some advantage in keeping Japanese forces under the pressure of a double attack." There was also a lack of accord between the Navy and the Army Air Force. Though this discordance had many ramifications, it was fundamentally the old disagreement about the way in which air power should be employed. The Navy believed that air forces should be primarily concerned with the security of naval bases and patrolling the sea communications, while the Air Force was convinced that it would be better employed, and more progress made toward winning the war, if it were allowed to develop to the full its unique offensive power.

The time had come, however, when it was necessary to adopt a

197

unified strategic policy. The Chiefs of Staff in Washington decided that the Japanese should be cleared out of the Philippines, and that the next step should be the capture of Mindoro, followed by that of Luzon, the largest and most northerly island of the group. After that had been done they would decide whether Formosa should be captured, as urged by the Navy, or neutralized by a concentrated air bombardment, as proposed by the Army. It was agreed that Formosa would have to be captured or neutralized before the important Japanese sea communications with Malaya and the Dutch East Indies could be cut, or a sea-borne invasion of Japan attempted.

On one matter the Army and Navy were in full agreement. Both were convinced that the final defeat of Japan could be accomplished only by a massive sea-borne invasion, and the destruction in battle of the two million troops estimated to be available for the defense of their homeland. And, indeed, the stubborn and heroic Japanese resistance which the Allied forces had encountered in the capture of numerous bases lent a good deal of support to this view.

Meanwhile the strategic air bombardment of Japan from bases in Saipan and Tinian, in the Mariana group, was getting under way. And in all the tangled complications of command and organization in the Pacific theater, none caused more difficulty than the control of the heavy bombers. When the B-29's were sent to China, Air Force Headquarters in Washington had been anxious to ensure that the XX Bomber Command should be employed in bombing Japan, and that its all too meagre strength should not be dissipated in tactical operations at the instance of local commanders. It was therefore decided that the B-29's should be controlled by the Joint Chiefs of Staff. They delegated the command to General Arnold, who by that time ranked for all practical purposes as a Chief of Staff, although in strict theory the Air Force was still a part of the Army. Arnold was a very busy man, with global responsibilities, and so he exercised command through a deputy in Washington, Brigadier-General Haywood S. Hansell. This system of remote control was not popular with the local commanders, and the Joint Chiefs of Staff were never entirely happy about it, but on the whole it achieved its purpose.

When in January 1945 it was decided to transfer the two B-29 wings in China to the Marianas and add them to the new Twentieth Air Force, now building up in the Pacific, Arnold was determined to make sure that the heavy bombers were not diverted from their task of bombing Japan to all sorts of local operations. He had seen how effectively the Navy in the Pacific Ocean Area had been able to acquire the operational control of all Army Air Force aircraft, by the simple expedient of incorporating them into joint task forces under naval command. All combat missions were flown on the orders of task force commanders responsible to the naval Commander-in-Chief, Admiral Nimitz, and at no time did the Commanding General of the Army Air Force in the area enjoy the operational control of his own aircraft. Arnold therefore himself assumed command of the new Twentieth Air Force and appointed Lieutenant-General Millard F. Harmon, the Commanding General, Army Air Forces, Pacific Ocean Area, as his deputy commander. This arrangement did not work well, because Arnold was reluctant to allow Harmon to direct operations, since he was, in the Pacific Ocean Area organization, subordinate to Admiral Nimitz. Harmon's responsibilities in this dual capacity were very involved and difficult, and put him in an almost impossible position. His tragic death in February 1945, when the aircraft carrying him disappeared without trace, occurred when he was flying to Washington in an attempt to clarify the situation. There were also difficulties with the Army. Although the Army Air Force had almost become a third Service in practice, it was not so in theory, and army commanders could, and did, claim it as part of their commands. Indeed, Lieutenant-General Robert Richardson, Commander of the land forces in the Pacific Ocean Area, considered that the Twentieth Air Force should be subordinated to him, as it was accommodated in his area.

Soon after the loss of General Harmon the whole command structure was radically altered and much simplified. MacArthur became the Supreme Commander for all land forces in the whole Pacific theater, and Nimitz for all sea forces. An exception was made to allow the Twentieth Air Force to be controlled by Arnold, who appointed Lieutenant-General Barney M. Giles, his former Chief of Staff, as his Deputy Commander, with headquarters on Guam.

A new formation, the XXI Bomber Command, was formed within the Twentieth Air Force to control the five wings, each consisting of some two hundred B-29's, now building up in the Marianas. Brigadier-General Hansell, who had been Arnold's Deputy Commander for the XX Bomber Command in China, was promoted to Major-General and appointed to the new Command.

The primary aim of XXI Bomber Command, in this phase, was the destruction of Japanese aircraft and engine factories. General Hansell was a firm believer in daylight precision bombing, but for various reasons his operations during the next two months were not very successful. The base facilities were still at an early stage of development, and the serviceability and reliability of the B-29's left much to be desired. Hansell had difficulty in raising more than a hundred aircraft for any mission, nor could he send out missions very often. Bad weather over Japan, and a high incidence of abortive sorties combined to reduce the effectiveness of the attacks, which were almost all failures. Arnold was impatient for results, and early in 1945 he decided to replace Hansell by LeMay. Hansell had certainly been unlucky; he was not responsible for the retarded development of the bases or for the unexpectedly bad weather, and another man might have done no better in the circumstances.

LeMay tried a few more high altitude precision bombing attacks, but achieved no greater success than did Hansell. An analysis made after the war by the U. S. Strategic Bombing Survey concluded that "the failure stemmed in part from a tactical error, the continued adherence to the conventional doctrines of precision bombing." There is no doubt that these methods can produce excellent results in good weather conditions, when the bomb-aimers can see their targets from a considerable distance. But these weather conditions occurred but seldom over Japan, and more often than not the target areas were obscured by clouds or bad visibility.

Arnold now sent a new directive to the XXI Bomber Command. Although the primary aim was still the destruction of Japanese aircraft and engine factories, missions were also to be directed against selected urban areas. If bomb-aiming had to be done by radar, attacks were to be made on Nagoya, Osaka, Kawasaki, and Tokyo, in that order. A large-scale experimental attack by night, using a high proportion of incendiary bombs, was to be made against an important Japanese industrial city. This took place on February 25 against Tokyo, and although capable of improvement the results were most encouraging. But before this could be followed up, a development occurred which temporarily diverted the B-29's from the air offensive against Japan.

Halfway between the Marianas and the Japanese mainland lies the small island of Iwo Jima. A number of B-29's had been destroyed on the ground, particularly on Saipan, and it was clear that Japanese aircraft operating from Iwo Jima were responsible. In addition, Japanese fighters based on Iwo Jima frequently attacked the B-29's on the way to and from their targets. Finally, as long as the island was occupied by the Japanese, the B-29's had a very long journey across the sea with no possible alternative to ditching if forced down by operational damage or mechanical failure. If Iwo Jima were in American hands, it would have great value as an intermediate landing place for B-29's in distress.

For all these reasons, it was decided to capture the island, and the date of the landing was fixed for February 19. After a heavy preliminary bombardment the troops got ashore without any great difficulty, but the Japanese put up a most strenuous resistance. The island had to be taken yard by yard in desperate hand-to-hand fighting. All available aircraft, including the B-29's, were called in to help. The American losses amounted to 4,590 killed, 301 missing, and 15,954 wounded; the Japanese lost 21,304 dead and 312 were taken prisoner. The cost had been high, but there can be no doubt as to the great value of Iwo Jima to the Americans. By the end of the war more than 2,400 B-29's had made emergency landings on its two airfields. And it enabled the U. S. air–sea rescue service to be made more efficient. It is unquestionable that, on balance, the capture of Iwo Jima saved many American lives.

During this diversion a very thorough analysis of the Tokyo incendiary attack had been made, followed by a careful consideration of the best tactics for weakening Japan by air bombardment. LeMay concluded that there was much to be said in favor of night bombing. The weather over Japan tended to be less cloudy at night, and radio aids to navigation worked better during the hours of darkness. A pathfinder technique for marking the aiming-points with incendiary or pyrotechnic bombs could be used, while the lower altitudes and reduced quantities of defensive ammunition permissible at night would allow much heavier bomb loads. LeMay decided to adopt incendiary attacks by night.

The first mission of this new series was against Tokyo on the night of March 9/10. Japanese opposition was slight and the results were startling. Air photographs taken on March 11 showed that just over 9,000 acres of the city had been burned out. Japanese records show that more than 267,000 buildings—about one-quarter of the total in

Tokyo—had been destroyed, and that over a million people had been rendered homeless. The official total of casualties was 83,793 dead, and 40,918 injured. The B-29 losses, from all causes, were 4.2 per cent.

This set the pattern for a number of heavy incendiary attacks against the six great industrial cities of Japan—Tokyo, Nagoya, Osaka, Kobe, Yokohama, and Kawasaki.

But the air bombardment of Japan was not to proceed without interruptions. The Navy had realized that Formosa had now been effectively neutralized by air attack and mine-laying, but they pressed for the capture of Okinawa, the largest island in the Ryukyu chain, which was only some 500 miles from the mainland of Japan. The landings began, on April 1, 1945, after suitable preparations, and by April 4 some 60,000 men were ashore. Though the actual landings met with only slight opposition, the capture of the island was to prove one of the toughest battles of the war. The Japanese fought back with desperate fury. For some months now, the Allied forces had been subjected to *kamikaze* attacks—suicide attacks in which Japanese aircraft, loaded with heavy bombs, had flown at full speed into their targets. At Okinawa, this practice was very prevalent, and no fewer than 1,900 *kamikaze* attacks were flown against Allied shipping, scoring 182 direct hits which sank 25 ships and damaged many more. The situation became so serious that every available aircraft, including the B-29's, had to be sent to assist the American forces. Between April 17 and May 11 more than 75 per cent of the total effort of XXI Bomber Command was devoted to the support of the Okinawa campaign.

On May 12 the Command was released from this task and returned to the attack of the Japanese mainland. By June 15, the six great industrial cities on their target list lay in ruins. The casualties ran into six figures, millions of people had lost their homes, and thousands of factories had been destroyed or burned out. In seventeen great attacks LeMay had dispatched 6,960 B-29's carrying a total of 41,592 tons of bombs. Losses had amounted to 136, an average of 1.9 per cent of the sorties flown, very much less than the average rate of loss suffered during the relatively ineffective daylight bombing. There followed a series of intensive attacks, sometimes by day but more often by night, against many of the smaller industrial cities and towns, and against a number of aircraft factories, arsenals, and oil storage depots. These were remarkably effective, and were accompanied by a mine-laying campaign which very seriously interrupted Japan's vital sea communications.

Meanwhile the Allied forces in Burma, consisting mainly of the British Fourteenth Army supported by a small long-range bomber force and the Third Tactical Air Force, had been advancing through a very difficult terrain. Owing to the poor communications, very great reliance had to be placed on air transport. By the end of May 1945, the reconquest of Burma had been accomplished, but it took a long time to clear up the many pockets of Japanese resistance in remote areas. After the fall of Burma, active preparations were made for the invasion of Malaya, but the Japanese surrender came before it could be begun.

The mainland of Japan, almost isolated from its main sources of supply, had suffered terribly from the effects of air bombardment. The problem now was to end the war quickly, humanely, and economically. The exceptional ferocity and determination shown in the defense of Iwo Jima and Okinawa, and especially the great increase in the number of *kamikaze* attacks, encouraged the belief that the fighting in the final assault on Japan would be inconceivably bloody and bitter. A long discussion now took place between the Army and the Navy as to the best way of carrying out the invasion, and who was to be the supreme commander responsible for this fearful task. Preparations on a massive scale were begun for an invasion in November of Kyushu, the southernmost island of the Japanese mainland.

On July 16 the first atom bomb was successfully exploded at Alamagordo, in New Mexico. On July 26, the Allied leaders in conference at Potsdam issued an ultimatum calling for the unconditional surrender of Japan, ending with the warning that "the only alternative for Japan is prompt and utter destruction." On July 28 the Japanese Premier told a press conference that his government would ignore the Allied ultimatum. It is not clear why he said this, as it is now known that at the time the Japanese Government had already realized that the war was lost, and was trying to find some means of negotiating an armistice.

The Premier's statement was regarded by the Allies as a rejection of their ultimatum. All was now ready for the *coup de grâce*. The atom bombs had arrived at Tinian, and specially selected and trained crews were standing by. A careful study had been made of the most suitable targets for the bombs, and Hiroshima, Kogura, Niigata, and Nagasaki were recommended. Everything awaited a decision by President Truman. On August 2, on his way home from Potsdam in the cruiser *Augusta*, the President authorized the atom bomb attack.

On August 6 the first bomb fell on Hiroshima, followed by a second one on Nagasaki on August 9. At Hiroshima the casualties and damage were very extensive, but it is worth noting that the area of destruction and the number of dead and missing, 71,379, were smaller than the comparable figures for the great incendiary attack on Tokyo on the night of March 9/10, though the number of injured was rather greater. The destruction and loss of life at Nagasaki were, for geographical reasons, much less than those at Hiroshima.

The effect, however, on Japanese public opinion, was profound, and within a few days the Imperial Government surrendered.

Although there is no doubt that the atom bomb attacks were the immediate cause of the surrender, they were only the last straw. The long series of battles in the Pacific and in Burma had weakened Japan, and the blockade of her communications by Allied sea and air power was slowly throttling her, but it was, above all, the intensive air bombardment by the B-29's which brought about her defeat. The Japanese Premier, Suzuki, under interrogation afterward, said:

It seemed to me unavoidable that in the long run Japan would be almost destroyed by air attack so that merely on the basis of the B-29s alone I was convinced that Japan should sue for peace. On top of the B-29 raids came the atomic bomb, after the Potsdam Declaration, which was just one additional reason for giving in. . . . I myself, on the basis of the B-29 raids, felt that the cause was hopeless.

To this Prince Fumimaro Konoye, who had been trying to enlist Russian aid in arranging an armistice, added, "Fundamentally the thing that brought about the determination to make peace was the prolonged bombing by the B-29's."

President Truman has been criticized in some quarters for authorizing the atom bomb attacks, on the grounds that the Japanese were already defeated and were seeking some way of making peace. But it is by no means certain that these overtures would have come to anything. The Allies were demanding unconditional surrender, and unconditional surrender does not require to be negotiated. It is indeed more than probable that matters would have drifted on until the invasion of Kyushu had started, and then the fighting, once begun, would have gone on to the bitter end. In any event, when President Truman gave his decision, he was not aware of any peace moves on the part of the Japanese Government, which, such as they were, were hidden under a cloak of secrecy.

There is no doubt that President Truman's decision was militarily and politically sound. He was right to take every possible step to avoid the horrors of a large-scale invasion of the Japanese mainland, against thousands of suicide attacks, and a desperate Japanese army fighting until almost the last man had been killed. If the atom bomb attacks made an invasion unnecessary—and no one can be sure that they did not—then they undoubtedly saved very many Japanese lives, and the saving in Allied lives has been officially estimated at about a quarter of a million.

So ended the bitter and savage conflict begun by Japan with a surprise attack at Pearl Harbor on December 7, 1941. Japan, in those days the proudest and most consciously military nation on earth, surrendered, with a powerful and unbeaten army standing ready to repel an invasion, because her air and sea power had been broken, and she faced a terrible threat of destruction and starvation to which she could find no answer.

Part V

AIR POWER:
PRESENT AND FUTURE

21 Air Power after the War

The immense part played by air power in the Second World War, and its massive contributions to the Allied victory, are even today imperfectly appreciated. In some instances this may be due to a fixed attitude of mind, still thinking of traditional warfarc in which only land and sea operations could be decisive, and to which all air operations were ancillary and subservient. It is also the result of a widespread lack of understanding of the ways in which air power must work, and a failure to appreciate the relevance of its operations to, and their profound impact upon, the grand strategy of the war. And to some extent it is due to the distaste still felt by some people when faced with the logical consequences of three-dimensional warfare, which makes them disinclined to take an objective view of air power. It is therefore worth interrupting the continuity of this narrative in order to make a simple analysis of the elements of air power, and summarize briefly the main achievements of air bombardment during the Second World War.

The vast salt-water seas and oceans cover nearly three-quarters of the earth's surface, and warships can move on or under the sea comparatively freely over wide areas. But the seas are bounded and divided by great land masses, and in narrow straits they can be dominated by land-based defenses. Shallow waters can be denied to warships by mine-fields, and it is possible to place obstacles, such as booms, in suitable places. Warships, therefore, cannot use every part of the sea, even if they are able to move under water. The ocean of the air, however, is all one, and covers both land and sea. There can be no barriers or obstacles in the air, and aircraft may fly at will to every corner of the globe. This confers on air forces ubiquity of operation, to which may be added great flexibility, an immense capacity for rapid concentration, and a remarkable power of penetration.

It is indisputable that wars can be won only by action that is strategically offensive. Defensive action, however successful, has in itself no power to achieve victory.[1] This basic fact, so often forgotten or ignored, cannot be emphasized too often. Many examples of failure to realize the limitations of the defensive have already been mentioned. The proposal in 1925 to equip the new Air Defence of Great Britain Command with fighters but no bombers; the decision to provide a fixed battery of huge guns at Singapore instead of a mobile, offensive, air force; the absorption of almost the entire French army into the Maginot Line; the plans put forward by the British Admiralty in 1942 to employ the whole of the long-range bomber force in the antisubmarine campaign; all these show a failure to understand the limitations of the defensive in war.

It is, however, true that although wars cannot be won by defensive action, victory cannot be achieved without it; because offensive action, if it is to succeed, must be conducted from a secure base. Not until the Battle of Britain had been won could Bomber Command undertake the strategic air offensive against Germany. Before that it had been almost exclusively employed in the strategically defensive task of disrupting the German preparations for the invasion of Britain.

Lord Trenchard frequently drew attention to the fact that it was possible to have an air force without possessing air power. Indeed, most of the limitations and restrictions on air forces debated in the various attempts, between the two world wars, to negotiate a disarmament agreement in the League of Nations were expressly designed to bring about that result.

It is not always easy for those who have not studied three-dimensional war to recognize that air bombardment is the strategically offensive element in air warfare. The bomber is the offensive weapon,

---

[1] It has happened on rare occasions that a prolonged and successful defensive campaign has caused a war to end in a draw.

though it must be capable of tactical defense. The fighter, on the other hand, is strategically defensive, though its activities are tactically offensive. Sir Winston Churchill made the point very clearly and concisely in his minute to the British War Cabinet on September 3, 1940, when he said "the fighters are our salvation, but the bombers alone provide the means of victory."[2]

Air power, therefore, is a product of air bombardment, and the agent of air power is the bomber, and especially the long-range heavy bomber.

During the First World War air power was largely ineffective. This was partly due to its technical immaturity, but the main reason for its relative failure was the general inability to understand how it ought to be used. The direction and control of air forces were almost entirely in the hands of armies and navies, whose senior officers had learned their business in the days of two-dimensional warfare, and who were imbued with the classical doctrine. They saw only air forces, and failed to realize the significance of air power.

Led by men of vision and courage, air power struggled during the years of peace against the apathy and conservatism, and sometimes even the opposition, of armies and navies. But the painful experiences of the Second World War, which affected all the belligerents to a greater or lesser degree, drove home the lesson that the days of two-dimensional warfare had gone forever. Sooner or later almost all the war leaders recognized that air power was able to dominate all warfare on land or at sea.

The three achievements of the long-range heavy bombers which had the most profound effect on the conduct of the war were the Allied air offensive against Germany; the preparation for, and the support of, the Allied invasion of France; and the American air bombardment of Japan.

The Allied air offensive against Germany was on a massive scale. The total weight of the German air attack on Britain, including flying bombs and rockets, was just over 72,000 tons. Bomber Command dropped just short of a million tons, including sea-mines, of which some 625,000 tons were on targets in Germany. The U.S. Eighth Air Force and Fifteenth Air Force dropped just over a million tons, of which two-thirds were directed against Germany.

[2] See Chapter 10.

Therefore the total weight of bombs dropped on Germany was approximately eighteen times as great as that of the German attack on Britain, and the accuracy of the Allied bombing, especially during the last two years of the war, was much greater.

Bomber Command mainly attacked the great industrial cities and towns, and by the end of the war the fully built-up area completely devastated amounted to over 50,000 acres, which included thousands of factories producing armaments or materials of direct value to the German war effort.[3] The B-17's mainly attacked individual factories or centers of communication, of which a very large number were destroyed or put out of action.

After the war, both the Americans and the British carried out a survey of the effects of this great bombing campaign. The results of these surveys were misleading, because they attempted to make a quantitative assessment of the reduction in German war production attributable to the Allied bombing. They were surprised to find that, on the whole, German war production had increased from 1941 to the end of 1943, and this fact has often been quoted as evidence that the air bombardment of Germany was a failure.

The mistake made by the bombing surveys was to assume that in 1941 German war production was operating at 100 per cent of its capacity. The truth is that the Germans had planned for a *blitzkrieg* —a lightning war—and their industrial capacity was not geared to the war production needed for a long war. Indeed, at the beginning of 1941 only about one-third of Germany's potential capacity was in fact producing war materials. There was, therefore, a very large margin in reserve. When, toward the end of 1941, it became clear to the Germans that the war on the Eastern front was not going to end in a quick victory, they began seriously to expand their war production. And in spite of the Allied air bombardment, Speer, the able German Minister of War Production, had not much difficulty in substantially increasing its volume. An increase in the volume of war production was not, however, enough. The Germans were now faced with a war on two fronts and, in the west, they had to reckon with the might of the United States. The test of Speer's success would be the expansion of German war production to meet the vastly increased demands made upon it, and to provide the weapons

[3] Much damage was also done outside the areas of complete devastation.

U. S. AIR FORCE OFFICIAL PHOTOGRAPH

Air Commander in the southwest Pacific, General George C. Kenney.

U. S. AIR FORCE OFFICIAL PHOTOG

U. S. Air Force attacks a Japanese airfield from a low height.

Railway center at Kassel after attack by Bomber Command.

IMPERIAL WAR MUS

U. S. AIR FORCE OFFICIAL PHOTOGRAPH

German factory bombed by U. S. Eighth Air Force.

Commander of the B-29's in the Pacific, General Curtis E. Le May.

The Super-Fortress: the B-29.

U. S. AIR FORCE OFFICIAL PHOTOGRAPH

Avro Vulcan with blue steel stand-off bomb.

AIR MINISTRY OFFICIAL PHOTOGRAPH

U. S. AIR FORCE OFFICIAL PHOT

Launch of Atlas intercontinental ballistic missile (ICBM).

U. S. AIR FORCE OFFICIAL PHOTOGRAPH

Launch of a Polaris missile from the ground at Cape Canaveral.

U. S. NAVY OFFICIAL PHOTOG

Polaris missile launched from a submerged submarine.

and equipment which could give the Germans victory over all their adversaries. On both counts Speer failed. The expansion of German production was severely checked by the Allied bombing campaign, and though it was not inconsiderable in absolute terms it was insufficient to meet the demands made upon it. The Germans were short of aircraft, guns, tanks, ammunition, locomotives, rolling stock, motor transport, oil, and clothing. And these deficiencies became worse as time went on. Though they were also short of manpower, they were compelled to allocate nearly a million men to passive air defense and repair work.

In addition, the defensive attitude forced upon the Germans by the Allied air bombardment caused them to modify the pattern of their war production in favor of defensive weapons. Thus they had to turn over almost the whole of their aircraft industry to the production of defensive fighters. They relied on the "V" weapons to replace the bombers that they could not build, but their armies everywhere were seriously starved of air support. So feeble did the German tactical air forces become that air superiority on the Eastern front passed into the hands of the Russians.

It has been alleged that the American daylight bombing, which was largely directed against the German aircraft and engine industry, was a failure because the German production of fighters was higher at the beginning of 1944 than it had been a year earlier. But it must be remembered that such things are a matter of priority. The Allied air offensive forced the Germans to give the highest priority to the production of fighters, at the expense of all other types of aircraft. But even this did not avail them, for the B-17's and their fighter escorts defeated the German day-fighters in combat, and reduced them almost to impotence.

The Allied air bombardment forced the Germans onto the defensive in the air, and with the failure of their air power they lost the initiative and were compelled to adopt the defensive on land. From this defensive posture they were never able to recover.

There can be no doubt that the general weakening of German military power—though it was certainly accelerated by attrition on the Eastern front—and the defeat of the German air force, were the two factors that made possible the invasion of the continent of Europe in June 1944. Nor can there be any doubt that they were the direct result of the Allied strategic bombing campaign.

It is hardly disputed by anybody that the thorough preparatory work done by the Allied heavy bombers insured the success of the invasion, and that their powerful support of the armies in the subsequent battles greatly facilitated their advance and saved the lives of many British and American soldiers.

The collapse of Japan, after her sea and air power had been broken, as a result of severe air bombardment by the American B-29's, marked a turning point in military history. No responsible airman, American or British, had ever claimed that an air offensive could bring about the defeat and surrender of a great Power, still in possession of a strong and unbeaten army. Yet that is precisely what happened in the war in the Pacific.

The versatility of the long-range bombers deserves some mention. A large proportion of the German heavy warships were destroyed or put out of action by bombs or sea-mines.[4] Although slightly outside the scope of this work, it is worth noting that out of the total of 997 German, Italian, and Japanese submarines sunk during the war, no less than 429 were destroyed by air action.[5] During the Second World War Bomber Command laid 47,307 sea-mines, about 80 per cent of all the mines laid by the British in all theaters of war. According to German records, 842 ships of all sorts were sunk in the areas mined by the Command, and many more were damaged. To this should be added the great German effort expended on mine-sweeping; the denial of many vital training areas to the U-Boats; and the serious delays to German sea-borne traffic. Finally the heavy bombers proved their ability to breach large dams and seawalls, to cripple rail transport and destroy inland waterways, to smash the heavy concrete roofs of the U-Boat shelters, and to defeat the German "V" weapons.

The heavy bombers, by the end of the war, had achieved air mastery, and they represented the ultimate development of offensive power. Sir Winston Churchill, in his important speech at Boston, Massachusetts, in 1949, said "For good or for ill, air mastery is today the supreme expression of military power, and fleets and armies, however vital and important, must accept a subordinate rank."

---

[4] See Appendix E.
[5] 366 destroyed by land-based aircraft, including those sunk by bombs or mines dropped by Bomber Command, and 63 by carrier-borne aircraft.

If there are any who still believe that air bombardment has made war more costly in lives, without any compensatory gain, they should study the figures of British casualties in the two world wars. It is fair to make this comparison, as in both wars Britain was involved from the first day until the last against the forces of Germany and a Mediterranean ally.

The First World War was fought in accordance with the doctrines of two-dimensional strategy. It lasted for four years and three months, and the total number killed in the armed forces and the air raids in Britain was 997,771. Of this number, 996,230 (99.8 per cent) were in the armed forces; selected, fit, younger men whose loss did much to cripple their generation. Most of them died in infantry battles, or under the horrible conditions of trench warfare, as a result of machine-gun, artillery, and mortar fire.

The Second World War lasted in Europe for five years and eight months, and the total number of British killed in the armed forces and in attacks by aircraft and "V" weapons, was 363,360. Of these 60,595 were killed in the air raids, and 302,765 (83.3 per cent) were selected, fit, younger men in the armed forces. Those killed in the air raids were a cross section of the population, including the old, the infirm, women and children. The total number killed in the Second World War in Europe, though it lasted seventeen months longer, and though Britain had to endure a fairly heavy scale of air attack, was little more than one-third of the total in the First World War. In addition, the loss was more evenly spread throughout the whole population.

It is a fact that the two-dimensional war of 1914-1918 was far more destructive of life, and killed a far higher proportion of younger men that the nation could ill afford to lose, than did the longer three-dimensional war of 1939-1945.

It has frequently been argued that the long-range bomber forces absorbed a very large share of the Allied war effort, which would have been more effective if it had been used to increase the strength of the land and sea forces, and the tactical air forces engaged in their support.

We have seen that long-range air bombardment was able to perform tasks, in Europe and in the Pacific, which could not have been undertaken by any other force, and without which victory would inevitably have been postponed, and might never have been gained at all. Apart from this, however, the proportion of the total resources devoted to the long-range bomber forces, with their supporting services, was in fact remarkably small. While such things are not very easy to calculate, it has been officially stated that the cost of Bomber Command, including the production of aircraft and equipment, and the training organization needed to replace casualties, amounted to approximately 7 per cent of the total British war effort.

It is safe to say that in the Second World War no branch of the armed forces gave a better return than did the long-range bomber forces for the resources allocated to them, or made a greater contribution to victory.

At the end of the Second World War, as at the Armistice in 1918, air forces were faced by a number of new problems. In wartime, years of concentrated scientific effort produce major advances, and important new developments are liable to appear too late to be fully tested in battle. By 1945 jet propulsion and nuclear weapons had completely revolutionized all previous ideas of air bombardment. But one thing was abundantly clear. The offensive power of the bomber, already great, had been enormously increased. In the past, the destruction of a large industrial area had required a concentration of many heavy bombers, and the cumulative effect of a number of attacks. One modern bomber carrying an atom bomb, flying at speeds and heights undreamed of during the war, could cause as much damage as a thousand Lancasters or B-29's could have done. And when the thermonuclear weapon—the H-bomb—became a practical proposition the destructive power of a single bomber became so great as to be almost beyond human imagination.

In these circumstances it was absurd to continue to regard air forces as subsidiary parts of armies and navies. The French, when they reconstituted their armed forces after the war, set up a third and separate Service, the Armée de l'Air. The Russians, though they did not publicly admit it, were deeply impressed by the results of the Allied air bombardment of Germany. Their air forces had hitherto been used almost entirely for the close support of military operations, but they now created a long-range bomber force, and started working intensively on the design of long-range rocket missiles.

In the United States several bills were submitted to Congress, aimed at providing a single Department of Defense to control three separate and equal Services. On May 13, 1946, President Truman instructed the Secretary of the Navy, James V. Forrestal, and the Secretary of War, Robert P. Paterson, to confer together and produce a plan. They were, however, unable to reach full agreement and the President had to make the final decision. He pronounced in favor of a single Department of Defense, controlling the Navy, Army, and Air Force. The Navy, as in Britain, was to retain only such air forces as could be embarked in ships.

This proposal was very strongly resisted by the Navy, and after further negotiations a new bill was drafted. This was finally passed on July 26, 1947. It set up a Department of Defense, headed by a Secretary, with three subordinate departments for the Navy, Army, and Air Force. The Navy was allowed to retain control of land-based aircraft for naval reconnaissance, antisubmarine warfare, and the protection of shipping. The Marine air units also remained under Naval control.

And so, at last, after a struggle that had continued for exactly forty years, the United States Air Force achieved complete autonomy, and parity with the two older Services.

After the defeat of Japan in 1945 Soviet Russia, in agreement with the Allies, occupied northern Korea as far south as the thirty-eighth parallel in order to accept the surrender of the Japanese forces in that area. Despite an agreement at Potsdam that Korea should become a free and independent nation, a "People's Democratic Republic" was organized in North Korea, under the firm control of Red China and the U.S.S.R., and the holding of free elections was not allowed.

In the southern part of the country a free and independent Republic of Korea had been set up as a result of elections held in 1948. By July 1949 the United States had withdrawn all their forces from South Korea except for a small military mission. The Communists made warlike preparations to overrun South Korea and on June 25, 1950, North Korean troops crossed the parallel and advanced southward. There was little to stop them. On June 27 the Security Council of the United Nations passed a resolution authorizing the members of the U.N. to "furnish such assistance to the Republic of Korea as may be necessary to repel armed attack and restore international peace and security in the area." It was possible to pass this resolution only because the Russians had temporarily withdrawn from the Security Council to mark their displeasure at something that it had done, and were not therefore in a position to use their veto.

Most of the forces needed to stem the Communist advance had to be provided by the United States, though later many other nations, including Britain, sent troops, air forces, and warships.

It was the first task of the air forces to slow down the Communist advance by direct attack and by interdiction. American troops were sent from Japan, and established a foothold in the southeast corner of the peninsula. Air superiority was gained without difficulty, and the position was stabilized. At this stage the B-29's, operating from airfields in Japan, were used in close support of the troops. The U.N. forces began to build up, and the heavy bombers were switched to the task of preventing the movement southward of North Korean reinforcements and supplies. By the end of July, they were attacking road and railway bridges, important centers of communication, power stations, and a number of industrial targets in North Korea. These attacks were successful, and by September 15, 1950, General Stratemeyer was able to report that "practically all of the major military industrial targets strategically important to the enemy forces and to their war potential have now been neutralized."

The U.N. forces now advanced and, once they had broken the Communist defense line, moved quickly northward. The government of the South Korean republic returned to its capital, Seoul, on September 29. By the end of October almost the whole of North Korea was in the hands of the U.N. forces. The Chinese then intervened, and sent a large army and air force to help the defeated North Koreans. Russian MIG fighters appeared in great numbers. The U.N. armies were compelled to retreat, and the air forces were once again called upon to do everything possible to slow down the Communist advance. The greatest weakness of the U.N. land forces in Korea was their dependence on a road-borne system of supply. Quite small bodies of Chinese troops, using mountain tracks, frequently worked their way round behind the U.N. forces and set up road blocks which cut their communications. Again and again the U.N. troops were compelled to retire when this happened, but they learned to stand their ground and rely on air supply until the

Chinese forces had been dislodged. As these were seldom in great strength and usually lightly equipped, this was not difficult.

By the end of 1950 the United Nations came to the conclusion that any further attempt to unify Korea by military action would involve the risk of a world war. They therefore adopted the policy of inflicting the maximum damage on the Communists in order to constrain them to seek an armistice. Severe air fighting ensued in which air superiority was regained, and the B-29's attacked bridges, railway centers, and other key points. This campaign dragged on until July 1953, when an armistice was signed at Panmunjom.

During the whole of this latter phase the U.N. long-range bombers were operating under a severe disadvantage. The Chinese had air bases and supply centers in Manchuria, north of the Yalu River, which the bombers were not allowed, for political reasons, to attack. It demonstrated very clearly the truth of the doctrine that air power cannot operate effectively unless it has freedom to attack the main sources of the enemy's military and industrial strength. The fear of widening the conflict restricted the action of the long-range bombers, and greatly reduced their effectiveness.

The Korean War ended in a draw, because both sides preferred to forego the chances of victory rather than take the risk of the conflict developing into a world war. Nuclear weapons were not used, but their shadow conditioned the operations, and induced a degree of caution on both sides that has perhaps set the pattern for similar wars in the future.

22 Missiles and Space Weapons

The German "V" weapons, though their effectiveness was largely nullified by the operations of the Allied air forces equipped with aircraft of conventional types, were remarkable achievements. They demonstrated the possibilities of an automatic, unmanned low-altitude missile powered by an air-breathing engine, and of a rocket-propelled ballistic missile. The work done at Peenemünde and related German establishments was of a very high order, and the development of all rocket missiles after the war, both in Soviet Russia and the United States, was based on test firings of captured V-2 weapons.

The new science of astronautics has made very rapid progress during the last fifteen years. It has a variety of applications, some of which are not strictly military, such as space research and improvements in tele-communications and terrestrial navigation. And, as the Russians have shown, it can be used to enhance national prestige and influence world politics. But its military applications, such as long-range nuclear bombardment and the defense against it, reconnaissance, and improved early warning systems are, at present, the most important, and it is significant that everywhere it is financed and directed almost entirely by military establishments.

Only those applications which are closely concerned with long-range bombardment and the possibilities of defense against it will be discussed in this chapter.

There are four groups of missiles which fall within this category. Two of them—surface-to-surface and air-to-surface—are strategically offensive; the other two—surface-to-air and air-to-air—are designed to destroy aircraft, or possibly missiles, and are therefore strategically defensive.

The only surface-to-surface weapons at present in existence are direct descendants of the German V-1 flying bomb and the V-2 ballistic rocket. There are long-range aerodynamic bomb-carriers—such as the American "Snark"—which can be automatic, guided, or homing, and which must operate at low altitudes. They do not appear to have many advantages over the manned bomber, and may not have much future. And there are long-range rocket-propelled ballistic missiles, such as the "Atlas," which follow a high trajectory far beyond the earth's atmosphere.

Surface-to-surface ballistic missiles can be fired from launching platforms on land or at sea. On land the launching sites of missiles using liquid chemical propellants must be fixed installations, but if solid chemical propellants can be developed for high-thrust rocket motors, it should be possible to make use of mobile launching equipment. At sea, medium-range missiles—such as Polaris—can be launched from surface vessels or submarines.

Since in all ballistic missiles accuracy is a function of the range, the indifferent degree of accuracy to be expected at intercontinental ranges will favor the use of thermonuclear war heads aimed at the largest possible targets. The NATO forces, with their large number of bases close to Soviet Russia, have a strategic advantage in this respect, because they can reach any target in Russia with a missile having a range of 2,000 miles, and most of them with a range of 1,500 miles. The Russians can reach targets in Europe and Britain with weapons of similar range, but to reach the vital targets in the United States, they must have missiles capable of reasonable accuracy at a range of at least 5,000 miles. It is mainly for this reason that Soviet Russia has concentrated on the development of long-range missiles and motors producing very high thrusts. This military necessity has enabled the Soviet Union to be the first nation to put a satellite into orbit, the first to strike the moon's surface, and the first to photograph the far side of the moon. It is not certain how accurate and reliable the Russian intercontinental ballistic missiles (ICBM) are, since it is obviously to their advantage to exaggerate their achievements in the development of these weapons, but it is probable that at present they are considerably ahead of the United States.

Air-to-surface missiles are carried in a manned aircraft with air-breathing engines and released at a distance of several hundred miles from the target. Examples of this type of weapon are the British "Blue Steel" stand-off bomb, and the more advanced American "Skybolt" which is now under development.

Surface-to-air missiles are antiaircraft weapons. They are rocket-propelled and may be guided to the target, or may home onto it by means of a device for detecting infrared radiation or other means. Examples of this type of weapon are the British "Bloodhound" and "Thunderbird," and the American "Nike" and "Hawk." Surface-to-air missiles may be equipped with a small-yield atomic war head fired by a proximity fuse. With electronic predictors and improved methods of guidance, they may be developed to the point at which it is possible to use them to intercept in flight and destroy surface-to-surface ballistic missiles, which are bound to follow a predictable trajectory.

Air-to-air missiles are small rocket-driven weapons, such as the British "Firestreak" and the American "Sidewinder," carried in fighters. They are effective at much longer ranges than any gun which can be installed in an aircraft. They also can be fitted with a powerful explosive war head and a proximity fuse.

It seems to be widely assumed that as soon as long-range rocket missiles reach a reasonable standard of accuracy and reliability, they will become responsible for all long-range nuclear bombardment. But it should be realized that, in all respects save one, the ICBM is at a disadvantage compared to the long-range manned bomber. When an alarm is given the bomber can take off and, if the warning should prove to be false, it can be recalled and no harm will have been done. If, however, a missile has been launched it cannot be recalled, but can only be destroyed in flight. It is not inconceivable that a bold aggressor, by the skillful use of feint attacks or radar deception methods, might at some risk to himself force a defender to expend his stocks of long-range missiles. Secondly, the missile, which is almost if not quite as expensive as the bomber, can be used only once, whereas the bomber can continue to deliver nuclear weapons until it is destroyed by the enemy defenses or by some mishap. In addition, it will be a long time before the mechanical reliability of the missile is equal to that of the modern manned heavy bomber.

The bomber is a more accurate weapon than the missile, for its accuracy is not a function of its range but depends on the skill and training of its crew and upon a number of other factors. A manned bomber, unlike a ballistic missile, need not follow a fixed trajectory between its starting point and its objective. It can plan its approach to suit the circumstances, taking full advantage of its power of maneuver, and its course cannot therefore be predicted.

It must not be forgotten that the long-range ballistic missile requires a large amount of supporting equipment, of which the most important are launching gear, special handling and transporting equipment, and provision for servicing and testing. If liquid fuels are employed elaborate arrangements must be made for rapid fueling.

The missile itself is only a part, though a vital part, of a guided weapons system. Such systems are, at present, relatively static, and cannot be mobilized and redeployed at short notice. It is true, however, that a missile of the Polaris type can to a large extent overcome this disadvantage. It can be embarked in an easily concealed mobile carrier such as a nuclear-powered submarine, which can move freely under the surface of the sea, and remain independent, at least for some time, of any main base facilities.

Only in its present immunity from interception by the defenses is the ICBM superior to the manned bomber. But this may be a very important factor, since it is possible that the development of the surface-to-air and air-to-air guided or homing missile will make it impracticable for the relatively slow bomber to penetrate a defended zone. The development of a rocket-propelled bomb, however, such as "Blue Steel" or "Skybolt," which can be released several hundred miles from the target, provides an opportunity of combining the tactical freedom and flexibility of the future manned bomber with the ability of the missile to penetrate the defenses. Since the defense organization could have no foreknowledge of the launching point of an air-borne missile, it would not be possible to predict its trajectory. Heavy bombers have the added advantage that they can be more rapidly deployed in any part of the world, and can carry a large and varied load of conventional weapons. They would thus be of great value in limited wars of the Korean type, in which the ICBM can play no part.

Since, under modern conditions, it would be impossible to win a full-scale war, in the sense that the victor could gain anything from it, the main object of armed forces nowadays is to prevent its occurrence. In military manpower, in conventional weapons, and in preparedness for war, the U.S.S.R. and Red China have a vast preponderance over any nation in the Free World, and even over the combined forces of any of its treaty organizations.

In the past, a deep and abiding hostility between two great groups of Powers having diametrically opposed interests in every part of the world, combined with an overwhelming unbalance of military power in favor of one side, would have created a situation of such instability that full-scale war would have been inevitable and indeed imminent. If that is certainly not the position today, it is because the military situation is unbalanced when conventional forces only are taken into account. But each side has, in addition, a nuclear capacity which is more than sufficient to annihilate the other. A new balance has therefore been created.

It is, however, quite clear that if all nuclear weapons were abolished western Europe and Britain could not be defended against Russian aggression. It would be impossible for the nations of the Free World to create and maintain land forces on the immense scale needed to provide an effective deterrent. Their peoples would fail to understand the need for them, and would refuse to serve in them or to face the colossal expenditure entailed. Land forces on this scale are nowadays possible only in totalitarian states, where the people have little or no effective voice in affairs. The Free World has therefore no choice but to rely on its nuclear capacity to prevent the outbreak of full-scale war, until such time as conventional forces everywhere have been reduced by agreement to a low level.

For the nuclear deterrent to be effective three conditions must be fulfilled. First, the Free World must have the power to destroy a potential aggressor, and this fact must be obvious to all concerned. Secondly, it must have the courage and resolution to use that power if necessary, and an aggressor must be convinced that it would not hesitate to do so. Thirdly, it must be able to deploy that power in such a way that it could not be destroyed in one devastating surprise attack. Since the Free World will never initiate an assault of this kind with nuclear weapons, it must be able to absorb a surprise attack and retain the capacity to retaliate in overwhelming force.

It is not by any means easy to fulfil these three conditions, but unless the Free World can do so the nuclear deterrent will not suffice to prevent a global war, and reliance upon it will prove illusory. But if they can be fulfilled there is no military reason why a conflict between the major Powers should not be prevented indefinitely through the balancing fears of mutual annihilation.

It can therefore be expected that the nuclear stalemate will continue, and that global war will be avoided, unless the Russians should succeed in achieving a technical break-through of such a nature as to lead them to believe that the Free World had been rendered defenseless. It is sometimes argued that a similar break-through by the United States would also endanger world peace. It is difficult to find any evidence to support this view, especially when it is remembered that for several years the Americans had the monopoly of the atomic bomb. During that period they used their power and influence in the interests of world peace, and indeed it is quite unthinkable that any genuinely democratic nation would resort to preventive war.

The danger of a technical break-through by the Soviet Union emphasizes the immense importance of scientific research and development. The Free World cannot afford to fall behind in the race.

This brings us to the consideration of space weapons and their potentialities. A number of satellites have been placed in orbit around the earth by Soviet Russia and the United States, and much has undoubtedly been learned from the information which they have transmitted. The most obvious and practicable military uses for these space vehicles are defensive. They can be employed for reconnaissance, using photographic and television equipment, with the object of guarding against a surprise attack. And they can supplement the terrestrial early warning system by means of instruments which could detect and report the launching of a long-range ballistic missile more easily than can be done from the earth's surface. It may not be long before such satellites become a permanent and indispensable part of existing early warning systems, and they may indeed largely supersede them.

Looking further into the future, space vehicles orbiting the earth may have important offensive possibilities. A vehicle may be placed in orbit carrying a thermonuclear weapon, which could be released by a signal from the ground. Such weapons could take the form of a rocket-propelled missile projected downward or merely decelerated and allowed to fall under the influence of gravity. Later, it is possible that such orbital launching platforms could be manned, which would make the whole system more flexible, accurate, and reliable.

There are two possible means of defense against such an attack system. The launching platform could be attacked directly by missiles fired from the ground, or by clouds of small pieces of matter, put into a similar orbit in the contrary direction, which would become artificial meteors capable of penetrating and damaging the launching platform. In order to reduce the danger from these two measures, it will be necessary for the launching platform to have the power of varying the pattern of its orbit.

Little is yet known about the effect on the human being of living in space, but there is no reason to believe that, if proper precautions are taken, it would be impossible to maintain a crew, relieved at suitable intervals, in a vehicle in orbit round the earth.

The next stage, already visualized, may be the establishment of early warning systems and even launching platforms on the surface of the moon. These would probably be unmanned and controlled from the earth, though in the more distant future it may be feasible to station men on the moon. Such lunar bases would be very difficult to attack and destroy by weapons launched from the earth, but it is not impossible to imagine that fighting to gain possession of them, or destroy them, might occur between rival garrisons on the moon itself. Such attempts would, however, give ample warning of aggressive intentions.

We have seen how the invention of the airplane and the submarine freed the conduct of war from the two-dimensional framework in which it had been confined for so long. Now the coming of satellites and space vehicles may carry the offensive, and the perpetual struggle to find means of defense against it, into the realms of space. Although many difficulties will have to be faced and overcome before this can become a reality, such problems are no more than an exciting challenge in our scientific age.

While it would be a grave mistake to suppose that sea, land, and air warfare as we have known them are things of the past, the military possibilities inherent in the conquest of space cannot be ignored, and should on no account be underestimated.

23 War in the Nuclear Age

In the last chapter we took a glance at the more distant future, and discussed briefly the possibilities of human armed conflict being carried into the realms of space. Now we may come back to earth and consider the forms that warfare could take in the immediate future, and the part that air bombardment—or its modern equivalent —is likely to play in it.

Apart from some miscalculation, which is not very likely to happen, full-scale war will not occur unless the rulers of Soviet Russia or Red China decide to invoke it. But if they should so decide, it could begin in one of two ways. It could start by a surprise attack in over-whelming force, using long-range bombardment by nuclear and thermonuclear weapons in an attempt to destroy, at one blow, the retaliatory power of the Free World. Or it could occur as the result of Communist armed aggression by conventional forces.

The possibility of a surprise attack cannot be ignored. An assault by long-range nuclear and thermonuclear missiles on a large scale would have immense destructive power, and a few minutes' warning is all that could be relied upon. If an attack of this kind should ever come, it will probably occur at the moment when it is least expected; when the statesmen of the Free World believe that they are making good progress in negotiations for disarmament; when a diminution of Communist truculence has brought about some relaxation of

world tension; on the eve of a summit conference, or the morning
of Christmas Day.

But even if such a surprise attack were to destroy many great cities
and devastate large areas with unimaginable loss of life, it would not
serve its purpose. Unless it were able to destroy all nuclear capacity
and thus inhibit the power to retaliate in force, it would merely mean
that, a few hours or even minutes later, the aggressor would suffer the
same fate.

The long-range missile can be protected against a knock-out blow
by dispersal, concealment, by putting launching sites underground
with heavy concrete cover, and by embarking a substantial part of it
in nuclear-powered submarines. Part of a long-range bomber force can
be kept permanently in the air, and a few minutes' warning would
suffice for more to take off before the attack could develop. A multi-
plication of bases helps to complicate the problem of knowing where
the bomber force is at any given moment. If vertical take-off and
landing can be developed in the near future—and nothing is more
urgently important—long runways will become obsolete and bombers
can be dispersed in small, easily concealed, or even improvised, sites.

Provided, therefore, that every effort is made to defend the deterrent, and that it is maintained in a genuine state of readiness, no
aggressor could ever feel confident that a knock-out blow would
succeed.

It is much more likely that full-scale war would begin by a massive
invasion of land forces using conventional weapons only. This might
be accompanied by a declaration abjuring the use of all nuclear or
thermonuclear weapons, and calling upon the Free World to do the
same. This would face the Western nuclear Powers with the necessity
of making a decision of great gravity. The choice would be between
military defeat and submission to Communist domination, or initi-
ating the use of nuclear weapons which might, and probably would,
lead to a disastrous competition in thermonuclear bombardment. The
Communist Powers would hope that the Western leaders might hesitate long enough to enable them to crush the land forces opposed to
them and demonstrate the futility of further resistance, and especially
of resorting to nuclear bombardment. To this end they would largely
rely on the protests, led by Communists, against the use of nuclear
weapons that would be raised in democratic countries by fellow-
travelers, misguided intellectuals, woolly-minded humanitarians, some

religious leaders, pacifists, and moral and physical cowards. To all these categories the Communists have given great encouragement in all countries except those under their own control.

If the Western nuclear Powers should decide not to employ nuclear weapons, or should hesitate for too long trying to make up their minds, nothing could save them from defeat. If they should decide to use them, their best plan would be to declare their intention of employing them only against strictly military targets, such as concentrations of troops and armor, supply dumps, railheads, and traffic bottlenecks, and take great care to observe this restriction.

The first task of the relatively small land forces of the Free World would be to check, using conventional weapons only, the initial Communist advance, and unless they are strong enough to do so they are useless. The object of this would be twofold. First, to force a pause, to give the Communists time for second thoughts, and to make them realize that any attempt to continue their advance would inevitably lead to the tactical use of nuclear weapons. Secondly, to compel the Communist land forces to concentrate in order to break through and thus offer rewarding targets for these weapons.

Some authorities believe that a full-scale war could be fought with tactical nuclear weapons without getting out of control. Others think that once nuclear weapons have been used, it would be impossible to draw the line anywhere, and that a disastrous exchange of thermonuclear bombs could not be avoided. They point out that the successful use by the West of tactical nuclear weapons, on a scale sufficient to stop a massive invasion of land forces, would involve the Communists in a military disaster of colossal dimensions. Their leaders would not accept defeat but would turn in anger, fear, and revenge, and even in desperation, to their thermonuclear weapons.

However this may be, it is clear that the danger of any large-scale war ending in a thermonuclear holocaust is very great. No aggressor toying with the idea of such a war could feel any confidence that it would not do so. The prospect would be so dangerous that no sane man would dare to take the risk. And, although, as Sir Winston Churchill has said, no system of deterrents is proof against lunatics, even the maddest dictators have relatively sane colleagues. And it is a fact that the rulers of Soviet Russia have never at any time shown a tendency to take undue risks. There is no reason to suppose that, in this respect, their policy will change.

The plain truth is that the thermonuclear balance must mean either the end of full-scale war or the destruction of the greater part of the civilized world. In a war fought with thermonuclear weapons there can be no distinction between civil and military targets, between combatants and noncombatants. The destruction would be on an unimaginable scale, and indeed such a war could end only in mutual annihilation. It is now useless as a means of settling international disputes, and it can no longer be regarded—as Clausewitz regarded it—as "a continuation of State policy by other means." Any continuation of state policy that leads directly and inevitably to national suicide is an absurdity.

Long-range thermonuclear bombardment has now made full-scale war too violent to be of any practical use. No war aim, no conceivable gain that full-scale war might bring, could have any value in the context of a thermonuclear holocaust.

It would, however, be too much to expect that a realization of the impracticability of full-scale war will lead the nations of the world to cease from quarreling, or to agree to settle all their differences by negotiation or arbitration. It is true that there is nowadays an increasing tendency to seek agreed solutions rather than to attempt to impose them by force of arms. This, however, mainly applies to economic and financial rivalries, which were certainly a frequent cause of armed conflicts in the past. But deep ideological differences are irreconcilable. It is impossible to negotiate an agreement between them, and one or other must in the end prevail. But international conflict will be carried on in future by methods which do not involve the use of unrestrained violence.

If, therefore, there is no likelihood of full-scale war, neither is there peace. The trend of international affairs seems to show that the rulers of Soviet Russia, though not yet perhaps those of Red China, have adapted their offensive against the Free World to meet the changed conditions. This new form of conflict is called the cold war, and its weapons are those of propaganda, subversion, political infiltration, and economic and industrial sabotage. The uninhibited use of these weapons in time of peace is a new phenomenon. It enables an aggressive nation, by means of trained agitators, industrial saboteurs, radio broadcasts, and the dissemination of literature, to damage the economy of another country, and to appeal directly to its people over the head of their government. The true democracies are very vulnerable to these forms of attack, as their cherished freedom of speech and opinion make it almost impossible to deal with them. In contrast to this, it is difficult for the Free World to gain the ear of people in Communist countries, where the state controls all sources of information, and has no compunction about jamming all foreign broadcasts.

In countries new to self-government—politically unstable, economically weak, and with a high level of illiteracy among the population—the Communists can hope to gain power by way of the ballot-box. In politically mature countries, the most promising tactics are infiltration into trade unions, taking advantage of the apathy of union members to win elections to key positions in the organization; and the penetration of left-wing political groups. Nowadays trade unions wield a great deal of power, and those in control of them have opportunities for damaging the national economy. The ultimate object would be to create widespread unemployment, and bring about the conditions in which a left-wing party, allied to or infiltrated by Communists, would be returned to power.

Once the Communists gain access to the levers of power, they will take care to reform the electoral system, so that no alternative government can ever be voted into office.

The United Nations, which takes an excessively legalistic view of international relations, does not recognize the operations of the cold war as aggressive. But if any nation, goaded beyond endurance by political and economic pressures, should resort to force of arms to save itself, it can and will be arraigned before the United Nations and branded as an aggressor, with those who engineered its desperate plight sitting in judgment upon it. Resort to force is thus possible for the victims of the cold war only at the cost of being denounced as aggressors, with world opinion and sanctions of various kinds mobilized against them.

As long as the cold war is yielding good results, the Communist Powers will be tempted to resort to force only in exceptionally favorable circumstances. They would need to be convinced that a quick military victory could be obtained, and that the conflict could be localized and kept under control. The most likely form of limited war would resemble that in Korea, in which a satellite Communist government, armed and encouraged by Moscow or Peking or both, would attempt to extend its rule over some free country.

Limited war, therefore, is not likely to be encountered very often in the future, but whenever such aggression does occur it will certainly be difficult to counter. The scene of the conflict will probably be remote, the situation confused, and the communications poor. Every day that passes before military reinforcements can arrive will reduce the chances of a successful defense, and increase the size of the force eventually needed to restore the situation. The Security Council will be unable to take action, because every attempt at positive action would be vetoed by Soviet Russia. It might well be that for several days the only effective action that could be taken would be long-range air bombardment. Air transport will be of the utmost value, both to carry troops and weapons to the battle zones, and to supply them after they have arrived. Tactical air forces will be required to support the land forces in battle. All these aircraft, with the possible exception of the long-range bombers, may have to operate from small or improvised bases, and a capacity for vertical take off and landing would be of first importance.

In order to prevent the conflict from getting out of hand and leading to full-scale war, it would probably be necessary to impose restrictions on the operations of the armed forces, and especially on those of the long-range bombers. Air bombardment may be limited by geography, and by the need to confine it to the attack of strictly military targets. For this reason manned bomber aircraft will be required, and in limited wars they cannot be replaced by ballistic missiles.

There remains the question of the use of nuclear weapons in limited war. The difficulty is that tactical atomic weapons delivered by short-range surface-to-surface, and probably air-to-surface missiles, and by guns and mortars, may soon become the standard equipment of conventional forces. The question, as yet unanswered, is whether it would be possible to use these weapons in a limited war without risking the expansion of the conflict into full-scale war. Clearly much depends on how small and "clean" such weapons can be made. But a civilized democracy, whose armed forces had been almost obliterated by nuclear attack in a limited war, might be so enraged that an irresistible popular demand for retaliation with more powerful nuclear weapons might arise. Governments, fully realizing the consequences of such action, might be firmly opposed to it, but public indignation might be so great that no democratic government could withstand it. The governments in Moscow or Peking, with their ability to suppress or minimize the news, might be more able to exercise restraint. But it may well be that this factor will exert an increasingly powerful influence against recourse even to limited war.

The latest developments of long-range bombardment armed with thermonuclear weapons, whether carried out by manned aircraft or ballistic missiles, have made full-scale war so violent and dangerous that it is now useless as a means of settling international disputes. And the tendency to arm conventional forces with tactical nuclear weapons makes it doubtful whether limited war, in future, will be a practical proposition.

The disappearance of war would be, in countless ways, a great boon to mankind, but it is not always realized that war, or the threat of it, has in all ages served an indispensable purpose in human affairs. If it is to be abolished, something must take its place.

The suppression, for all practical purposes, of the reality or the threat of war will remove the means by which, in the past, aggressive, dishonest, and treacherous rulers and governments were compelled to conform to an acceptable standard of behavior. They knew that if they went too far they would be faced with the threat of war and, if they persisted in inflicting injury upon others, with war itself. Nowadays that sanction has largely disappeared, and already a grave deterioration in the standards of international behavior has occurred. Some states indulge with impunity in flagrant treaty breaking and damage to the major interests of others which, before the days of nuclear weapons, would not have been tolerated. Since the end of the Second World War many countries have had to submit to outrageous misconduct on the part of their neighbors. And, since the United Nations is powerless to help them, and because they feared that any attempt to assert their rights by force might lead to full-scale war, they have been compelled to endure—under the name of peaceful co-existence—a measure of hostile interference and international mischief-making that would have been unthinkable in former times.

If nuclear weapons should get into the hands of the irresponsible leaders of backward and aggressive countries the situation will undergo a further rapid deterioration. The threat of nuclear attack from such a source would be a very potent instrument of inter-national blackmail.

It is clear, therefore, that two problems of great urgency and importance will have to be solved in the near future. It will be essential to insure that nuclear and thermonuclear weapons are concentrated under responsible control. This is as much in the interests of the U.S.S.R. as of any other country, and it is perhaps not too much to hope for Russian cooperation in the solution of this problem.

Finally, and most important of all, some way must be found of restoring a satisfactory standard of international behavior. There is a strong tendency to assume that this duty should be undertaken by the United Nations. This might be possible if the United Nations resembled in any way a world court of justice, and was prepared, and had the ability, to deal with powerful evildoers. But this is unfortunately not so. The Security Council is reduced to impotence by the use of the Russian veto, and the recommendations of the General Assembly have no mandatory force. And some of its members do not cast their votes in accordance with equity or justice, but as part of a bloc, or in order to further their own national interests. But if the United Nations cannot undertake this vital task, some other machinery must be created which is capable of doing so.

The abolition of war will never be achieved by agreement or by disarmament, or by a renunciation of armed conflict for reasons of morality or humanity. It will disappear because its violence has made it an anachronism and, under modern conditions, it can serve no useful purpose. It will have to give place to some sensible and effective means of settling international disputes.

The disappearance of war will make it all the more necessary to protect the peoples of the world from the horrors and miseries caused by riots, rebellions, and civil conflicts. These, provoked by inflamed minorities, encouraged and supported by international communism, have cruelly afflicted very many countries during the last twelve years. They have caused more human suffering and material losses than many great wars have done in the past. Mankind will gain but little if international war is to be replaced by unending civil strife, violence, and intimidation. Ordinary people everywhere long for peace with justice, security, and good order, and means of restoring it must be found.

Although the logical evolution of long-range bombardment has at last brought us to the point at which the suppression of war is in sight, the story cannot end there. If the civilized world is to survive, it must eventually succeed in setting up some form of world judicial authority, independent of national threats and pressures, and clothed with sufficient power to make its rulings effective.

In this direction, and not in futile attempts to put the clock back and abolish modern weapons, lie the best—perhaps the only—hopes of mankind.

Appendix A

Summary of Bomb Development

EARLY DAYS. The development of bombs to be dropped by aircraft followed much the same lines in all countries aspiring to air power. The first bombs to be dropped, by the Italians in 1911, were modified hand grenades of Swedish manufacture, weighing about 4½ lbs. In the early days of the First World War, improvised bombs converted from shells or hand grenades were used. In addition, steel darts were used for the attack of troops in the open. These were followed by explosive bombs of 16 to 20 lbs. in weight, specifically designed for air use. Further development during the war resulted in a range of high-explosive (H.E.) bombs from 20 lbs. to 550 lbs. in weight. These had a heavy cast-iron case, with an explosive content of about 30 per cent. During the last few months of the war a few larger bombs, up to 1,650 lbs. in weight, were developed.

Generally speaking, simple direct action fuses were employed.

ARMOR-PIERCING BOMBS. Development of armor-piercing bombs began soon after the end of the First World War. In general, development produced two types of bomb; semi-armor-piercing (S.A.P.) and armor-piercing (A.P.) S.A.P. bombs were mainly of 250 lbs. or 500 lbs. in weight, of good ballistic shape with steel bodies hardened at the nose. They were capable of penetrating about 3½ inches of armor plate when dropped from 7,000 ft. or over. The explosive

237

content was low, about 12 per cent. A.P. bombs were up to 2,000 lbs. in weight, and were of strong steel construction with a very thick hardened nose with progressive toughening of the body toward the tail. The 2,000 lb. bomb, dropped from 7,000 ft. or over, was capable of penetrating 7 inches of armor plate.

All British S.A.P. and A.P. bombs were originally fitted with elaborate shuttered fuses, but these proved so unreliable that the bombs were redesigned during the Second World War to use a simple pistol-detonator combination.

GENERAL PURPOSE BOMBS. A range of G.P. bombs was also developed soon after the First World War. Mainly they had strong cast-steel bodies of good ballistic shape, and were in various sizes up to 1,000 lbs. in weight. They could be fused at either end and delay action fuses could be used, giving delays of up to 48 hours. Owing to the strength of the steel body, the explosive content was no more than about 25 per cent.

At the beginning of the Second World War an improved range of British G.P. bombs was introduced, up to 1,000 lbs. in weight, simpler to produce, with an explosive charge of about 60 per cent.

The German G.P. bombs had, from the beginning, a very high explosive content.

HIGH CAPACITY BOMBS. The Germans were the first to use bombs of this type, made from converted sea-mines, the descent of which was checked by a parachute. During 1941 the British introduced a range of high-capacity bombs, commonly known as "block-busters," in weights of 4,000 lbs. 8,000 lbs., and 12,000 lbs. The heavier ones were multiples of the 4,000 lb. design. These bombs were simple welded cylinders of ¼ in. mild steel plate, with a simple drum-shaped tail unit, and an explosive content of 80 per cent. Although the ballistic shape was crude, the bombs proved to be reasonably stable in flight. Nose fusing only was possible with so light a case, and toward the end of the war a diaphragm pistol was developed which detonated the bomb just before contact with the target, to obviate any risk of the body breaking up before the explosive charge could be initiated.

DEEP PENETRATION BOMBS. In early 1940 it was clear that a bomb was required that could destroy certain types of target by detonating large H.E. charges deep in the earth to set up destructive earthquake shocks. The requirements for such a bomb were a good ballistic shape, to obtain a high striking velocity, the highest practicable H.E. content, and sufficient body strength to stand up to the impact and subsequent penetration. Tail fusing only was required.

Dr. Barnes Wallis, who also developed the weapon which destroyed the Möhne and Eder dams, designed a bomb of 12,000 lbs. in weight, of streamline form with offset fins inducing rotation to give stability in flight, for the bomb approached or even exceeded the speed of sound when dropped from high altitudes. The body was a high quality steel casting of ingenious design, giving great strength and allowing an explosive content of 50 per cent. Toward the end of the war a similar bomb of 22,000 lbs. in weight was used in small numbers.

Although not designed to penetrate hard targets such as armored ships or massive concrete structures, these bombs proved to be very effective against such targets. They were employed successfully in the sinking of the *Tirpitz*, the destruction of German submarine pens with heavy concrete roofs, and the massive "V" weapon concrete structures which the Germans attempted to build in northern France.

INCENDIARY BOMBS. During the First World War two types of incendiary bombs were developed. Small magnesium bombs, of about 2½ lbs. in weight, and larger bombs of 20 lb. weight, containing a variety of incendiary compounds, were employed with some success.

The most successful type used during the Second World War consisted of a small 4 lb. bomb, of hexagonal section to save space when stowed in a container carried in an aircraft. The bomb was made of magnesium, with a hollow center filled with an incendiary composition. The bomb was detonated by a simple inertia fuse in the tail.

Owing to their shape and light weight these bombs had poor ballistic qualities. This was overcome by dropping the bombs in a container of good ballistic shape, designed to open at about 2,000 ft., and allow the small bombs to scatter.

During the Second World War several designs of larger incendiary bomb, with liquid or solid incendiary fillings, were developed and used. One of these, known as the "Napalm" bomb, filled with a jelly composed of a metallic salt of naphtha mixed with gasoline, was especially successful.

NUCLEAR BOMBS (THE A-BOMB). During the later stages of the Second World War work had been proceeding in America and Britain on the development of an atomic bomb. It was decided to concentrate this development at Los Alamos in the United States. On July 16, 1945, at Alamagordo in New Mexico, the first atomic bomb was detonated. Two of these bombs were dropped during the war; one on Hiroshima, on August 6, and one on Nagasaki on August 9. The explosive force of these bombs was about 20 kilotons, i.e. equal to 20,000 tons of H.E.

Since then atom bombs of greater power, for strategic bombardment, and of smaller yield, for tactical use, have been developed.

THERMONUCLEAR BOMBS (THE H-BOMB). By using the detonation of an atom bomb to initiate a fusion of hydrogen atoms, a weapon with an explosive force many times as great as that of an atom bomb has been developed.

Appendix B

Summary of the Development of Marker Bombs and Flares

EARLY DAYS. During the First World War simple marker bombs for use at sea were developed, which spread a patch of powdered aluminium on the surface of the water. Smoke bombs were also developed which could be used on land or as smoke floats at sea. Their main use was to mark the place where a submarine had been seen to dive.

From 1917 to 1940 all air forces relied for the illumination of targets at night on small parachute flares, which were effective only at very low altitudes.

GROUND MARKERS. In the early days of the night bomber offensive in the Second World War the need was felt for some means of marking visually a point on the ground, to enable the less experienced crews to see and concentrate on the aiming-point. This requirement resulted in the production of a series of pyrotechnic marker bombs, employing several different colors and combinations of colors. This variety was needed to overcome attempts by the defenses to mislead the bomber force by igniting imitation markers in the wrong place. Information as to the color or combination of colors to be used for marking was included in the orders for each attack.

These marker bombs were generally of about 250 lbs. in weight, with burning times of from 5 to 15 minutes.

SKY MARKERS. Ground markers could usually be seen through fog, mist, or thin cloud, but in order to deal with heavy cloud over the target area some sort of aerial beacon, placed in the correct position by radar methods, was needed. These sky markers could be used to mark the point of bomb release, though they were subject to drifting with the wind and required frequent renewal. They were a form of parachute flare, produced in a wide variety of colors, to avoid confusion due to star-shells or other deceptive measures. These markers were initiated by fuses operated by barometric pressure, and had a relatively short period of burning.

Appendix C

Summary of Bombsight Development

EARLY DAYS. At the beginning of the First World War bombs were dropped over the side by hand, and aimed by guesswork. Later they were released from carriers fixed under the aircraft, but were still aimed by eye, or by some very simple improvised aiming device.

HIGH-ALTITUDE DRIFT SIGHTS. Toward the end of the First World War, bombsights were developed to meet the requirements of aircraft bombing from heights of up to 18,000 ft. These were simple open sights, usually fitted on the side of the aircraft. Settings were available for height, air-speed, and bomb trail-angle. Fore-and-aft and lateral levels were provided. A simple drift-wire, which was adjustable to measure drift when flying at right angles to the wind, was fitted. The drift, applied to an ordinary navigational computer, enabled the ground speed of the aircraft to be calculated, and the air-speed setting was adjusted accordingly. The great drawback to this type of sight was that bombing runs could be made only up or down wind.

COURSE-SETTING BOMBSIGHTS. These sights appeared about 1924. They incorporated a compass-bowl coupled to the drift-wires, in addition to the normal height, air-speed, and bomb trail-angle settings. The direction and velocity of the wind could be determined by one or more of three methods. With this vector set on the sight the bomb-

243

aimer directed the pilot to fly the aircraft so that the target approached along the drift-wires, and adjusted his compass-bowl so as to keep the compass needle pointing at the wind heading on the verge ring. By this means the sight compensated for the wind vector on any course, and afforded the great tactical advantage of making it possible for the aircraft to approach the target from any direction without loss of accuracy.

AUTOMATIC BOMBSIGHTS. Automatic sights were developed in the early 1930's. They were tachometric sights, which relied upon the determination of the ground speed through a constant speed electric motor driving, through simple gears, cross-hairs optically projected against the ground below. An approximation of the ground speed was set on the instrument and the cross-hairs set on the target. If they remained on the target, the ground speed setting was correct. Any error in the ground speed setting would cause the cross-hairs to lag behind or move ahead of the target. The bomb-aimer would then bring the cross-hairs back on to the target, thereby resetting the gears and accelerating or retarding the movement of the cross-hairs. After two or three such adjustments the instrument would have absorbed the correct ground speed.

Similarly for drift, the bomb-aimer would set an approximate drift angle. If the cross-hairs departed from the target to one side or the other, he would reset them, thereby giving a signal for the aircraft to turn. After two or three adjustments of this nature the correct drift would have been fed into the instrument.

Having the correct ground speed and drift angle, the bombsight would then calculate the correct release angle and automatically drop the bombs at the right moment.

This type of sight, though very accurate in the hands of an experienced bomb-aimer in ideal conditions, had two serious drawbacks. It relied, as did all previous sights, upon the aircraft remaining in a horizontal plane, which required extremely accurate flying. In addition, all changes of course had to be made by means of "flat" turns. This became increasingly difficult, because faster and "cleaner" aircraft continued to skid sideways after the heading had been changed. Secondly, any errors arising from inaccurate flying were greatly magnified in an automatic sight, as distinct from the course-setting type of sight.

STABILIZED AUTOMATIC BOMBSIGHTS. It was clear that in order to get the best results the sight itself, rather than the aircraft, would have to be stabilized. This led to the development of an automatic sight, gyroscopically stabilized in pitch and roll. The first of these was the American Norden sight. A British sight, on the same lines, was developed independently two or three years later. While these instruments were capable of far greater accuracy than any previous design of bombsight, they had serious limitations under operational conditions. They required the recognition of the target from a considerable distance, with a continuous clear view during the whole of the approach, which had to be straight and at a constant height. Avoiding action against fighters or A.A. fire was therefore impracticable. In expert hands, however, in good weather in daylight against light opposition, these sights made it possible to drop bombs with a remarkable degree of accuracy.

STABILIZED CONTINUOUSLY SET VECTOR SIGHTS. There was an obvious need for a sight which would always indicate the point on the ground where a bomb would fall if released at that moment, no matter what maneuvers the aircraft might be carrying out. This would enable an aircraft to take avoiding action during the approach to the target. Although the target itself might not be identified until the last moment, if the bomb-aimer could bring his sight to bear on it for an instant and release his bombs, the attack could be successfully completed. These requirements were met by a stabilized continuously set vector sight. Information regarding air-speed, heading, and height were continuously fed into a computer, which adjusted by means of servo-mechanisms the settings of the bombsight. The cross-hairs in the sighting head were optically projected on the ground at a point where the bombs would fall if released at that moment.

This type of bombsight could never be as accurate, under ideal conditions, as a tachometric sight, because the wind vector had to be pre-set, and any errors in estimating the direction and velocity of the wind over the target appeared in the bombing and drift angle. But owing to the tactical freedom allowed to the aircraft during the approach, it proved in practice to be the most accurate sight under operational conditions.

These sights came into use toward the end of 1942.

BOMB RELEASE MECHANISM. Concurrently with the development of
bombsights, release mechanisms were developed which enabled a
bomb-aimer to drop all the bombs in one salvo, or to release a suc-
cession of bombs at intervals that could be pre-set.

Appendix D

Summary of Development of Radar Aids to Night Navigation and Bombing

GEE. Gee is an accurate fixing system. Three ground stations, A, B, and C are situated as widely apart as possible with A at the apex. A and B and A and C transmit pulse signals simultaneously and the instrument carried in the aircraft measures the difference in time of receipt between A and B and A and C. It then converts this into a difference in distance between A and B and A and C. These differences are the lines of constant path differences along which the aircraft is flying between A and B and A and C and the aircraft position is at the point of intersection. The fix is instantaneous, and the two readings from the instrument can be readily plotted on a special chart, known as the Gee Lattice Chart. The limit of range is about 400 miles at 20,000 ft.

The first operational trials of Gee were undertaken on the night of August 11th/12th, 1941. All Gee equipment was then removed from aircraft flying over Germany until a sizable force could be equipped and trained.

First large scale operational use occurred on the night of March 8th/9th, 1942, in an attack on Essen.

OBOE. Oboe is an extremely accurate method of controlled bombing. Two ground stations, based wide apart, transmit pulse signals to the aircraft, which receives them and transmits them back again. By measuring the time taken for each pulse to go out and return the distance of the aircraft from each station can be continuously measured. If the distance of the target from Station A is known, the aircraft can be guided along the arc of a circle circumscribed by the radius, the length of which equals this distance with center at A. This will take the aircraft over the target. If the bomb release point is calculated, its position on this arc can be determined and measured from Station B. When the aircraft reaches this point it can be instructed to release its bombs. The effective range of Oboe is about 350 miles at 30,000 ft. Only one aircraft can be controlled at a time by one pair of ground stations.

The first operational trials of Oboe took place in late December 1942. The first operational use occurred on the night of March 5th/6th, 1943, in an attack against the Krupps Works in Essen.

H 2 s. H 2 S is an equipment carried in the aircraft to assist in night navigation, target location, and bombing. It transmits pulse signals toward the ground, and receives back the "echoes" which are displayed on a cathode ray tube. This display is in the form of a series of spots of light of varying degrees of brightness which together form a picture comparable to a map of the area over which the aircraft is flying. Water gives very little reflection and appears dark; land gives a fairly bright response, and built-up areas a very bright reflection. Contrast between land and water is very marked; rivers, lakes, and coast lines show clearly. Built-up areas can be identified with experience. The area covered is a radius of about 25 miles around the aircraft from 20,000 ft.

The first operational trials of H 2 S took place on the night of January 30th/31st, 1943, against Hamburg. The equipment was gradually introduced into Bomber Command until all aircraft were fitted with it and all crews trained to use it.

GEE-H. Gee-H is a very accurate system of blind-bombing. It is the exact reverse of Oboe, the aircraft transmitting pulse signals to the two ground stations, which receive the pulses and transmit them back. The aircraft can therefore continuously measure its distance from two known points and can track itself over any target within range of the system, and determine its release point with great accuracy. The limit of range is much the same as Oboe, some 350 miles at 30,000 ft.

The great advantage of Gee-H over Oboe is that 80 aircraft can simultaneously operate one pair of ground stations.

The first operational use of Gee-H occurred on the night of November 3rd/4th, 1943, in an attack on the Mannesman Steel Works near Düsseldorf.

Appendix E

FATE OF THE EIGHTEEN PRINCIPAL GERMAN WARSHIPS
1939–1945

Name	Deep load Tonnage	Date and cause	Agent
Bismarck	52,700	Sunk 27/5/41—Naval action in Outer Bay of Biscay.	Navy
Tirpitz	52,700	Sunk 12/11/44—R.A.F. attack near Tromso.	Bomber Command
Schleswig-Holstein	14,800	Scuttled 28/4/45 as a blockship at Gdynia.	
Schlesien	14,400	Beached 4/5/45 after mine damage off Swinemunde.	Bomber Command
Graf Spee	15,600	Scuttled 17/12/39 after Naval action off River Plate.	Navy
Von Scheer	15,650	Sunk 9/4/45 by R.A.F. air raid on Kiel.	Bomber Command
Deutschland-Lutzow	15,206	Sunk 16/4/45 by R.A.F. air raid on Swinemunde.	Bomber Command
Scharnhorst	37,000	Sunk 26/12/43—Naval action off North Norway.	Navy
Gneisenau	37,000	Scuttled in Gdynia 28/3/45. Sustained very heavy damage in Feb. 26/27th 1942 R.A.F. air raid on Kiel and never subsequently repaired. Pre-	Bomber Command

		vious to this she had been damaged by torpedoes, bombs, and mines.	
Admiral Hipper	19,000	Scuttled in dock 3/5/45 after serious damage in R.A.F. air raid on Kiel 9/4/45.	Bomber Command
Blucher	19,000	Sunk 9/4/40 by Norwegian shore batteries in Oslofjord.	Norwegian artillery
Prinz Eugen	19,000	Surrendered intact in May 1945.	
Konigsberg	8,200	Sunk 10/4/40 by Fleet Air Arm at Bergen.	Fleet Air Arm
Karlsruhe	8,200	Sunk 9/4/40 by H.M.S. Truant off Kristiansand South.	Navy
Koln	8,200	Sunk 30/3/45 by U.S.A.A.F. air raid on Wilhemshaven.	U.S. Air Force
Nuremberg	9,114	Surrendered intact in May 1945.	
Emden	6,931	Sunk 9/4/45 by R.A.F. raid on Kiel.	Bomber Command
Leipzig	8,600	Badly damaged by Soviet naval action in Baltic during April 1945 and found in Aabenraa on 10/5/45.	Soviet Navy

Note

Six destroyed by R.A.F. Bomber Command	*Tirpitz* *Schlesien* *Von Scheer* *Deutschland/Lutzow* *Gneisenau* *Emden*
Four destroyed by British Navy	*Bismarck* *Graf Spee* *Scharnhorst* *Karlsruhe*
Two severely damaged by R.A.F. Bomber Command	*Admiral Hipper* *Scharnhorst*
One destroyed by U. S. Air Force	*Koln*

One destroyed by British Fleet Air Arm *Konigsberg*

One sunk by Norwegian shore batteries *Blucher*

One severely damaged by Soviet Navy *Leipzig*

Two surrendered intact at end of war *Prinz Eugen*
Nuremberg

Index

253

About the Author

Born in 1896, Robert Saundby was a Second Lieutenant in a territorial infantry battalion when World War I broke out and in 1915 he transferred to the Royal Flying Corps. He served in two famous fighter squadrons on the Western front and destroyed several enemy aircraft. In May, 1917, he was awarded the Military Cross for his part in the destruction of Zeppelin airship LZ48 over Britain. At the end of the war he was awarded the Air Force Cross for his work in flying training units. In 1919 he was given a permanent commission in the RAF. He transferred to bombers and spent five years in Iraq, Aden, and Egypt, gaining the Distinguished Flying Cross during air operations near Aden.

Returning home he was appointed to the RAF's first squadron of heavy night bombers. Passing the staff college course in 1928, he went to the staff of the bomber headquarters in Britain, and two years later joined the Air Staff of the Air Ministry. He graduated from the Imperial Defence College, and then for three years was the senior instructor at the RAF Staff College. Returning to the Air Ministry in 1937 he was succesively Deputy Director of Operations, Director of Operational Requirements, and Assistant Chief of the Air Staff (Technical). Appointed Senior Air Staff Officer of Bomber Command in November 1940, he became Deputy Commander-in-Chief in February 1943, remaining in that post until the end of the war. In 1946 he was invalided from the RAF as the result of injuries sustained in France in 1917.

Since his retirement he has devoted himself to lecturing and writing about air power and to voluntary work with the RAF Association, the RAF Benevolent Fund, the Air League, and the Territorial, Auxiliary and Cadet Forces.